MALLARMÉ AND THE POETICS OF EVERYDAY LIFE

FAUX TITRE

Etudes
de langue et littérature françaises
publiées

sous la direction de Keith Busby,
M.J. Freeman, Sjef Houppermans,
Paul Pelckmans et Co Vet

No. 198

Amsterdam - Atlanta, GA 2000

MALLARMĒ AND THE POETICS OF EVERYDAY LIFE
A Study of the Concept of the Ordinary in his Verse and Prose

Hélène Stafford

The paper on which this book is printed meets the requirements of "ISO 9706:1994, Information and documentation - Paper for documents - Requirements for permanence".

Le papier sur lequel le présent ouvrage est imprimé remplit les prescriptions de "ISO 9706:1994, Information et documentation - Papier pour documents - Prescriptions pour la permanence".

ISBN: 90-420-1314-1
©Editions Rodopi B.V., Amsterdam - Atlanta, GA 2000
Printed in The Netherlands

CONTENTS

Introduction: the Poetics of the Prosaic	9
Syntax	63
Vocabulary: 'Les aptes mots'	107
Metaphorisation of the Ordinary	151
An Ideology of Ordinary Life	181
Conclusion	209
List of Works Consulted	227
Index	241

ACKNOWLEDGEMENTS

I would like to thank my thesis supervisor Professor Malcolm Bowie for his advice and assistance during the writing of the original project. I would also like to thank Mike Freeman for all his help, first of all with reading the original draft, but also with the publication of this book. My thanks go to Claire Lewis for her willingness to offer her word-processing expertise, to Vicki Statham for her careful proofreading and to my husband Geoff for his patience and tireless support.

CHAPTER I

Introduction: the Poetics of the Prosaic

The reader of Mallarmé might not, in the first instance (or possibly in any other instance), describe his work as the expression of the ordinary truth of a common human experience; the initial impression of difficulty, obscurity and opacity, is more likely to engender a sense of alienation and the feeling that here is a level of complexity and mystery which has little to do with the routine of everyday life.[1] Even if we feel very strongly that Mallarmé's poetic achievement resides to a large extent in his difficulty and that Mallarmean difficulty is indeed an art, we must at some point ask the question: what is it in Mallarmé's work that speaks to the ordinary reader? Can it be claimed that either beyond, behind or underneath the shimmering constellations of words, at the source of even his most intricate and unyielding material, one might discover either a common experience reworked with appropriate complexity to render a complex reality, a mixing and re-organising of different levels of reality, or a playing with the basic structures which undergird our apprehension of the poetic world as well as our perception of quotidian life?

In this book, I shall seek to rehabilitate the ordinary within the Mallarmé corpus, responding to a challenge set out in the texts themselves and identifiable in a number of relevant features. I shall reconsider at length Mallarmé's use of syntax and vocabulary, highlighting the frequent occurrences of ordinary syntax and the extensive use of a lexis derived from the quotidian. I shall give special attention to the poet's use of the word *ordinaire* and its cognates, and analyse a number of important metaphors linked to the world of the everyday. I shall also examine Mallarmé's ideological engagement with the artistic and socio-political environment that formed part of ordinary life in nineteenth-century *fin-de-siècle* Paris. At the heart of this project

---

[1] I shall occasionally refer to everyday life, or the concept of the ordinary, or banal experience, or quotidian routine as 'the ordinary', 'the everyday', 'the banal', 'the quotidian'. Although this might not strike the British reader as standard usage, I have found that for the sake of economy and conciseness, this would be convenient. The context within which the phrases are used will make it clear whether I am referring to 'the ordinary', 'the everyday', 'the banal' or 'the quotidian' as ordinary life or experience, or as a concept and frame of reference.

is a specific problematic that aims not only at contributing to Mallarmé studies in content terms but also in a mode of analysis that will produce a number of conclusions which differ from those of recent critical studies developed along similar lines of inquiry.

The density of references to the ordinary in the corpus is a feature that has been neglected and deserves, because of the very challenge it presents, a thorough analysis. This project therefore rises from the textual peculiarities of the works themselves, from a linguistic solicitation that has been hitherto overlooked. This invitation to implement a new dynamic dialectic based on a study of the concept of the ordinary within the texts points to Mallarmé's creativity in his use of language as it relates to the ordinary and to his inventiveness in the expression of his engagement with, and his response to, a dimension that is at once inescapable and all-pervasive. My inquiry is stimulated by a number of simple observations: the insistent use of a clutch of words and cognates explicitly naming the ordinary, their positive or negative charge, the way in which Mallarmé himself in his usage of specific quotidian vocabulary marks out a terrain for exploration, putting the concept firmly on the agenda.

My main task will therefore be to make sense of, and to analyse, these initially strange references. On the one hand we must recognise Mallarmé's difficulty, yet we must also acknowledge the closeness of the Mallarmean imagination to the ordinary world. This area of inquiry is indeed, as it seems, divided and made complex by the dichotomy between linguistic and conceptual difficulty and ordinary, easily comprehensible circumstances which lead us back to the ordinary. The first imperative will therefore be to establish a suitably *nuancé* yet appropriately structured working definition of the ordinary as conceptual tool.

The avenue of inquiry I propose to follow is one that will study the ordinary from the inside out, from within the texts. I shall not therefore be primarily studying Mallarmé's own everyday world from a biographical point of view, although that in itself would bring illuminating insights into his concept of the ordinary. A number of writers have indeed capably assembled fascinating biographies, not least the author of the most recent book on Mallarmé's life by Gordon Millan.[2] His premise which he describes as 'treating Mallarmé's life and work as an organic whole' (p.2) is a legitimate and genuine attempt to bring back the

---

[2] Gordon Millan, *Mallarmé: A Throw of the Dice* (London: Secker & Warburg, 1994).

poet's everyday into the critical arena, and to show the indissoluble links between his ordinary, real, lived life and his literary achievements. My own project can be situated at the other end of the spectrum, as a part of the same endeavour to rehabilitate the ordinary as it relates to the poet. Whereas the biographer will proceed by beginning with the outward and tangible material which testifies to the reality of the writer's everyday life, and work as it were from the outside in, I intend to take the texts themselves as my starting point, to extract out of their very density, difficulty and opacity, evidence of the crucial role of the world of the ordinary in the Mallarmean corpus. I am therefore proceeding inversely, from the inside out.

The creative use of language involves an awareness of the polysemic quality of terms such as *ordinaire* or *banal*, and the production of rich ambiguities and uncertainties in the process. I shall study the rich evaluative colouring of the use of the words and of the ordinary within the Mallarmé workshop, tracking it down through the texts in an attempt to redefine the concept from within the fabric of the texts themselves, with the sense of unearthing and isolating a number of unusual items, and establishing a kind of 'curiosity shop' of Mallarmean usage. The job of sifting and sorting lexical and syntactical linguistic matter has been done most competently by Jacques Scherer.[3] Yet the high incidence of the material I am focusing on has escaped his otherwise thorough analysis. My study is an attempt to circumscribe and analyse a feature that has essential relevance to our reading of the poet.

Having reconsidered Mallarmé's use of language in the light of the concept of the ordinary based on a number of philosophical approaches and theoretical frameworks in the course of this chapter, I intend then to study the poet's response to the manifestations of the ordinary and his elaboration of a number of measures by which he either owns and appropriates the quotidian, or rejects it. My approach will inevitably involve a narrow focus, an intense relationship to the material and an investing in the textual detail of linguistic, semantic and conceptual relevance. It will also gain stimulus from Julia Kristeva's important study, *La Révolution du langage poétique*, 1974, particularly from her illuminating syntactical analysis of *Un Coup de dés*.

---

[3] Jacques Scherer, *L'Expression littéraire dans l'œuvre de Mallarmé* (Paris: Droz, 1947).

As a first step, I shall situate my project within the present landscape of Mallarmé studies. I shall briefly discuss past and present tendencies, and highlight a new and dynamic current which departs from traditional Mallarmé criticism and seeks, by a fresh reading of the totality of the poet's output, to reclaim him from the superb isolation and impenetrable obscurity where so many past critics have respectfully and firmly relegated him. The present study situates itself within this latest current, whilst focusing on an aspect of Mallarmé's writing that has not been given particular attention. Secondly, this introductory chapter will be concerned with the analysis of a number of theoretical models of the ordinary, derived from philosophers and critics. These models are evaluated in relation to their potential when applied to Mallarmé's *œuvre*. The concept of the ordinary, studied in the light of Mallarmé's reputed difficulty, will then be relocated within the texts and applied to Mallarmé's use of language. It will be helpful to analyse the nature of Mallarmean difficulty in the light of our definition of the ordinary and for this purpose I shall draw on George Steiner's four categories of difficulty as described in his essay 'On Difficulty' (1978).[4] The four modes of difficulty devised by Steiner, contingent, modal, tactical and ontological, will provide a useful framework within which to develop constructively a strategic analysis of Mallarmé's constant intertwining in his texts of the ordinary and the difficult.

I. A brief survey of Mallarmé studies as they relate to this project

On the subject of the poet's own apprehension of reality, Mallarmists have in the past been divided into two irreconcilable camps: on the one hand, those who would have him entirely devoted to an uncompromising Platonic ideal whose aim is to abstract the concrete, dissolve tangible reality and escape from the world of mere phenomena; on the other, those who argue that Mallarmé's work is rooted in everyday concrete reality to a large extent, as his use of domestic objects and familiar surroundings and images might suggest. The poet himself has to some degree encouraged an almost mythical image of himself, as Millan points

---

[4] George Steiner, *On Difficulty and other essays* (Oxford: Oxford University Press, 1978). Steiner presents his essay as an attempt at 'a classification, a typology, of some of the principal modes of difficulty as one meets them in poetry, notably in Western poetry since the Renaissance. From such a classification could derive a "theory of difficulty" which remains one of the *desiderata*, made urgent by twentieth-century practice, in the more general aesthetics of executive forms' (p.19).

out: 'he was deliberately creating a myth which was to go unchallenged in his lifetime and, for the most part, ever since'.[5] He has been described as the most extreme of idealists, absorbed in the temptation of a parallel and distant world which eventually proves to be a threatening void. However, the image of Mallarmé as a priest and martyr to his poetic vocation, entirely removed from the world of the everyday, engaging in the somewhat hermetic and exquisitely irrelevant task of pursuing a form of poetry reserved for a select sophisticated few, away from the ordinary pleasures and anxieties that befall the greater part of mankind, has had its day.

The changes in critical standpoints have moved from the *tour d'ivoire* view of the poet to much more *nuancé* accounts of his relationship with the world of the everyday. The range and quality of the early critical body is impressive; nevertheless, perceptive and thorough critics such as Albert Thibaudet and Emilie Noulet, as well as Henri Mondor,[6] have been surprisingly quick to subscribe to the *tour d'ivoire* myth of the poet, and simply have not noticed Mallarmé's immersedness in the facts and the vocabulary of the ordinary world. However, even in earlier criticism, a number of writers have developed new critical avenues that follow less docilely the model of the poet in his ivory tower. A.R. Chisholm writes in *Mallarmé's Grand Œuvre* (1962):

> An idealist. But not a lover of abstractions. His poetry is not abstract, nor is it a mass of word-puzzles. The starting-point of his transcendental flight is to be sought in the domain of physical realities, including of course people, works of art, landscapes, sunsets... He is preoccupied with the essence of things; but an essence has to have an object, has to be the essence of something (p. 12).

Within the broad division mentioned above, the dizzying variety of interpretative traditions to which Mallarmé's work has been submitted is not the least puzzling symptom of his unique ability to engender in the reader the need somehow either to justify or ignore his difficulty, and to attach himself to one clearly stated response. On the one hand, the optimists, possibly hastily,

---

[5] Gordon Millan, *Mallarmé: A Throw of the Dice* (London: Secker & Warburg, 1994), p.8.

[6] Albert Thibaudet, *La Poésie de Stéphane Mallarmé* (Paris: Gallimard, 1926). Emilie Noulet, *L'Œuvre poétique de Stéphane Mallarmé* (Paris:Droz, 1940). Henri Mondor, *Vie de Mallarmé*, (Paris: Gallimard, 1941).

do not doubt the ability of the patient reader armed with glosses to reach a satisfactory level of elucidation and understanding of Mallarmé's work; on the other, the pessimists might either ignore or bemoan a feature which might be seen as spoiling an otherwise near-perfect production. The beginnings of Mallarmé criticism, which I have already mentioned, first with Albert Thibaudet (*La Poésie de Stéphane Mallarmé*, 1926), and then with Emilie Noulet (*L'Œuvre poétique de Stéphane Mallarmé*, 1940), still held out the promise of a form of 'consensus reading'. It is no longer possible to adopt such a stance when the field of Mallarmean studies has exploded into a variety of approaches, from the grammatical work of Jacques Scherer (*L'Expression littéraire dans l'œuvre de Mallarmé*, 1947), the thematic reading of Richard (*L'Univers imaginaire de Mallarmé*, 1961), to the semiotic studies of Kristeva (*La Révolution du langage poétique*, 1974).

The present book is written in a context in which a great deal of attention has been lavished on the circumstances of production of works such as *Vers de circonstance*. A number of critical texts are of particular interest to this study in that they relate to the poet's everyday life and to his engagement with his own time. The community of Mallarmé critics has shifted its emphasis, focusing on new and challenging features of the texts: the study of the poet's notorious obscurity has gained much from the psychoanalytical approach of Charles Mauron, the careful linguistic and prosodic analyses of Malcolm Bowie and more recently from the studies of the poet's sustained inventiveness and creativeness by Roger Pearson. Mallarmé's difficulty has been perceived, in different ways, as a positive, indeed an essentially creative feature by all three critics. Pearson, Michael Temple and Graham Robb bring a new microscopy to the works at a time which has seen fresh and innovative ways of exploring the texts in an attempt to get Mallarmé out of the study, one might almost say out of the closet and back into a wider world as a frame for biographical, linguistic and conceptual reference. In the present study, however, the poet's famed obscurity will provide a different set of challenges, as the dimension of the ordinary, both within and without the texts forces on the poet linguistic constraints, metaphysical tension and an ideological balancing act with an inevitable risk of sudden and fatal fall into vacancy.

With the studies of Bertrand Marchal (*Lecture de Mallarmé*, 1985), the use of language and the relevance of everyday life in its historical and individual dimension have been given greater prominence. So have a number of texts which had drawn little critical attention, texts that are of particular interest to this study as they relate to the ordinary circumstances of the

INTRODUCTION: THE POETICS OF THE PROSAIC   15

poet's life, such as the *Vers de circonstance*, or to the life of a society undergoing irreversible changes, as in the texts on the *expositions universelles*. Marian Zwerling Sugano in *The Poetics of the Occasion: Mallarmé and the Poetry of Circumstance* (1992) has focused her study on Mallarmé's occasional writings, and builds her analysis upon her opening remark that '[...] with few exceptions, all of Mallarmé's works after 1873 manifest a reinvestment in the world subsequent to the metaphysical crises of the 1860's and the years of silence that followed'(p.15). However, Sugano does not analyse the role and status of the ordinary within Mallarmé's texts, and never problematises the concept itself.

Roger Bellet in *Stéphane Mallarmé: l'encre et le ciel* (1987) accounts for the poet's obscurity by drawing a causal link between a particularly simple and limpid everyday life and the poet's need to disguise it, but this 'simplicity theory' does not have adequate complexity and flexibility to account for the rich ambiguities in the mallarmean response to the ordinary. At the heart of Vincent Kaufmann's study *Le Livre et ses adresses* (1986) is a fascination with the place of the reader of Mallarmé, his real or virtual existence, his necessary or ignored presence. The positing of a 'dispositif symbolique', if it does answer a number of questions and offer solutions to some of the puzzles created by the poems themselves, clearly sets up a different framework and agenda to the one this book intends to focus on, as does the further study of some of Mallarmé's correspondence in Kaufmann's *L'Equivoque épistolaire* (1990) which offers a fascinating insight into specific aspects of Mallarmé's. In *Mallarmé: la Politique de la sirène* (1996), Jacques Rancière formulates a simple but challenging programme: 'L'idée de secret suppose que la vérité est cachée quelque part derrière la surface que l'œil et l'esprit appréhendent. La révélation de cette vérité s'effectue alors selon deux logiques inverses et complémentaires: trouver l'extraordinaire sous l'ordinaire et l'ordinaire sous l'extraordinaire' (p8). This leads to the debatable implications that behind every potential secret lurks a potential truth and that the concepts of the ordinary and extraordinary are two sides of the same coin. However, Rancière points out that Mallarmé's difficulty and his immersedness in the society of his time are linked. Mallarmé's awareness of the historical moment, his enthusiasm for industrial progress and production as well as his fear of the loss of the rare and the unique and his undoubted interest in the lives of his contemporaries make him far more than a distant witness. It is within the everyday of his time, as this study will attempt to show, that Mallarmé's texts reveal a new and dynamic potential at the linguistic, metaphorical and ideological levels.

That the work of one writer should generate such a range of critical approaches is part of the fascination that Mallarmé holds for many. His odd ability to draw his readers into passionate debate seems in its scope almost unique. None of his near-contemporaries, even where they have generated as large and distinguished a body of critical studies, have engendered views quite as intense and divergent. At the end of a century that has seen immense historical and economic changes, Mallarmé attracts more attention than he ever did in the first fifty years following his death. One can only speculate that it is the richness and variety of the material itself, its ambiguity and its very difficulty that has stimulated this vast and contrasted critical activity. Most promising for a project with a particular interest in the concept of the ordinary in Mallarmé is the relatively recent interest in Mallarmé's immersion in the local surrounding culture, in his journalistic endeavours, the studies of his occasional verse and the renewed interest with his large correspondence, particularly in the book by Roger Dragonetti.[7] The present study is indebted to all the authors mentioned, and endeavours to travel further down avenues of inquiry along which much of the more recent research has been conducted. However, the density of reference to everyday life within the Mallarmé corpus is a feature that has been largely neglected, yet has important consequences on our reading of the texts and on the author/reader relationship. The changing socio-economic conditions in the late nineteenth century have a crucial bearing on the status of the poet, and therefore on his experience of the quotidian as well as on his perception of the ordinary life of his contemporaries. Inevitably, this will affect the very fabric of his writing, the words on the page. It is therefore and foremost with the texts, rather than with biographical events, that this study will be concerned.

In human life and experience, there is a general need and desire to make things clear and simple, and one of the ways of achieving this aim is to refer to the ordinary as the lowest common denominator for accessibility and reliability. The experience of the ordinary becomes a marker of stability and a dimension that allows easy communication and shared experience. This is not the case with the ordinary as we encounter it in the works of Mallarmé; the ordinary world within the corpus appears

---

[7] Roger Dragonetti, *Un Fantôme dans le kiosque: Mallarmé et l'esthétique du quotidien* (Paris: Seuil, 1992).

to be deeply ingrained but also constantly shifting. On the one hand, we can readily identify a thematic current that focuses attention on the clutter of bourgeois life. On the other hand, there exists also a sense that everyday objects and circumstances matter only as a trampoline used to distance oneself from the ordinary world. In either case, the concept and the world of the ordinary are crucial to the poet and they are abundantly gestured towards, both implicitly and explicitly, they are named and even cherished. The ordinary in the Mallarmean corpus cannot be reduced to any one defining and stabilising element, but acts both as a 'vaporisation' of the concept and also as a centralisation of this concept. At its centre, we therefore find a double disposition, a creative ambiguity, a rich and unstable element that feeds on a paradoxical understanding of the everyday and constantly undermines its recognisable, safe and transparent status. The ordinary becomes opaque, palimpsestic, alternately invested with positive and negative qualities, forcing the reader to go back to his or her original understanding of the term in order to readjust his or her expectations.

In order to give new inflexions and nuances to our definition of the ordinary, an analysis of a number of possible models offered by theorists and philosophers of the ordinary will provide rich and diverse material which will subsequently be used to elaborate a syntactic, lexical, metaphorical and ideological study of Mallarmé's works. By interlinking different facets of the ordinary into a network of everyday experiences, I hope to uncover patterns of linguistic, psychological and ideological responses and habits that will provide a new and dynamic view of Mallarmé's texts. My trajectory will proceed from a general discussion of the concept of the ordinary and its relocation within the Mallarmé corpus to an empirical close study of the texts. I shall also briefly place Mallarmé within a tradition of writing about the quotidian, with special reference to Charles Baudelaire as one of the most significant and ongoing influences in Mallarmé's own works.

II. Theoretical models of the ordinary

If Mallarmé's texts have, in the past, gained a reputation for almost insurmountable difficulty, and for a rather remote diction disengaged from the world of the everyday, more recent research has endeavoured in a rather general way to demonstrate that he nevertheless offers to the ordinary reader absorbed in modern routine the challenge of rediscovering his relevance. The challenge is indeed daunting. The concepts of 'the banal', or 'the quotidian' are in an important sense complex constructs evolving from a deliberate departure from everyday experiences. Ordinariness, routine, pattern of habits in the ordinary world do not possess the same meaning as their literary counterparts; the word 'ordinary' would lead most people to think in terms of the dull, the trivial, the prosaic, the vicissitudes of daily commuting, for instance; and yet it is also possible to examine the concept of the ordinary as valorised positively. In his fascinating book, *Sources of the Self: the Making of the Modern Identity* (1989), Charles Taylor traces the origin of what he calls 'the affirmation of ordinary life' (p.13). He argues that it is with the Reformation that ordinary life became central to good life, or the life of contemplation, and that previous concepts of higher forms of life were dethroned. He sees this important change in attitude as providing the inspiration for widely divergent views of society: it underlies both bourgeois politics and revolutionary ideology. Taylor equates ordinary life not with the dull and the trivial but with an acceptable and valuable alternative to what had been hitherto perceived as a higher form of existence. This antithetical use of the concept of the everyday demonstrates the richness of the concept and its potential value as a positive theoretical model.

The concept of the ordinary has a far wider and more complex semantic and philosophical range than might at first appear; it is often far easier to define what it isn't than what it is, and to set up a number of oppositions that on closer examination prove not to be oppositions at all. The central question is therefore to do with the way in which we go on to reconcile the wildly idealistic, the strange, the almost unintelligible, the obscure, the extraordinary, the uncanny, as a set of opposing terms, with the domestic, the familiar, the everyday world. How does the one set of terms relate to the other within Mallarmé's poetic discourse? There is of course a sense in which the ordinary world is a necessary resource for all poets, and is therefore both imminent and endemic in poetry. Even Dante, in *The Divine Comedy*, draws on a number of metaphors and images of the ordinary in order to characterise and describe the transcendental.[8] The difficulty lies not in establishing the links between poetry and the ordinary, but in defining them in the context of the dangerous versatility and the chameleon like qualities of the ordinary. Can there exist a

---

[8] See *The Divine Comedy 3: Paradise*, for instance, in 'Canto V', where souls are compared to fish in a pond rising towards food:
> As in a fish-pond clear and still, the fish
> Draw to some dropped-in morsel as it moves
> Hoping it may provide a dainty dish [...], p.93, trans. Dorothy L.Sayers and Barbara Reynolds (Penguin, 1962).

relationship other than crude antithesis, an interaction more complex and rewarding than mutual exclusion between the poetic and the ordinary? In Heidegger's 'Der Ursprung des Kunstwerke',[9] written in 1935-6, the philosopher develops a concept of the ordinary which will bear particular fruit when applied to the poetic, and will release us from a rather sterile antithesis into a new understanding of the ordinary. Heidegger writes:

> Im nächsten Umkreis des Seienden glauben wir uns heimisch. Das Seiende ist vertraut, verläßlich, geheuer. Gleichwohl zieht durch Lichtung ein ständiges Verbergen in der Doppelgestalt des Versagens und des Verstellens. Das Geheure ist im Grunde nicht geheuer; es ist ungeheuer.[10]

> We believe we are at home in the immediate circle of being. That which is familiar, reliable, ordinary. Nevertheless, the clearing is pervaded by a constant concealment in that double form of refusal and dissembling. At bottom, the ordinary is not ordinary; it is extra-ordinary, uncanny.[11]

The fact that terms like the ordinary or the banal exist in their more complex meaning, and have come to be used as conceptual tools to reassess the political but also the poetic, a domain that seems at first so removed from everyday life, is testimony to a malaise. The more elaborate meanings have been generated not from everyday experience itself - indeed the unquestioning inhabitant of the world of the everyday has little use for the concept - but by art and philosophy. After Taylor's positive valorisation of ordinary life, Heidegger offers us a more complex understanding of the familiar. The relationship between what is ordinary and what seems its opposite indeed goes well beyond a merely antithetical one. It posits an interfusedness and an interdependence which cannot simply be described as two sides

---

[9] For a translation of the essay, see Martin Heidegger, *Poetry, Language, Thought* trans. Albert Hofstadter (New York: Harper and Row, 1975).

[10] Martin Heidegger, *Holzwege, Gesamtausgabe*, Band 5 (Frankfurt am Main: Vittorio Klostermann, 1977). This quote is taken from the essay 'Der Ursprung des Kunstwerkes' (1935-6), from the section entitled 'Das Werk und die Wahrheit', p.41.

[11] Translation by Albert Hofstadter in *Poetry, Language, Thought*, p.54.

of a coin, but rather as a double strand appearing and disappearing in alternate and unpredictable patterns. To the question, 'what is the ordinary?', Heidegger's concept of concealment, in the form of refusal and dissembling, defines it not in the rather simple positive terms of Taylor, but in a negative apprehension that uncovers unfamiliar, even unknowable depths.

Stanley Cavell, in his collection of essays *The Quest of the Ordinary: Lines on Skepticism and Romanticism* (1988), redefines both the poetic and the ordinary in terms of quest and inquest: 'The ordinary is always the subject of a quest and the object of an inquest' (p.149). He is closer to Heidegger in the sense that he does not take the ordinary as a given, as an unproblematic state, but as a dynamic and mobile concept that needs exploring. Poetry, and in particular Romantic poetry, for Cavell is an exercise in retrieval and restoration, a recovery of the ordinary, a reconstruction, and, one might be tempted to add, sometimes a deconstruction of everyday experience. The ordinary is not seen as a betrayal of the poetic, nor the poetic as irretrievably alien to the ordinary, but the two are seen as mutually useful and enhancing concepts, interwoven in more complex and subtle ways than might at first seem possible.

'Consentir au mystère d'être matière'[12] in the words of Joël Pourbaix, is one poet's way of describing the interplay between the everyday, material world and the poetic world. And indeed, for Mallarmé, this was to prove a struggle and the object of constant questioning. 'The difficulty of Mallarmé comes chiefly from his attitude towards the world of phenomena', writes Chisholm.[13] The subject matter of Mallarmé's work is almost always drawn from everyday life. Yet the immediate qualifying words when reading Mallarmé tend to point to the mysterious, the ambiguous, the complex, the extraordinary in his writing. These characteristics would also be applicable to the familiar according to Heidegger, and we will therefore argue later on in this chapter that the philosopher's concept of the ordinary will prove particularly useful when brought into relationship with the Mallarmé corpus.

The ordinary has become more and more the subject of an ongoing inquiry, and the main theme of modern literary and media pursuits. Scientists as well as writers are researching its structures, its manifestations, its reality as a concept and as a

---

[12] Joël Pourbaix, *Le Simple Geste d'exister* (Québec: Noroît, 1989), p.15.

[13] A.R. Chisholm, *Mallarmé's Grand Œuvre* (Manchester: Manchester University Press, 1982), p.18.

necessary condition for day to day life, and the reactions it provokes. In his article 'Er lebe den Alltag',[14] Steffen Jacobs points to the many facets of the everyday, and to its attraction for the modern poet:

> Die Welt des Alltags ist nicht nur banal und vorhersehbar, sie ist auch exotisch und faszinierend. Statt von Banalität spräche man daher besser von unterschiedlich hohen Dosierungen des Alltäglichen. Was aber machen die Dichter, jedenfalls die Antimaterialisten unter ihnen? Sie glauben seit geraumer Zeit, ihr tägliches Brot sei das Schreiben. Und so hat sich mit den Jahrzehnten eine sehr spezifische Form der Alltagslyrik entwickelt, der das Schreiben von Gedichten über das Schreiben von Gedichten als Hauptmotiv zugrunde liegt. (p.27)[15]

Both Martin Heidegger and Ludwig Wittgenstein reflected on the meaning, the effect and the nature of the everyday. Both are forced to recognise its power and its all-pervading quality. Both eventually acknowledge the impossibility of disengaging from it, and the necessity to confront it and own it. In his article on 'Die Pharmakologie des Banalen',[16] Dieter Thomä compares and underlines the attitude of the two philosophers:

> Statt sich auf den Alltag als ein leichtes Opfer zu stürzen, sahen sich die Philosophen am Ende gezwungen, seine Immunität anzuerkennen. In diesem Jahrhundert waren die zwei leitenden - und miteinander streitenden - Immunologen des Alltags Martin Heidegger and Ludwig Wittgenstein. [...] Heidegger und Wittgenstein sind Nachkommen des Odysseus - und der Alltag ist ein Nachfahre Ithakas. Die Philosophen, die ihre Reise einst

---

[14] Jacobs, Steffen, 'Er lebe den Alltag', *Neue Rundschau* 107, 1996, in a special edition dedicated to 'Die Schönheit des Banalen', pp22-34.

[15] The following translations of extracts from the *Neue Rundschau* are mine, with the help of my German speaking father Gérard Mog. 'The world of the quotidian is not just banal and predictable, it is also exotic and fascinating. Instead of speaking of banality, it would be better to speak of a greater or lesser measure of quotidian. But what are poets about - if only those amongst them who are antimaterialists? - They have long held the belief that writing is their daily bread. Thus, over the past decades, a specific form of lyricism of the quotidian has emerged as a principal motivation in the writing of poetry'.

[16] Article published in *Neue Rundschau*, 1996, pp.15-21.

> notgedrungen beim Alltag begonnen haben, stehen ihm fern und landen dann doch wieder bei ihm; sie unternehmen eine Odyssee, die schließlich an den Ort ihrer Herkunft zurückführt. (pp.16-7)[17]

Both discover the inevitability of the everyday, and the impossibility of escaping it. The point of departure is also the point of arrival, despite the tremendous journey they have undertaken in between. The question that remains is therefore one of response to the inescapability of the everyday. As Thomä writes, there are two possible responses: an attempt to disturb and destroy it, or an attempt at understanding it and taming it:

> Zwei Gifte gibt es gegen den Alltag: Mann kann ihn zerstören oder verstehen. [...]
> Das zweite Gift gegen den Alltag ist die Einsicht. Wer das, was er gerade tut und was ihm gewohnheitsmäßig widerfährt, zu verstehen beginnt als sinnvolles Geflecht von Begebenheiten, wer hinter fast gedankenlos vollzogenen Handlungen geheime Beweggründe und hinter halbherzig beibehaltenen Gewohnheiten versteckte Zusammenhänge entdeckt, bringt den Alltag, indem er ihn versteht, zum Verschwinden. (p.15)[18]

He argues that by understanding and taming the everyday, one is able to alter it to such a degree that it will not be ordinary

---

[17] 'Instead of throwing themselves on the everyday as on an easy prey, the philosophers have eventually found themselves obliged to acknowledge its immunity. In this century, the two leading immunologists of the quotidian, who were also in disagreement, are Martin Heidegger and Ludwig Wittgenstein. [...] Heidegger and Wittgenstein follow on in their own Odyssey, and the quotidian is a disciple of Ithaca. The philosophers, who, driven by contingency, had started their journey from the quotidian, have moved away from it but are now coming back to it. They undertake an Odyssey, which brings them back eventually to their point of departure'.

[18] 'There are two ways of getting rid of the quotidian: one can either destroy it or one can try to understand it. [...] The second way is to try and dissect it. The person who begins to understand his own actions at the time of their execution, who understands the nature of routine, and who sees it as an intertwining of meaningful events, the one who searches for hidden motives in relation to actions done almost without thought, the one who looks behind habitual acts carried out half-heartedly and who discovers connections, he is the one who, by understanding the quotidian, will be able to make it disappear'.

anymore. Yet what the historian Paul Veyne[19] identifies in Heidegger and other writers is not a sense of wanting to tame the ordinary, but a sense of helpless rage at the all-pervading nature of the everyday, and a quixotically exaggerated and useless response to it:

> Was man da bei Heidegger und vielen anderen untergründig spürt, ist eine schimärenhafte Wut auf die unüberschreitbare Alltäglichkeit; diese Wut äußert sich dann als Kritik an der bestehenden Gesellschaft und als satirischer Angriff auf unsere angebliche Dekadenz; wie Don Quijote gegen die Windmühlen kämpft man gegen das Zeitalter der anonymen Massen, gegen den Individualismus, der keine Ideale mehr habe, oder gegen die angebliche Mittelmäßigkeit der Demokratie. (pp.13-4).[20]

It seems that the response to the concept is as complex as the concept itself, and that its ambiguous nature evokes a range of often-paradoxical thoughts, feelings and emotions. The rage evoked in Heidegger and others is expressed in their critique of society, their ferocious satirizing of the prevalent social order and political system. The parallel with Mallarmé's own response, as expressed in particular in *Divagations* and a number of texts focused on social, philosophical and economic issues, has to be made and will uncover a close fellowship in attitudes between the philosopher and the poet. Mallarmé's mode of writing, and even of being, seems to be one of constant questioning of reality, of the phenomenal world, of the way human consciousness relates to the structures and recurring patterns of nature, and manages (or not) to make sense of it all. The obscurity is born of a sense of tremendous struggle, a wrestling which has its source in a perception of reality which endeavours to go beyond as well as behind the solid materiality of things, 'motifs, aspects, figures

---

[19] 'Das Alltägliche und das Interessante', article published in *Neue Rundschau*, 1996.

[20] 'What emerges in Heidegger and in many others is a rage of mythical proportion against the inescapable quotidian. This rage is then expressed as a critique of contemporary society and as a satirical attack on our so called decadence; like Don Quixote fighting against windmills, one fights against contemporary ideas produced by anonymous masses, against individualism, which is said to lack idealism, and against the so called mediocrity of democracy'.

qu'il s'efforce d'apercevoir en filigrane, derrière tout événement sensible' in the memorable words of Jean-Pierre Richard.[21]

It would indeed be useful to re-assess the domestic dimension of Mallarmé's world, for instance, and his 'immediate circle of being' in the light of the extraordinary side of the familiar. And if, as Ernest Sturm writes in the preface of his English translation of Jean-Paul Sartre's posthumously published *Mallarmé: La Lucidité et sa face d'ombre* (1986),[22] Mallarmé's mode of perceiving reality is dissonant, one might argue, as Heidegger does, that reality in its most ordinary manifestations might also have its dissonances, its uncanniness, its epiphanic moments and its own puzzling complexity. The language we use to speak of the ordinary world and the language used in poetry both originate in a *décalage* with ordinary experience. It is this very *décalage* that reveals to us the existence of those domains both as separate and as interfused. The poet Yves Bonnefoy draws out the links in *Entretiens sur la poésie*: 'La poésie en somme, fut longtemps le dire commun porté à son intensité la plus grande' (p.299). The difference is one of degree, not one of essence. But he also points out 'la primauté du fait d'être sur l'écrit, du dehors sur ma langue toujours close' (p.299). Yet the two cannot be separated or even studied or considered as separate entities. Biographical realities, as well as literary ones, legitimately reflect one aspect of the ordinary, which inevitably influences another aspect.

We discover in Mallarmé's writing the powerful pull of the craving to escape commonness, ordinariness, but also a need to rejoin it and to explore its positive possibilities (as in Taylor's 'good life') and negative potential (the possibility of encountering a threatening void). Henri Lefèbvre, in his *Critique of Everyday Life* (1947),[23] develops a dialectic of the concept of everyday based on an opposition between routine and celebration,

---

[21] Jean-Pierre Richard, *L'Univers imaginaire de Mallarmé* (Paris: Seuil, 1961), p.15. Richard's essential and distinctive work rests on an occult interpretation of Mallarmé's perception of the material world, including that of the quotidian. Materiality is therefore but a superficial layer covering and sometimes obscuring a reality which has far greater depth and complexity.

[22] Sartre, Jean-Paul, *Mallarmé or the poet of Nothingness,* trans. Ernest Sturm (London: Pennsylvania State University Press, 1986). This translation is based on the authoritative French edition established by Arlette Elkaïm-Sartre and published posthumously in 1986 in Paris by Gallimard in the 'Collection Arcades' under the title *Mallarmé: La Lucidité et sa face d'ombre.*

[23] I am using the translation of Henri Lefèbvre's book because I have been unable to access the original in French, now out of print.

emphasising the necessary acknowledgment of the ambiguous nature of ordinary life: 'Man must be everyday or he will not be at all' (p.127). Epiphanic moments, if they mark a break in the banal routine, also give it a new sense of value and potential. They add to it a perspective that leads us from a feeling of surface perception to an experience of depth, sometimes negative as well as positive.

Why should the concepts of the everyday and the banal as a single informing perception present such a challenge when applied to Mallarmé? Why should it be at all rewarding to bring together such widely and seemingly alien worlds as that of the ordinary and that of the poetic in general, and more specifically the ordinary and Mallarmé's world? One might initially argue that all great writers seem to follow a pattern of either using the ordinary world as point of departure or returning to it by means of a detour via the extraordinary. This is not a feature unique to Mallarmé's writing. Although the concept has indeed broadened and gained in meaning and application since the Reformation, and has become immensely rich and complex with the further analyses of Cavell and Heidegger, a relocation of the concept within the works of the poet has not yet been attempted in Mallarmé studies. What does make Mallarmé's case so much more challenging is his seeming eclecticism, which appears to remove him completely from the world of the ordinary, yet contains within its very remoteness a call back to the everyday. One of his favourite images, the star, for instance, can be interpreted as a reference to alien, unfamiliar worlds light-years away, or as reference to the familiar night sky present just beyond the window, a part of the ordinary night, integrated in the rhythm and pattern of everyday life. It is the contrast between the exotic and the everyday, cause of such tension, which lends particular fascination to the analysis of the corpus of Mallarmean texts in the light of the concept of the ordinary.

Neither Victor Hugo, whose firm grasp of reality in its most ordinary manifestations is apparent even in his most visionary moments, nor Charles Baudelaire whose use of the trivial and the prosaic in his work is one of his major successes, display in their writing the same tension between ordinary and extraordinary, familiar and strange. Mallarmé, walking as he does 'a tightrope between perfection and banality',[24] in the words of Rosemary Lloyd, between confusion and clarity, between extraordinary complexity and almost frightening simplicity,

---

[24] Rosemary Lloyd, *Mallarmé: Poésies* (London: Grant & Cutler, 1984), p.25.

entertains a particularly difficult, tense, almost perverse relationship with the world of the ordinary and everyday life. His use, indeed love of artifice, what has often been described as preciosity, if it can be seen as a device to hide, transform or destroy the ordinary, can also be interpreted as a way of returning to ordinary experience, a complex approach to the everyday life in its most hidden structures, using a contrastive process, and one that often starts not with a Heideggerian familiar 'circle of being' but with the hidden depths in order to reach via the exploration of concealment and refusal, the everyday world.

In Mallarmé's use of the banal object (furniture, flowers, etc.) which has often been commented upon, objects are revealed both as ordinary and extraordinary, as part of the banal fabric of life and yet given a new and mysterious status within the texture of everyday living. The point of departure here is indeed the familiar, and so is the point of arrival, but changes have taken place: the object is the same and yet not the same, its value, both positive and negative, enhanced within its familiar environment.

Mallarmé's use of language, both in his poetry and his prose, seems especially to portray his perverse relation to the ordinary. In the course of this project, I shall study the relationship between familiar and unfamiliar vocabulary, its place in the sentence, its juxtaposition with unusual qualifiers. I shall analyse the problems and excitement of the ordinary in the context of lexis and syntax. Mallarmé's syntax is given important performative tasks: it has a particularly close relationship to the world of the ordinary. I shall establish that it is to syntax that the task of manipulation backwards, forwards, to and from the ordinary falls, and its moulding power over vocabulary and themes cannot be overemphasised. It gives imaginative fullness to a vocabulary which might otherwise slip into abstraction, but it also performs a constant subversion of the ordinary, a rejection not of grammatical rule but of its unquestioned application, and a rejection at the same time of readers unwilling to take up the syntactic challenge of much of Mallarmé's work. Kristeva[25] interprets the expression of this rejection as morpho-syntactic destruction. Yet one can also argue that subversion, rather than destruction, is at work in Mallarmé's innovative use of syntax, and that subversion is a far more creative literary principle than destruction.

---

[25] 'Ce rejet est impliqué dans le jugement affirmatif (*Bejahung*) (tel est le texte de Lautréamont), ou dans la morphologie et la syntaxe linguistiques (tel est le texte de Mallarmé), c'est-à-dire qu'il est manifesté par le symbole de la négation ou par la destruction morpho-syntaxique', *La Révolution poétique*, 1974. p.150.

INTRODUCTION: THE POETICS OF THE PROSAIC

The ordinary and the poetic are not only compatible worlds but display great similarities; the everyday and the extraordinary can be reconciled and their very differences make for a closer interaction. We can therefore move on to say that the ordinary as a conceptual tool is indeed useful and particularly challenging when applied to the works of a poet as seemingly removed from everyday reality as Mallarmé. But the problem and risks of such an approach are great: Mallarmé's own claims for a poetry removed from a bourgeois understanding of the world of the everyday have to be taken into account, and his undeniable difficulty, esoterism and opacity have to be preserved rather than pseudo-elucidated. The temptation to categorise and straighten one's argument is ever-present, and the difficulties that arise from trying to work within and with rather than against the contradictions and complexities of the texts cannot be dismissed. The question of the relationship between the world of the everyday and the poetic, particularly in the works of Mallarmé, has all the teasing qualities of a Chinese *rébus*. The question is often more captivating than the answer, and especially so when it focuses on a poet whose mode of writing is one of questioning. Is a poetic world as complex and opaque as Mallarmé's merely a particularly complex vision of everyday life by a poet who feels himself a stranger in the familiar world, or an ordinary account of a particularly extraordinary reality? Does it express, in the words of Bonnefoy (*Entretiens sur la poésie*, 1983, p.74),

> un effroi sur le rapport le plus fondamental qu'on peut entretenir avec le réel, celui qui nous révèle le caractère étranger, transcendant à nos représentations, et qui nous rejette donc dans le néant?

Mallarmé himself has been much preoccupied by the threat of potential nothingness, and there is no lack of evidence of this concern at the thematic, metaphoric and syntactic level in the poet's works.

Mallarmé's poetry is profoundly metaphysical, in the sense that it engages with different levels of reality and the difficulty of representing the various layers in language. Robert C. Coburn, in *The Strangeness of the Ordinary: Problems and Issues in Contemporary Metaphysics* (1990), gives the following definition of metaphysics:

> Metaphysics is the discipline that is concerned with a variety of questions and problems that arise when one reflects upon certain notions that pervade everyday

thought and discourse, notions such as time, space, object, property, necessity, possibility, existence, fact, God, consciousness, causality, truth, proposition and value (p.x).

One might argue that a poetry that is deemed metaphysical cannot also embrace the world of the domestic and the ordinary, that metaphysical obscurity excludes the familiar and the everyday. And yet even a poetic mode as seemingly obscure as Mallarmé's is nevertheless, maybe in its very difficulty, concerned with everyday thought and discourse.

III. Steiner's classification of difficulty

In order to make progress it will be useful to return to the categories of difficulty established by George Steiner, to apply the classification to Mallarmean difficulty in order to discover its nature and its compatibility with, or its distance from, the ordinary. Steiner himself makes, unsurprisingly, several references to Mallarmé in the course of his essay 'On Difficulty' (1978). To illustrate his first category, contingent difficulty which he defines pragmatically as '[...] a word, a phrase or a reference which I will have to look up',[26] Steiner uses the word *ptyx*, from the famously difficult sonnet 'Ses purs ongles très haut' (pp.68-9): 'To this day, Mallarmé's famous *ptyx*, one of the indispensable sovereign rhymes in the sonnet on *ix*, appears neither in the Littré nor in the *Nouveau Larousse* (but it *can* be unmasked, via Greek and via liturgical art and this, as we shall see, is a key point)' (p.59).

The reader of Mallarmé could quote a restricted number of instances of such terms: *septuor, lampadophore* in the same poem, but also *nonchaloir, hoir* and *tisonne*. The occasional use of rare words is not by any means the most important or relevant aspect of Mallarmé's difficulty. Where the poet uses archaic terms, the context often justifies his choice, and the difficulty is explained by the poet's attempt 'to anchor the particular word in the dynamic mould of its own history, enriching the core of its present definition with the echo and alloy of previous use' (p.21). Mallarmé has expressed a very similar view in his 'Notes':

> Enfin - les mots ont plusieurs sens, sinon on s'entendrait toujours - nous en profiterons - et pour leur sens principal,

---

[26] Steiner sees contingent difficulty as one that can always be solved if the reader is in possession of the appropriate tools: 'this is a word, a phrase or a reference which I will have to look up. In the total library, in the *collectanae* and *summa summarum* of all things, I can do just that. And find that a *ptyx* is a conch.' *On Difficulty and Other Essays,* 1978, p.27.

INTRODUCTION: THE POETICS OF THE PROSAIC   29

> nous chercherons quel effet ils nous produiraient prononcés par la voix intérieure de notre esprit, déposée par la fréquentation des livres du passé (Science, Pascal), si cet effet s'éloigne de celui qu'il nous fait de nos jours [OC, 852].

In the well-known 'Le Tombeau d'Edgar Poe' [P, 60][27] Mallarmé uses *oyant*, anchoring not only the word, but also the centuries of language use into a constantly evolving past, and highlighting by an appropriate and strategic use of 'contingent difficulty' the memorable simplicity of the following line: 'Donner un sens plus pur aux mots de la tribu'. Contingent difficulty is also linked by Steiner to the use of polysemic terms, which enrich and complexify the linguistic tissue and is one of the cornerstones of poetic writing. The definition given by Steiner can easily be applied to Mallarmé's poetry and prose:

> An energized field of association and connotation, of overtones and undertones, of rebus and homophone, surround its motion, and break from it in the context of collision (words speak not only to the ear, but to the eye and even to the touch). Multiplicity of meaning, 'enclosedness', are the rule rather than the exception.' (p.21)

Mallarmé himself, as a poet and theorist of language, has described words in not dissimilar terms, exploring the various aspects of their complexity and their relationships:

> Les mots, d'eux-mêmes, s'exaltent à mainte facette reconnue la plus rare ou valant pour l'esprit, centre de suspens vibratoire; qui les perçoit indépendamment de la suite ordinaire, projetés, en parois de grotte, tant que dure leur mobilité ou principe, étant ce qui ne se dit pas du discours: prompts tous, avant extinction, à une réciprocité de feux distante ou présentée de biais comme contingence. [OC, 386][28]

Up to this point, it is clear that Steiner's category of difficulty is applicable to Mallarmé's work. Indeed the concept of

---

[27] All quotes from Mallarmé's verse are taken from *Poésies* (Gallimard, 1992).

[28] All quotes from Mallarmé's prose works are taken from *Œuvres Complètes* (Pléiade ed., Gallimard, 1945).

contingency as linked to that of language and of words is central to both Mallarmé's fascinated view of the dynamic effect of words, and to Steiner's apprehension of one form of linguistic difficulties, 'the most visible, they stick like burrs to the fabric of the text' (p.27). Both perceive words in terms of movements, changes, transformations, and mystery but also as visual and tactile. 'The context of collision' is a violent image that Mallarmé has himself used in the well-known 'Crise de vers' [OC, 360-8]: 'L'œuvre pure implique la disparition élocutoire du poète, qui cède l'initiative aux mots, par le heurt de leur inégalité mobilisés'. Where it becomes more problematic is in Steiner's distinction between poetry and prose: 'lexical resistance is the armature of meaning, guarding the poem from the necessary commonalties of prose.' (p.21) Although on a superficial level, the sentiments expressed might well appear similar to some expressed by Mallarmé in early texts, the poet's prose is fully as 'armoured' as his poetry, and his poetry displays the same 'commonalties' as his prose if one studies their respective lexes. The category of contingent difficulty is therefore applicable just as much to Mallarmé's prose as to his poetry, the more interesting point being the way in which his texts combine the other categories that Steiner elaborates: modal, tactical and ontological.

Modal difficulties are in many ways less clear to detect and define, partly because they 'lie with the beholder' (p.33) and belong therefore to the realm of the personal sensibility of the reader, and partly because Steiner himself is at pains to give a clear account of the difficulties: they function 'centrally', they are not attached to the use of one single archaic term or obscure reference, but are evaluated according to our comprehension and response to the poem, 'the operative distinction between surface understanding or paraphrase on the one hand, and penetrative comprehension on the other' (p.29). There is of course a sense in which the vast majority of Mallarmé's œuvre falls into this category. His poems and his prose works are generally demanding, exacting from the reader extensive and sustained participation. If we do not acknowledge the central difficulty of many of his writings, we might well run the risk of being described by Mallarmé as someone who doesn't know how to read.[29] The sonnet 'Mes bouquins refermés' [P, 72][30] displays examples both of contingent and of modal difficulties: *Paphos*,

---

[29] 'Je préfère, devant l'agression, rétorquer que des contemporains ne savent pas lire' [OC, 386].

[30] The sonnet was published in 1887 in *La Revue Indépendante*.

Hyacinthe, nénie, guivre and *tisonne* might all need some research and elucidation. Once the careful reader has taken that step, he or she is still confronted with a sense of difficulty. This, according to Steiner, could be described as modal, 'the poem in front of us articulates a stance towards human conditions which we find essentially inaccessible or alien' (p.28). The poem is difficult not because of the lexis, not even because of syntactical ambiguities, but because it fails to provoke in the reader a deep and confident sense of full understanding. Are the experiences described in the poem so removed from everyday life that they are no longer of any relevance to the twentieth-century reader?

Yet the interaction between imagination and the routine of home on a winter's day are clearly identifiable as part of ordinary life, or at least as part of the poet's ordinary life. The difficulty stems from the complex currents and undercurrents, tensions and paradoxes that run under a seemingly calm linguistic surface. The relationship between absence and presence, between the supreme power of the imagination to make real the unreal, and to abstract the present whilst retaining a sense of chronology and context create in the reader an uneasy and disorientating awareness of his or her exclusion from the private, whether real or unreal, world of the poet, who, whilst ostensibly opening windows into his dreams, immediately shuts them again in the face of the bemused onlooker. The difficulty resides in the mode, or even the mood of the poem, which sets up alternative ways of living, dreaming and reading parallel to those of the everyday world.

The third category of difficulty identified by Steiner is described as 'tactical': 'it is the poet's aim to charge with supreme intensity and genuineness of feeling a body of language, to "make new" his text in the most durable sense of illuminative, penetrative insight' (p.34). Indeed this ambition cannot find better expression than Mallarmé's 'donner un sens plus pur aux mots de la tribu'. As a labourer whose material is words, Mallarmé worked relentlessly at just that kind of difficulty, not to eradicate it but to exploit it, not necessarily to invent new words but to use 'les mots, aptes, quotidiens'[31] in innovative ways and in relationships that would reveal unusual facets. The task of the poet is to re-energise, to inject new vitality into ordinary syntax and lexis:

---

[31] 'Surprendre habituellement cela, le marquer, me frappe comme une obligation de qui déchaîna l'Infini; dont le rythme, parmi les touches du clavier verbal, se rend, comme sous l'interrogation d'un doigté, à l'emploi des mots, aptes, quotidiens'. [OC, 648].

> He will reanimate lexical and grammatical resources that have fallen out of use. He will melt and inflect words into neological shapes. He will labour to undermine, through distortion, through hyperbolic augment, through elision and displacement, the banal and constricting determinations of ordinary, public syntax. (p.35)

This of course applies to Mallarmé's poetry and to his prose. Yet he always saw himself as *syntaxier*, keen to respect the 'guarantee' offered by grammar: '[...]il faut une garantie - / La Syntaxe' [OC, 385], whilst admitting that '[...]l'artifice excelle pour convaincre', and acknowledging that 'Le débat - que l'évidence moyenne nécessaire dévie en un détail, reste de grammairiens.' [OC, 386] The category of tactical difficulty is displayed in the following quote taken from the 'Médaillons et portraits' and written in honour of Villiers de l'Isle-Adam:

> Sait-on ce que c'est qu'écrire? Une ancienne et très vague mais jalouse pratique, dont gît le sens au mystère du cœur. Qui l'accomplit, intégralement, se retranche.
> Autant, par ouï-dire, que rien existe et soi, spécialement, au reflet de la divinité éparse: c'est, ce jeu insensé d'écrire, s'arroger, en vertu d'un doute - la goutte d'encre apparentée à la nuit sublime - quelque devoir de tout recréer, avec des réminiscences, pour avérer qu'on est bien là où l'on doit être (parce que, permettez-moi d'exprimer cette appréhension, demeure une incertitude). Un à un, chacun de nos orgueils, les susciter, dans leur antériorité et voir. Autrement, si ce n'était cela, une sommation au monde qu'il égale sa hantise à de riches postulats chiffrés, en tant que sa loi, sur le papier blême de tant d'audace - je crois, vraiment, qu'il y aurait duperie, à presque le suicide.[32] [OC, 481]

There are no contingent difficulties and arguably no modal difficulties. But the number of tactical difficulties is high. This has mainly to do with the use of ellipsis, condensation, a number of enclaves, a predominance of the infinitive and generally a non-linear use of syntax. What is the grammatical function of *soi*? Why is the subject inverted in 'demeure une incertitude'? Why is there

---

[32] This was a conference given six times in Belgium in 1890, and eventually in Paris at Berthe Morisot's. It was published in *L'Art Moderne* in Brussels on 16 February 1890.

INTRODUCTION: THE POETICS OF THE PROSAIC

no conjugated verb in the following sentence? How do we construct or reconstruct the last sentence? Mallarmé has made some clear choices in this extract: on the one hand a refusal to conform to a linear syntax, and to express his thoughts within the ordinary conventions of French grammar. On the other hand, the unusual syntax and the carefully worded-sentences (we must remember that the tribute was read aloud at a conference) re-enact in their complexity the work of the writer, its difficulties, its uncertainties, and fittingly express the struggle of Villiers' life. The deliberate choice of tactical difficulty seeks in this case not to obscure the meaning of the tribute or to exclude the reader from full comprehension, but on the contrary to demonstrate within language itself the doubts and the hardships that assailed a fellow-writer, and by extension all writers.

Steiner proposes as a last category of difficulty 'ontological difficulty'. This can only be understood in the context of a 'contract of ultimate or preponderant intelligibility between poet and reader, between text and meaning' (p.40). The difficulty is really a philosophical one, as it questions a number of generally accepted presuppositions: that a written work has first and foremost a communicative function and must be accessible to a majority of readers. 'Ontological difficulties confront us with blank questions about the nature of human speech, about the status and significance, about the necessity and purpose of the construct which we have, with more or less rough and ready consensus, come to perceive as a poem.' (p.41) In Mallarmé's *Un Coup de dés*, we have a fine example of ontological difficulty, an experimental attempt to question a number of preconceptions about the nature of language and poetry, of communication or its eventual failure. Mallarmé's preface to the poem opens up with a significant and revealing appeal to the reader:

> *J'aimerais qu'on ne lût pas cette Note ou que parcourue, même on l'oubliât; elle apprend, au Lecteur habile, peu de chose situé outre sa pénétration: mais peut troubler l'ingénu devant appliquer un regard aux premiers mots du Poëme pour que de suivants, disposés comme ils sont, l'amènent aux derniers, le tout sans nouveauté qu'un espacement de la lecture. Les "blancs" en effet, assument l'importance, frappent d'abord; la versification en exigea, comme silence alentour, ordinairement, au point qu'un morceau, lyrique ou de peu de pieds, occupe, au milieu, le*

> *tiers environ du feuillet: je ne transgresse cette mesure, seulement la disperse.*[33] [OC, 455]

Mallarmé is keen to underplay the innovative character of his poem, and to reassure his reader that he has not strictly abandoned the conventions of poetry writing. In a clear and uncharacteristic effort to explain his intentions to his reader, he also cleverly flatters him by implying that an astute reader will only need his or her own keen sensibility to read the poem. To an extent of course he is right, and Mallarmé's wish that the poem should be read like a musical score, *une partition*, will give the reader a hint as to the effect pursued. But this is not enough to turn a complexly experimental poem into a simple text. The difficulties of the poem belong to several categories: possibly contingent if one assumes that there might well be within the poem a number of references to treatises of alchemy or magic, to some of his own previous work, to the work of contemporary poets, to astronomy, possibly to Homer. It is also a prime example of modal difficulty, often leaving the reader (despite the reassuring words of the author) feeling alienated and disorientated not only by the pagination but by the sheer multiplicity of events and chronologies, and the number of characters that appear and disappear in what reads like a space odyssey or a cosmic shipwreck. The intricacies of the relationships between the words on the page well exceed the boundaries of syntax. All it seems to guarantee is that the superficial grammatical anarchy which appears to reign in *Un Coup de dés* does in fact 'vaincre le hasard mot par mot' in the meticulous positioning of each noun, verb, adjective and adverb, and that the tactical difficulty here is indeed due to the choices made by a supremely clever word strategist in control of his material.

The ontological difficulties in the poem are of several types: a questioning of the nature of language in general and poetry in particular, with reference to an ongoing debate in Mallarmé's mind about the respective qualities of music and poetry, and his attempt to appropriate and claim the supremacy for poetry, an attempt to go beyond the limits of conventions and to push back some of the accepted barriers, a quest for a new, more meaningful and more crafted form of writing, an exploration of space and the effect of a spatialisation of words, a reflection on the interaction of the visual, the poetic and the philosophical.

---

[33] In italics in the text.

If we accept that the difficulty of Mallarmé's texts is diverse, and can be helpfully analysed and classified according to Steiner's taxonomy of difficulty, how can we relate the complex interaction of different categories of difficulties with the concept of the ordinary? Do difficulty and the everyday necessarily exclude each other? And is the self-removal from the world of the ordinary, often through the deliberate exploitation of one or more of the categories of difficulties described earlier necessarily and always a symptom of profound antipathy and complete and final avoidance?

IV. The challenges of the concept of the ordinary as applied in Mallarmé's work

The work of the poet is not so much one of self-removal from everyday life as one of transmutation, even in a poetry that could be described as the most removed from the ordinary, Surrealism. The goal both for Mallarmé and the Surrealists, if it is couched in very different language, has similarities: the one seeks a Hegelian absolute, the other what is called in the *Manifesto* 'real life'. In his preface to Lefèbvre's *Critique of Everyday Life,* Michel Trebitsch writes:

> In the Surrealist experience, in the revolt of the poetic against the 'prose of the world', there is the idea that subverting the everyday will open the way to what, on its first page, the *Manifesto of Surrealism* calls 'real life' (p.xx).

What seems to be the most outrageous subversion of the everyday world and perception, attained by systematically looking for the surprising, the marvellous, the extraordinary, proves in the end to be a detour, a tortuous and fascinating way back to reality: 'Ce qui importe dans le fantastique, c'est qu'il n'y a plus de fantastique, il n'y a plus que le réel', writes André Breton in *Les Manifestes du Surréalisme.*[34] The circle is complete, and yet reality rediscovered via the fantastic cannot be exactly the same reality as the initial point of departure. The discovery, and it is one of importance, is that the fantastic is indeed part of everyday life, invasive and interfused. The poetic game has uncovered one of the structuring features of the everyday world: its alien quality, 'the surrealism of the habitual, the sense of the human as

---

[34] André Breton, *Les Manifestes du surréalisme* (Paris: Editions du Sagittaire, 1946) note 1 p.30.

inherently strange, say unstable, its quotidian as forever fantastic' writes Cavell.³⁵ It is tempting to attribute Mallarmé with exactly the same process, but his *démarche*, if it is familiar with detours, alternative routes and even shortcuts in his use of extraordinarily condensed language is one that depends far more on the artist as organising power and simplifier of reality. Nor did Mallarmé subscribe to his forebears' view of reality. Chisholm writes:

> His predecessors, not entirely excluding Baudelaire, had taken the physical world for granted, as something existing independently of mind. The Romantics did indeed recognize a relationship between objects and consciousness, but they often looked on nature as an extension and magnification of their own ego, whereas Mallarmé adopted a diametrically opposite view-point; for him, consciousness was the one thing that gave nature coherent form and therefore made it real.³⁶

Both fantasy and reality, ordinary and strange are part of the everyday world. The everyday world is therefore not a given, but a task, a reconstruction in the Cavellian sense, a restoration, a re-creation. It is in some of Mallarmé's descendants, the poets of the OuLiPo, for instance, that we can usefully and comparatively trace, in their extreme removal from reality, the way Mallarmé related to everyday life, how he fused the phenomenal world and the absolute, and the risks inherent to such a project. Raymond Queneau and George Perec, in developing and playing with abstract patterns, went much further than Mallarmé in taking poetry away from the routine of everyday life. The problems and successes of their work are often obvious. The risk of total unintelligibility and ultimate vacancy is ever present. Indeed the negative, damaging side of extreme removal from the ordinary world, in the discipline of philosophy of mathematics, for instance, could be illustrated by the example of Bertrand Russell, of whom it is biographically reported that he felt permanently scarred because of the level of abstraction which he had reached. The severing from ordinary life left him with the inability to fully re-integrate the everyday. This frightening experience of vacancy, described earlier by Bonnefoy, seems to be one of the prices to pay for self-removal from the world of the everyday.

---

35 Stanley Cavell, *The Quest of the Ordinary: Lines on Skepticism and Romanticism* (Chicago, London: University of Chicago Press, 1988) p.118.
36 A.R.Chisholm, *Mallarmé's Grand Œuvre*, p.158.

INTRODUCTION: THE POETICS OF THE PROSAIC   37

Mallarmé's poetry is of course riddled with such negatively epiphanic moments, sudden awareness of void, of nothingness, dissolution, disappearance, and vacancy. We do not feel, as with the poetry of Vigny, for example, in *La Maison du berger*,[37] that the poet takes us back to a reality that we already know, that we are reintegrating a familiar world, albeit re-worked by the poet. Our own sense of security is not challenged and disturbed in the way it is when reading Mallarmean poetry. We experience a satisfying sense of knowing where the starting-point was and of finding our way back. And yet the difficulties, contradictions and ambiguities of Mallarmé have more to do with the structure of reality itself than with a failure on the part of the poet to engage with reality. For Bertrand Marchal, in his *Lecture de Mallarmé*,

> Mallarmé n'est pas de ceux qui dissertent sur le peu de réalité de la réalité; il y a au contraire réalisme profond. Il sait le poids des choses et l'inconsistance du rêve (p.298).

The ways to and from the world of the ordinary, it seems, are many, all leading away or back to an everyday which we have demonstrated is far from simple and perfectly and immediately knowable, but many-layered, veiled by a form of Heideggerian concealment and ultimately ambiguous. Ambiguity is seen by Lefèbvre as yet another category of everyday life, and perhaps an essential category. The fact that Mallarmé's work bears the stamp of ambiguity can be interpreted not as a sign of divorce from the everyday world but as a sign that, at the level of structure and organisation, poetic and everyday display resemblances.

At the level of the language, it is often the syntax, in its ambiguity, that mirrors and reasserts the claims of everyday life, a way of keeping in contact with the language of the tribe, 'les mots de la tribu', whilst at the same time experimenting and renewing its usage to the point of almost rewriting French grammar (and hence enabling Jacques Scherer to write a *Grammaire de Mallarmé*). It is syntax which anchors the text in the spatio-temporal, which allows for the micro-movements of 'Sainte' [P, 41] and for the everyday drama and the cosmic drama to merge in 'Le vierge, le vivace et le bel aujourd'hui' [P, 57]. Ordinary, linear time is only one aspect of temporality, a process that describes only one aspect of time. Mallarmé's poetry often evokes

---

[37] Vigny, *Œuvres complètes*, (Gallimard: Bibliothèque de la Pléiade, 1986), pp.119-28.

time as a fragmented multiplicity of instants, a yearning for simultaneity, which could express a fear of the objective, uniform passage of time. His preference for the use of substantives rather than verbs, or for very static verbs, (in 'Sainte' the main verb is simply *est*) is one way in which Mallarmé manipulates time sense. In 'Le vierge, le vivace et le bel aujourd'hui', ordinary time is treated from every possible angle, at every possible level: the *temps logique* of the poem on the page, the *temps vécu* of the swan's experience, the inner and outer perception of temporality, moving backwards and forwards from a concrete picture of a present experience back into a lost paradise and springing forward into a future that extends into eternity. The whole structure of the poem is dependent on this complex treatment of time, from the role of memory and the intrusion of the past into the present, to a re-interpretation of the present in the light of that past and of an immediate as well as hypothetical and eternal future.

'La poésie n'est rien d'autre, au plus vif de son inquiétude, qu'un acte de connaissance' writes Bonnefoy in *La Présence et l'image* (1983, p.51). Poetry is described as a way to know and apprehend the world of the phenomenal, the emotional and the spiritual. The quest of knowledge is one of its central functions. This is where some of the concepts used in the philosophy of science, for instance, as they appear in Thomas S.Kuhn's seminal work *The Structure of Scientific Revolutions* (1970), can help not only to extend our vocabulary as far as describing some of the processes present in the reconstruction and representation of reality in the poetic and the everyday world is concerned, but also to formulate a new approach to the description of space in poetry, for example. Mathematical imagination and poetic imagination seem at first remote from each other. Yet both in a work such as *Un Coup de dés* and in the work of non-Euclidean mathematicians, three-dimensional space is problematised. If it is Euclidean space, which describes the properties of everyday space, and is therefore perceived as real, it is non-Euclidean geometry, which has been used to develop the theory of relativity, a geometry not based on everyday experience but on an imaginative rethinking of models. *Un Coup de dés* frustrates our concepts of literary space. One needs of course to acknowledge the great differences between mathematics and poetry: geometrical imagination is rooted in arduous and meticulous work, the demands of which are recognised and quite different to the work involved in the production of poetic metaphoric worlds. And yet some of the criteria applied to poetry are also applied to geometry. Scientists have been known to call their theorems beautiful, when theory has been able to go back to the substructure of quotidian living, to explain our everyday experience. From an initial movement away from the ordinary world, it finds a route back in a rhythmical pattern characteristic both of the artistic and the scientific domain. The investment in the investigative process is an emotional one which, beyond the major differences, aligns both scientific and poetic imagination with ordinary perception.

Central to both is the recognition that metaphor and reality are two inseparable halves of the cognitive and investigative process. Mary B. Hesse, in *The Construction of Reality* (1986), argues that not only poetry, religion and myths for instance, make extensive use of metaphor and symbol, but that all language, including scientific language is metaphorical. She gives metaphor cognitive status, a status reflecting the facts of ambiguity and change in language, of inadequacies and complexities which are also a source of poetic creativity. The 'puissance infirme du langage' that Bonnefoy alludes to in his *Entretiens sur la poésie* is present both in science and in poetry, two fields of human activity described as 'two extremes of a continuum with regard to types of controlled interpretation of their various linguistic and symbolic resources' by Hesse.[38]

The understanding and describing of the phenomenal world is indeed a common agenda both for poetic and scientific experiment. Whether the poet explores space, as in *Un Coup de dés*, for example, setting artistic space against locomotive space, seeking to explore the complexities of a reality which also concerns a science such as topology, or whether he grapples with the problems of expressing the various facets of time in its present, futurity, retrospection and simultaneity, the poet also rejoins the scientist in his concern with structures and organisation, his struggle with matter, chaos and void. The last line of 'Sainte', for example, is poised and balanced in quasi-mathematical, equation-like clarity. *Un Coup de dés* already questions the traditional mechanistic paradigm that is only recently being challenged by alternative scientific paradigms. In an age when the most popular games are called 'virtual reality', where illusion and the real world are expected to merge and overlap in the closest possible way to provide an escape from 'real reality', the claims of poetry as well as science are equally acceptable as constructors, or de-constructors of reality and of the ordinary. The Surrealists' way to

---

[38] Arbid and Hesse, *The Construction of Reality* (Cambridge University Press, 1986), p.181.

'une sorte de réalité absolue' as described by Breton[39] via total removal from the everyday world is in a way as legitimate as the scientist's or the mathematician's equally removed approach, and if one might argue that the resulting dimension is a kind of surreality or anti-reality which has little to do with the ordinary, the very contrast and discrepancy promotes the everyday as a valid tool acting as a revelator, a point of departure and possibly an eventual point of arrival.

The dimension of the everyday as it appears from a scientific and from a poetic point of view plays a role which is often understated or overlooked. In the psychoanalytical field, Bruno Bettelheim deliberately re-reads Freud with an emphasis towards an everyday rather than a scientific experience. His emphasis on Freud's everyday vocabulary privileges an aspect of Freud's writing which has often been completely obscured in a deliberate attempt to make his language more scientific, particularly in translation. Freud's perception of the ordinary fabric of life and experience showing the unconscious as intermittently visible provides yet another helpful concept with which to analyse both the ordinary and the poetic: intermittence of clarity and mystery is one recurring feature of Mallarmean writing. The line before the limpid and well known 'donner un sens plus pur aux mots de la tribu' in 'Le Tombeau d'Edgar Poe' [P, 60] has indeed all the contrastive complexity that will lend memorability to the alexandrine, and underline its clarity. As Leo Bersani, in *The Death of Stéphane Mallarmé* (1982), somewhat optimistically writes:

> We should, I think, find him [Mallarmé] close to the most familiar moves of ordinary consciousness. His writing is really neither hermetic nor exotic; indeed Mallarmé even re-introduces us to what might be called the energetic domesticity of desiring representations, a domesticity which no amount of exegesis will tame (p.ix).

Indeed the sense of mystery, which is, undoubtedly, present in Mallarmé's work is not directly interpretable as obscurity. Not only does Mallarmé as a craftsman, aware of the 'gloire ardente du métier'[40] stay in touch with the imperatives of his material, that is words, he also builds into his poetry the various concrete facets of reality by using much concrete vocabulary.

---

[39] Breton, *Les manifestes du surréalisme*, p.28.
[40] In 'Toast funèbre', [P, 42], line 12.

Mallarmé's use of artifice is far more than 'une esthétisation du quotidien'.[41] In 'Hérodiade', for example, a work he prized above any other, the linguistic procedures and the thematic repertoire interact in a way which is both paradoxical, shot through with contradictions, and harmonious. The tension which is sustained to a high degree throughout the poem has the effect of pulling the reader in two opposite directions: a feeling of strangeness, and alienation, of removal from the ordinary, but also a sense that this is nevertheless one expression of someone else's perception of everyday life in its endless circularity, a recognition of a basic and unavoidable set of choices and questions worked into the very structure and diction of the poem. Bonnefoy comments:

> Et certes, ce qu'il veut susciter dans ce poème, ce qu'il veut y ouvrir à la pénétration poétique, c'est bien la réalité comme telle, si même il l'emblématise une fois de plus dans l'historique par une figure de femme.[42]

We are aware of the sheer materiality of the poem, as we are in 'Le vierge, le vivace et le bel aujourd'hui'. Malcolm Bowie writes in *Mallarmé and the Art of Being Difficult*:

> Awesome generalities are checked, kept in focus and given delicate gradations of sensuous appeal by single complex image: the image not of a poet with the emblems of his craft, but of the white plumes and the muscular neck of an ice-bound swan. This is where Mallarmé begins and where his finely differentiated debate finds its equilibrium (p.13).

Mallarmé's work is indeed dependent on objects, often banal objects, even if they are vaporised or if they disappear. If the familiar object is rendered extraordinary in an unfamiliar environment, as in 'Sainte' where the not unusual *harpe* proves to be the wing of an angel, le *plumage instrumental,* the opposite process also occurs: the *lampadophore*, the *ptyx*, the *septuor* take on an almost familiar resonance in the context of the 'Sonnet en-yx' [P, 59].

---

[41] Michel Lemaire, *Le Dandysme de Baudelaire à nos jours* (Montréal: Presses de l'Université de Montréal, 1978), p.78.
[42] Preface of Yves Bonnefoy in the Gallimard edition of *Poésies de Stéphane Mallarmé*, p. xiii.

V. Departures from the ordinary in Mallarmé's work
The concept of the ordinary as apprehension of the world and as metaphysical postulate will help to light Mallarmé's own use of the everyday world, either in his images of banal objects, his use of ordinary vocabulary or his adherence to orthodox syntax. Nevertheless, how do we account for the spectacular departures from the ordinary for which Mallarmé is renowned? We have already analysed the variety of difficulties (using Steiner's taxonomy) that account for some of the departures. Moments of revelation present within the ordinary fabric of life are yet another possible answer and a Mallarmean characteristic. The Romantic theme of the transfiguration of the ordinary world and experience was indeed a common one, with the metaphor of alchemy recurring in many works. But this is quite different to the concept of epiphanic moments woven into the fabric of the ordinary. The resulting synthesis, often ambiguous and complex, displays the qualities not of an altogether new and alien product but of a disorientating mixture of the banal and the extraordinary. This everydayness encompasses both the seamless texture of the quotidian, not as simple background but as integral part of man, and also the element of extraordinary event and perception, of revelation, of mystery. For Heidegger, the uncanny, the extraordinary is always present just beneath the surface of the familiar. One needs nevertheless to break through the surface of concealment and refusal to come face to face with the reality of the familiar: its unfamiliarity. Mallarmé's expression of his own experience of the ordinary is closer to Freud's model of the intermittent visibility of the unconscious, with spectacular textual departures from ordinary syntax or lexis as an intermittent appearance of nodal points of difficulty and tension. This would bring together and transform what seem to be antithetical and mutually exclusive aspects of experience.

Formulating a definition of the quotidian, in the poetic realm or in any other realm also leads, as we have already remarked, to an exploration of what appears to be its antithesis: the extraordinary, the mysterious, the uncanny. Drawing on Heideggerian concepts, Cavell writes:

> The ambiguity in the idea of the unnatural matches an ambiguity in the idea of the ordinary as what the natural (in language) reveals. The ambiguity concerns whether the ordinary, or say the human habitat, is something that thinking is to take us back to (as Wittgenstein seems to

INTRODUCTION: THE POETICS OF THE PROSAIC

imagine), or something thinking is to take us onwards to (as Heidegger seems to imagine).[43]

The question with Mallarmean poetry is also one of moving in two opposite directions: we move from the ordinary to the mysterious as in 'Sainte' for instance, only to find in 'Tout orgueil fume-t-il du soir' that we move back to the familiar, but a familiar world that has revealed in its very banality a potential for transformation and strangeness which contains frightening possibilities. This exemplifies, in the words of Naomi Segal, 'the banal object in which there lurks a perpetually potential ability to metamorphosis. These are everyday, ordinary-looking objects, but they are infinitely threatening'.[44] If the ordinary contains within it the potential for positive, creative epiphany, 'le mystère qui nous fait nous émerveiller de la chose, de l'événement le plus ordinaire' in the words of Bonnefoy, the 'extase pur' of the Chinese artist in 'Las de l'amer repos', 'l'ivresse belle' in 'Salut', it also contains, hidden in the very fabric of the banal, the destructive and the vacant. We move towards moments of impending catastrophe when ordinary experience proves to be disempowering and banality threatens to engulf and alienate, as in 'Brise marine'.

Which particular aspects of Mallarmé's writing will benefit most interestingly from a relocation of the concept of the ordinary within the text, a concept which has gained richness, complexity and diversity from a close examination and from the study of a number of its theoreticians? What is the link between what seems to be just one aspect of reality, and the words on the page of *Poésies* or *Divagations*?

It will indeed be with the words on the page, the choices in lexis and syntactic structures, and the use of ordinary language within poetry and prose that this project is concerned. The everyday experienced as life, world and concept not only inhabits language, language also inhabits the everyday. Mallarmé's use of language offers a particularly fascinating challenge, both in terms of vocabulary and syntax. At the level of lexis, the characteristic Mallarmean use of straightforward vocabulary with spectacular exceptions warrants particular attention, as does the syntax.

---

[43] Stanley Cavell, *The Quest of the Ordinary: Lines on Skepticism and Romanticism*, p. 149.

[44] Naomi Segal, *The Banal Object: Themes and Thematics in Proust, Rilke, Hofmansthal and Sartre* (London: Institute of Germanic Studies, Bithell Series of Dissertations, 1981), p. 70.

Mallarmé of course described himself as a great *syntaxier*,[45] and here again we find a teasing mixture of unusual and everyday usage. His use of metaphor reflects the tension between familiar and unfamiliar worlds, between a need to make the world more habitable, and a desire to escape from it. As a consequence, the poet constructs a complex rhetoric about the ordinary, particularly in the prose works and the journalistic writings. It is within these areas of interest which arise from the Mallarmé corpus of texts that the concept of the ordinary acquires its edge, its focus and its usefulness as a tool for the study of a rich and puzzling literary *œuvre*.

VI. The ordinary in poetry and Mallarmé's indebtedness to Baudelaire

When reflecting on Mallarmé's involvement in and with the world of the everyday, it would be near impossible to understand how he could have written and explored the themes he chose to focus on without the galvanic shock of his early encounters with contemporary poets, in particular with Baudelaire.[46] He was part of a powerful contemporary movement which swept like a wave over the poet and his work, and is the essence of modernity. As Millan points out in his biography of Mallarmé, the desire to be part of a modern trend was '[...] a major preoccupation of Mallarmé's mature works: a quest for something modern to replace the currently outmoded myths and rituals of the past'.[47] The exploration of the ordinary, reinvesting it with a new 'divine' quality, is apparent not only in literature but also in art (see Bonnard,[48] for instance) and highlights within the

---

[45] The term *syntaxier* is attributed to Mallarmé by Maurice Guillemot: '[...] si l'on arrive avec une âme vierge, neuve, on s'aperçoit alors que je suis profondément et scrupuleusement syntaxier, que mon écriture est dépourvue d'obscurité, que ma phrase est ce qu'elle doit être et être pour toujours...' in *Villégiatures d'Artistes* (Flammarion, 1898), quoted in Mondor's *Vie de Mallarmé*, pp.506-7.

[46] The Baudelaire secondary bibliographical corpus is now so extensive that I am not proposing in this brief survey to look at other contributions.

[47] Gordon Millan, *Mallarmé: A Throw of the Dice*, p.34.

[48] Pierre Bonnard (1867-1947) was part of the modern trend and its interest in everyday life. In the arts as well as in literature, this focus on the ordinary is evident. Bonnard for instance majored in painting interiors, including bathrooms. He reinvented this most banal of places, painting it as laboratory, temple to hygiene, space where unusual optical effects take place, always emphasising the sense of a shifting and constantly renewable ordinary, posing yet again the question of the nature of the everyday, which on the one hand has

ordinary the sense of the religious. We are back to a Taylorian 'good life', where contemplation finds sustenance within the ordinary environment. Although Mallarmé himself seeks to resist this trend, or at least seems to in the later sonnets and the *Coup de dés*, he is part of the historical flux, as is Baudelaire, a flux which ends with Ponge and the life of the end of the second millennium, where we escape from our own ordinary into other people's ordinary via Eastenders and Coronation Street. Stimulated by the irresistible trend, which started in the nineteenth century, the ordinary has now become the privileged subject and object of art, literature and film, making it the quintessential modern theme. It is indeed an indication of the richness of Mallarmé's writing that he takes us right into the heart of modernity with a specific and unique contribution amongst the contemporary trends, such as Naturalism for instance, that seek to rehabilitate the ordinary against the Romantic stance. He was a great admirer of Zola, as his answer to Jules Huret' *enquête* clearly indicates:

> J'ai une grande admiration pour Zola. Il a fait moins, à vrai dire, de véritable littérature que de l'art évocatoire, en se servant, le moins qu'il est possible, des éléments littéraires; il a pris les mots, c'est vrai, mais c'est tout; le reste provient de sa merveilleuse organisation et se répercute tout de suite dans l'esprit de la foule. Il a vraiment des qualités puissantes; [OC, 871]

Not only is he well aware of the social impact of Zola's novels, he also isolates a realist principle: an openly stated lack of self-reference, a will to describe reality in all its intricacies, richness and ugliness, in a form that immediately brings to the reader's mind the very object or person described:

> Son sens inouï de la vie, ses mouvements de foule, la peau de Nana, dont nous avons tous caressé le grain, tout cela peint en un prodigieux lavis, c'est l'œuvre d'une organisation vraiment admirable! [OC, 871]

This implies of course a real confidence in the solid materiality of things, in the unproblematic presence of an everyday that can be mastered as well as described by words which are themselves unproblematic. To this 'unquestioning' of the everyday and to

---

to be worked for because of its quality of strangeness, but also worked away from to try and escape from the oppressive solidity of things.

the prolific response of a Zola or a Flaubert, Mallarmé opposes his sense of the literary and his uncertainty vis-à-vis an ordinary that is just as present in absence and emptiness as in an accumulation of things and characters. And yet he is also able to distinguish the other side of realism and naturalism, the lyrical, the poetic, the romantic echoes which resonate clearly in *Madame Bovary*, in what he calls 'les grandes œuvres de Flaubert, des Goncourt et de Zola, qui sont des sortes de poëmes' [OC, 871]. Although his own writing was influenced by Romantic poets rather than Realist and Naturalist novelists, he was clearly aware of their impact on contemporary society as well as of their ambition to paint a larger picture of reality.

Mallarmé's own style, themes and approaches to the task of writing developed in the wake of formidably original poets, in particular Victor Hugo and Charles Baudelaire. It is inevitably within the literary folds of his predecessors that his own authorial originality evolves, and it is with a ready made set of inherited notions about the ordinary world that he moves on to explore the area of everyday life in ways, scriptural, philosophical, metaphorical and rhetorical which both acknowledge and disown his patrimony. As a sensitive, intelligent adolescent, it is unsurprising that he should have been greatly influenced by the most renowned poets of the time, and that he fell under a double spell. It is particularly in the area of his perception of the ordinary world, and use of the concept of the ordinary that I propose to trace the influence of these predecessors, in particular Baudelaire, in order to establish the measure and nature of Mallarmé's borrowing. I shall explore his indebtedness to the imaginative world of the poet in his relationship to the ordinary, not so much at the level of themes as at the level of the fabric of the verse and the complexity of the poet's response. The surface indications of borrowings, reworkings and further exploration of themes and approaches to the ordinary are necessarily betrayed by a use of common jargon, of clichés and stereotypes that can be traced back to the poet. This study will therefore be both comparative and contrastive, a combination of a diachronic and synchronic account of Mallarmé's grappling with the ordinary as theme and as method within the Baudelairian literary genealogy.

The ten poems published in the *Parnasse contemporain*[49] bear, to a greater or lesser extent, the marks of Mallarmé's early

---

[49] The ten poems published in *Le Parnasse Contemporain* on 12 May 1866 were: 'Les Fenêtres', 'Le Sonneur', 'A celle qui est tranquille', 'Vere Novo', 'L'Azur', 'Les Fleurs', 'Soupir', 'Brise Marine', 'A un pauvre', 'Épilogue'.

enthusiasm for Hugo's[50] and Baudelaire's[51] poetry. One is tempted to see in several of the poems, 'Le Guignon' [P, 4-5], 'Aumône' [P, 24-5] and 'Angoisse' [P, 15], for instance, a straight pastiche or paraphrase of Baudelaire, a testimony to Mallarmé's predictable admiration for a master of the craft. Some of the early poems, from *Entre quatre murs*[52] to some of the *Parnasse contemporain,* owe much to Hugo in the domain of imagery, syntax and versification. And yet Mallarmé's boundless initial reverence for both Hugo and Baudelaire, his adopting a set of notions of reality and a set of stereotypes on the poet and his relationship with the ordinary world is far from unadulterated borrowing. If he is indeed indebted to Hugo's and Baudelaire's imaginative worlds, to their approaches to reality, to their apprehension of the everyday and their perception of the poet's task, from the *Parnasse contemporain* onwards he does develop a diction, treatment of themes and network of metaphors which transforms the clichés and borrowings into uniquely Mallarmean, complex, multi-layered creations.

The relationship between the everyday and the poetic, between a reality experienced within the quotidian and a reality represented within the poetic undergoes a shift in the nineteenth century. The ordinary becomes an acceptable literary theme and its treatment is characterised by a relatively ordinary use of syntax and lexis. The adolescent Mallarmé was a self-avowed Lamartinian,[53] and it is perhaps with Lamartine in 'La Vigne et la

---

[50] For an account of Hugo's influence on Mallarmé's early poetry, see *The Early Mallarmé*, Austin Gill, particularly chapter 9 of vol. I.

[51] See L.J.Austin's 'Mallarmé et le Rêve du Livre' in *Mercure de France*, January-April 1953.

[52] Early poems written by Mallarmé in 1859-1860 when he was still at the Lycée in Sens. In volume I of *The Early Mallarmé*, Austin Gill writes: 'The title may be taken to refer to the walls of a class-room, but I believe a literary allusion is also intended, to the most engaging of Hugo's nature poems, 'Ce qui se passait aux Feuillantines en 1813'. I would suggest that the reference might be to the Baudelaire poem 'Sur le Tasse en prison' in *Les Fleurs du mal*: 'Ce rêveur que l'horreur de son logis réveille,/ Voilà bien ton emblème, Ame aux songes obscurs,/ Que le Réel étouffe entre ses quatre murs!' (p.182). The manuscript consists of forty-one pieces of verse, and is now at the Bibliothèque Jacques Doucet.

[53] See 'Autobiographie': '[...] d'âme lamartinienne avec un secret désir de remplacer, un jour, Béranger, parce que je l'avais rencontré dans une maison amie' [OC, 662].

maison'[54] in its dramatic recreation of undramatic events of ordinary human existence that the reality and the poetic potential of the quotidian are explored at length, and that the young Mallarmé's sensitivity is first awakened to the fertility of the concept. Sainte-Beuve[55] and later on Coppée[56] were already committed to exploring the poetic possibilities of the prosaic. We need therefore to replace Mallarmé firmly within a strongly developing tradition to gain an illuminating perspective on the poet's own response and choices to the ordinary world. 'Les Rayons jaunes',[57] Sainte-Beuve's masterpiece, has some of the elements of Mallarmé's 'Les Fenêtres' [P, 10-1] without the metaphysical dimension and the oneiric imagery. Sainte-Beuve's windows open on to a street peopled with 'ouvriers en habits de fête'[58] and do not reflect 'le matin chaste de l'infini'.[59] And

---

[54] In Œuvres Complètes (Gallimard: Bibliothèque de la Pléiade, 1963), pp.1484-94.

[55] For a study of Sainte-Beuve's writings and his influence, I shall refer the reader to Barlow's *Sainte-Beuve to Baudelaire: a Poetic Legacy*, 1964.

[56] See his 1872 poems, 'Les Humbles' in *Œuvres Complètes: Poésies* vol.I (Paris: Hébert, 1885), pp. 219-86. Mallarmé, who corresponded avec Coppée, also published one of his poems in *La Dernière Mode* in the seventh issue, on 6th December 1874. He also advertised the forthcoming publication in the sixth issue, dated 15 November 1874:

> Nombre des morceaux qui composent ce recueil prochain de François Coppée [*Le Cahier rouge*] ont été applaudis par des mains aristocratiques ou charitables dans les réunions de bienfaisance, véritables clubs des dames, avant de captiver, imprimés, le regard, à la clarté familière d'une lampe de boudoir. La sympathie reste la même; car le vers du jeune poète populaire, s'il frappe tout de suite et à jamais par la justesse de son intonation, supporte la rêverie et exhale, pour qui s'y appesantit ou s'y laisse aller, toute une atmosphère de sentiments rares: double don presque contradictoire des œuvres décidément parfaites! [OC, 803-4].

[57] For a study of 'Les Rayons jaunes', see the first two chapters of Barlow's *Sainte-Beuve to Baudelaire, a Poetic legacy*, pp. 3-58. Barlow ascribes to necessity Sainte-Beuve's choice of the intimate and the prosaic as subject matter for his poems, as 'the field of poetic distinction was largely occupied by three poetic giants, Lamartine, Hugo and Vigny [...]' (p.6). And Barlow continues: 'Sainte-Beuve saw the restricted field of his own poetic inspiration as in marked contrast with the lofty soarings of the lyric veterans' (p.7).

[58]   Les dimanches d'été, le soir, vers les six heures,
       Quand le peuple empressé déserte ses demeures
           Et va s'ébattre aux champs,

INTRODUCTION: THE POETICS OF THE PROSAIC   49

instead of turning his back on life ('tourner l'épaule à la vie'),[60] his solution is to mingle with ordinary people:

> je descends et bientôt dans la foule inconnue
> J'ai noyé mon chagrin.[61]

Mallarmé is clearly following a growing trend in nineteenth-century writing, and reworking at the level of theme, syntax and lexis, a set of concepts inherited from a number of predecessors. Mallarmé's fervent admiration for Baudelaire is reflected at several levels within his own early poems: choice of themes, vocabulary, use of Baudelairian correspondences. What one might call the Baudelairian phase (from 1859-65), also privileges the ordinary world as a major theme, treated either with Baudelaire's directness and vehemence as in 'Le Sonneur' [P, 18], or with an already uniquely personal use of both syntax and transformed and reworked Baudelairian style, as in 'Brise marine' [P, 22], for instance, where, below the borrowed stereotypes we discern a typically Mallarmean obliqueness. The young poet's uncertainties about his own poetic voice together with his unsurprising deference towards Baudelaire would seem to condemn him to the trap of borrowed diction and derivative language. But his own perception of reality, in its everyday manifestations, from his responses to spring in 'Renouveau' [P, 14] to his account of

---

> Ma persienne fermée, assis à ma fenêtre,
> Je regarde d'en haut passer et disparaître
>   Joyeux bourgeois, marchands,
>
> Ouvriers en habits de fête, au coeur plein d'aise;

in 'Vie, poésies et pensées de Joseph Delorme', *Poésies complètes*, vol.I (Paris: Lemerre, 1929), pp. 95-9.

[59] Stanza 7, l.4 of 'Les Fenêtres'.
[60] Stanza 7, l.2.
[61] In the one but last stanza:

> - Ainsi va ma pensée, et la nuit est venue;
> Je descends et bientôt dans la foule inconnue
>   J'ai noyé mon chagrin:
> Plus d'un bras me coudoie; on entre à la guinguette,
> On sort du cabaret; l'invalide en goguette
>   Chevrote un gai refrain.

In *Poésies complètes*, p. 99.

maternity in 'Don du poème' [P, 26] are departures from the Baudelairian imagery, themes and techniques, or adaptations which bear little resemblances to the master's work and can hardly be called paraphrases or pastiches. The differences go deeper than simple reworkings of similar imagery; they have to do with an attitude of mind, a way of handling the dimension of the ordinary that has entirely different qualities.

In the following analyses of poems by both poets, I shall focus on their attitude to the perceived vacuity of the ordinary world, a vacuity which constantly overshadows Mallarmé, but which stimulates in Baudelaire the energy to fight back. Against the interfusedness and obliqueness of Mallarmé, the straightforwardness and directness of Baudelaire make a striking contrast. The effect of those qualities inevitably affects the poets' perception of the ordinary, and their expression of a dimension that evokes such diverging responses. A comparative study of the poets' handling and use of everyday life within their own imaginative worlds, tracing back poetic genealogy specifically by focusing on the ordinary, and highlighting a number of important points of departure from straightforward imitation will emphasise a radical reorganisation of themes linked with the ordinary, the establishment of a new set of relationships between images, themes, and at a syntactical level, between words on the page. It will also establish their major similarity: both poets are risk-takers, willing to explore in new, innovative, extraordinary ways an everyday environment which is subject matter and inspiration for the one, referent and potential emptiness against which to measure the power of words for the other.

Mallarmé's early poems seem to be constructed around a set of borrowed notions, and quite obviously on the theme of spleen and ideal. 'Angoisse' [P, 15] has been described, and rightly so, as the most Baudelairian of Mallarmé's poems:[62] Woman is seen as a *bête impure*, accustomed to 'noirs mensonges'; the poet follows a Rousseauesque theme in 'Une nuit que j'étais près d'une affreuse juive', where the woman is attributed with 'majesté native'. The image is of vice or remorse eating away at the poet's heart. Baudelaire in 'L'Irréparable' (p.79) writes:

L'Irréparable ronge avec sa dent maudite

---

[62] See the article by L.J.Austin, 'Mallarmé disciple de Baudelaire: "Le parnasse Contemporain"', vol. 67, in *Revue d'Histoire Littéraire de la France*, 1967, pp.437-449.

Notre âme, piteux monument,

In both poems, the abstract is given concrete presence by everyday imagery and vocabulary. In 'Le Léthé' (p.164), Baudelaire expresses a desire for sleep as a means to total oblivion similar to Mallarmé's wish for 'le lourd sommeil sans songes':

> Je veux dormir! Dormir plutôt que vivre!
> [...]
> Pour engloutir mes sanglots apaisés
> Rien ne vaut l'abîme de la couche;
> L'oubli puissant habite sur ta bouche.

The presence of woman is seen by both poets as the provider of a state of complete oblivion and insensibility. But Mallarmé also draws on Baudelaire's 'Le gouffre' (p.201) when he describes his fear of death linked with the experience of night and sleep; Baudelaire writes: 'J'ai peur du sommeil comme on a peur d'un grand trou', and Mallarmé develops this into: 'Ayant peur de mourir lorsque je couche seul'. Both poets describe a common experience possibly going back to a childhood fear of the dark alleviated by a maternal presence. But already Mallarmé's approach to the description of what might well be seen as a common human fear is marked by a very Mallarmean recourse to the negative, presence suggested through absence ('les rideaux inconnus du remords' for example), by a reworking of the link between vice (in its archetypal meaning) sterility and fear of death, introducing into the Baudelairian pastiche a more developed account of a common fear of solitude.

The reformulation of Baudelairian themes is also apparent in 'Le Guignon' [P, 4-5], concerned as it is with a major Baudelairian theme of the poet and his relationship with the ordinary world. Here it is the syntax which already bears the marks of Mallarmean uniqueness and creativity, despite a generally Baudelairian lexicon: the use of a generalising singular ('le pied dans nos chemins'), of substantivised adjectives ('le nu de son glaive'), and a typically Mallarmean complement of the adjective ('ces héros excédés de malaises badins'). There is already a hint of Mallarmean complexity and obscurity which has been noted in a number of exegetical studies of the poem.[63] The 'rois de l'azur' of Baudelaire's 'L'Albatros' (p.38), appearing in

---

[63] See Thibaudet, *La Poésie de Stéphane Mallarmé*, p.32; Mondor, *Vie de Mallarmé*, p.37.

'Le Guignon' as 'mendieurs d'azur', and the clearly allegorical pattern of many of Baudelaire's poems, including the well-known 'Le Cygne' (p.107) are transformed by a satirical network of images which end not in a second comparative term as in many of Baudelaire's sonnets, but with a kind of 'morale', or rather 'anti-morale' as found at the end of a fable, for instance. 'Le Guignon' ends with a deprecating and ironic reference to a real poet (Nerval) and his all too real suicide. The last line of the poem, set as it is in isolation and in opposition to the *terza rima* verses, has the deflating and sobering quality of a brutal return to reality.

Baudelaire has been praised for his ability to seize upon everyday themes and images and to transform them into works powerfully invested with poetic charge. 'Tableaux parisiens' in particular focuses on what seems to be essentially removed from the poetic, the beautiful, the noble. The opening poem 'Paysage' (p.104) uneasily mixes reality, everyday and imaginary world. The cohabitation of the banal

> Les deux mains au menton, du haut de ma mansarde,
> Je verrai l'atelier qui chante et qui bavarde;

and of the dream-world 'pour bâtir dans la nuit mes féeriques palais' nevertheless finds justification and a coherent explanation of the poet's thought process through the concrete description of

> Les tuyaux, les clochers, ces mâts de la cité,
> Et les grands ciels qui font rêver d'éternité.

The process is one that goes from observed reality to inner reality. As in 'Renouveau', Baudelaire also acknowledges winter as the season for poetic creation, a self-reflexive, reclusive time, which exploits inner resources rather than sense experience. Marcel Raymond writes in *From Baudelaire to Surrealism:*

> One of Baudelaire's great distinctions is to have made the urban landscape, houses, rooms, interiors, objects of his contemplation, and to have perceived in their shabbiness and incongruities, secret analogies with his own soul.[64]

Baudelaire himself describes the poet's task as that of the sun in 'Le soleil' (p.104):

---

[64] Marcel Raymond, *From Baudelaire to Surrealism* (London: Peter Owen, 1957), pp.18-9.

Quand, ainsi qu'un poète, il descend dans les villes,
Il ennoblit le sort des choses les plus viles,
Il s'introduit en roi, sans bruit et sans valets,
Dans tous les hôpitaux et dans tous les palais.

This is a very optimistic account of the artist's ability to transform 'boue' into 'or', to operate magically a romantic alchemy, an account to which Mallarmé in 'Les Fenêtres' [P, 10-1] does not subscribe. He gives a far more pessimistic account, one which reveals him to be more of a realist than the Baudelaire of the 'Tableaux parisiens', even though Baudelaire's poems teem with concrete detail and down-to-earth descriptive touches. Mallarmé does not believe in a poetic magic wand or an alchemical formula, but he does go beyond as well as remain within a Baudelairian conception of the poetic function and its link with the ordinary. The sun in 'Les Fenêtres' does indeed open up an alternative world of beauty and imagination for the moribund, but this is not a transformation of the real world but an altogether new, created, alternative world. Similarly, 'Les croisées' do not open onto a transformed reality, but on to a totally new 'ciel antérieur où fleurit la beauté'.

The reality described in 'Tableaux parisiens' is at once alien and alienating, the poet both identifying and distancing himself from the observed inhabitants of an everyday which encompasses, behind and underneath its sordid banality, a spectral reality; Paris itself, a living, breathing reality[65] ('colosse puissant' p.109) with a desperate ordinariness akin to an actor's soul ('décor semblable à l'âme de l'acteur' p.109) is itself inhabited by beings who belong to their environment yet are alien to it ('Hostile à l'univers plutôt différent' p.109) and extraordinary because of the very quality which might have made them ordinary, their numbers (as in 'Les sept vieillards' and 'Les petites vieilles'). The nightmarish quality has invaded an ordinary Parisian morning, revealing the tightly interwoven strands both of a horrifying kind of banality and of a banal strangeness.

In contrast, the reality described in 'Aumône' [P, 24-5], if it also draws on an urban decor and focuses on a city dweller, already recreates a reality removed from the ordinary at several levels: at the level of imagery, where it is not the nightmarish and the sordid but the banal that is transformed by the altered perception of the *mendiant* into poetic reconstruction; at the level

---

[65] 'Les sept vieillards', pp.109-10.

of the language, the syntax, leaving Baudelairian symmetry and orthodoxy, already has the performative moulding role which is displayed in Mallarmé's more mature works. The rhythm of the Mallarmean alexandrine also displays surprise elements and unpredictability which underline the thematic transformations from banal to poetic, from quotidian and concrete detail to metaphorically constructed world:

> Et quand tu sors, vieux dieu, grelottant sous tes toiles
> D'emballage, l'aurore est un lac de vin d'or
> Et tu jures avoir au gosier les étoiles!

Nevertheless, the ordinary is present throughout the poem, in the form of sketched-in concrete detail and vocabulary but not, as in Baudelaire's poetry, in its almost surreal quality of nightmare world, alien and alienating but as a constant enveloping presence transcended only by two perceptions which produce a reality at twice removed: the *mendiant*'s own altered perception because of the alms, and the poet's own perception of the beggar's reality through a dramatic and poetic reconstruction.

There are nevertheless some clear indications of surface borrowings, at the level of jargon, clichés and stereotypes of the everyday world. 'Brise marine', with its quite unmistakably Baudelairian resonance, might provide a helpful example to demonstrate the level and importance of Mallarmé's borrowings, but also to point to specific departures from Baudelairian diction and imagery. The theme of 'Brise marine' [OC, 38] seems to centre on the poet's longing to escape the banality of his own everyday routine: his work and his domestic situation. The opening line sounds as if it has been borrowed directly from Baudelaire, but describes a form of spleen which has more to do with intellectual repletion and an almost Biblical awareness of the inadequacies of the flesh to provide contentment of a spiritual nature rather than a Baudelairian debilitating mood. Quotidian and exotic dimensions are contrasted yet not altogether mutually exclusive, and voyage is not perceived as the ultimate answer to lassitude of body and spirit. The outcome is uncertain, and the negative potential of staying within the quotidian is more than matched by the negative potential of leaving. The interpretation of voyage is therefore less conventional than that of Baudelaire in 'Parfum exotique' (p.52), for example, where the dreamland is seen in conventional terms of abundance and pleasure. The last line of 'Brise marine' is borrowed almost word for word from the last line of 'Parfum exotique', but has acquired, set as it is in opposition to the preceding lines, a quite different tone and meaning, a restless longing which is absent from the synaesthetic Baudelairian lines. The kind of spleen expressed in Mallarmé's 'Brise marine' and the bitter disillusionment with the quotidian and the exotic in Baudelaire's 'Le voyage' (p.150) are indeed fundamentally different, despite some similarities in images and vocabulary: Mallarmé describes the birds as 'Ivres / D'être parmi l'écume inconnue et les cieux!', Baudelaire speaks of the travellers in similar terms: 'ils s'enivrent / D'espace et de lumière et de cieux embrasés'; the word 'ennui', used with a capital in Mallarmé's poem as a poetic and universal representation of a personal feeling, appears throughout Baudelaire's poem as a much more concrete and threatening reality, characterising both the quotidian life and environment and the exotic and faraway lands:

> Et, malgré bien des chocs et d'imprévus désastres,
> Nous nous sommes souvent ennuyés, comme ici.

And further on, he adds:

> Amer savoir, celui qu'on tire du voyage!
> Le monde, monotone et petit, aujourd'hui,
> Hier, demain, toujours, nous fait voir notre image:
> Une oasis d'horreur dans un désert d'ennui!

The unfamiliar and the exotic are not the answer to escape the banal world; it is indeed within the banal itself that escape in the form of the extraordinary and the alien might well be found for Baudelaire. The restless search for the strange and exotic experience as panacea to the all-pervasive and deathly ennui does not end in success but in the complete loss of even the faintest glimmer of hope. In Mallarmé's 'Brise marine' the hope to find a more habitable reality, even perhaps in the very possibility of death and final disappearance, in the banal yet momentous 'adieu suprême des mouchoirs', is the very thread that guides the reader from familiar, domestic environment and scenery to the heartfelt rather than actually heard 'chants des matelots'. In 'Le voyage', the Mallarmean steamer which 'lève l'ancre pour une exotique nature' is eventually named as death itself, the only escape from both a quotidian and an exotic reality perceived eventually as identical. Mallarmé, borrowing thematically from Baudelaire, also makes a much more veiled parallel, the considered possibility that 'L'exotique nature' is either unattainable or does not exist.

The relation between the description of the everyday and the description of escape in voyage rests therefore on the same perception of ultimate unknown and emptiness rendered real and tangible by the concrete detail of the white paper, the lamp, the breast-feeding woman, the steamer, the handkerchiefs. Again syntax lends power and shape to the poet's imaginative reworking of thematic and lexical material partly borrowed: the threefold repetition of the negative *ni* gives gradual focus and importance to the main elements of the poet's everyday, both describing and cancelling the quotidian in the very description, acknowledging it and dismissing it, the use of repetition giving, together with a liberal and indeed Baudelairian use of exclamation marks, emotional emphasis and vehemently expressive visual impact to the symmetrically constructed poem.

Desire and reality, mediated through the transforming perception of the poet, plunge their roots deep into the ordinary world; both in the Mallarmé and the Baudelaire poems, they shape in their intertwining upon the 'canevas banal de nos piteux destins' (Baudelaire, 'Au lecteur' pp.33-4), in the complex imagery and mythological references of the longer poem, in the simple and gracefully balanced evocations of the shorter one, the very pattern of poetic longing oscillating between the seduction of the siren-like 'chants des matelots' and the awareness that without the quotidian, the most likely outcome is 'naufrage'; weighing the anchor of the everyday carries the inherent risk of no return to an ordinary dimension which provides the very texture of life.

Mallarmé's use of metaphor and imagery owes much to Baudelaire. The use of apposition, for instance, frequent in Baudelaire, is also present in Mallarmé, and becomes more and more frequent in the more mature works. But already, Mallarmé's own voice is discernible. In 'Las de l'amer repos' [P, 16-7], the last line reverses the usual sequence of the metaphoric apposition ('trois grands cils d'émeraude, roseaux'). In 'Le Pitre châtié' [P, 9], the compound 'Yeux, lacs' makes a striking use of apposition, and allows, because of its simplicity and the unusual proximity in terms for a number of metamorphoses of the image. In 'Don du poème' [P, 26], 'Palmes' introduces a new and unexpected image which has the effect of bringing into the quotidian an exotic note harking back to the escapist longings of 'Brise marine'. The equilibrium and subsequent development of the poem is altered by a term which equates dream with the unfamiliar and the illusive, reality with the cold, menacing and revealing light of dawn, a return of awareness of unexotic yet alien rather than familiar domesticity. Baudelaire frequently introduces unusual, even painfully realistic or repulsive terms of comparison, thereby undermining the sense of the familiar or of known and expected stereotypes. In 'Le crépuscule du matin' (p. 124), Baudelaire describes the dawn in terms that are not altogether different in Mallarmé's 'Don du poème': he writes of 'les combats de la lampe et du jour' and he also introduces an element of visual horror:

> Où, comme un œil sanglant qui palpite et qui bouge
> La lampe sur le jour fait une tache rouge;

The general atmosphere of the poem is one of unpleasantness evoked by the concrete comparisons and images:

> Comme un sanglot coupé par un sang écumeux,
> Le chant du coq au loin déchirait l'air brumeux;

The everyday described in the poem is inhabited by the less appealing sights and sounds of suffering humanity, governed by a sense of inescapable evil and hopelessness. If Mallarmé does indeed borrow from Baudelaire some decidedly repulsive images, as in 'Le Guignon', for example, he seems to abandon an obviously borrowed stance and diction to find in 'Don du poème' a more subtle mixture of strange and familiar, of quasi-gothic and domestic. 'L'enfant d'une nuit d'Idumée', product of 'une horrible naissance' recalls Frankenstein's experiment with creation and its monstrous, unnatural results. Set against the description of the inhabitants of a dawn-revealed reality, mother and daughter engaged in natural activity, their innocence concretely symbolised by 'Pieds froids', the dark 'child' of the night has the effect of uncovering, within the dimension of the ordinary, layers of the strange and the incomprehensible, of initiating a questioning of the everyday and of investing it with the alien quality which belongs to the 'enfant d'une nuit d'Idumée'. Yet in jumping from one register to another, Mallarmé also acknowledges the irreducible nature of bodily functions, and the deeply felt parallel between an organic experience displaying a basic life giving operation, and the poet's task, also in its basic physical effort and inescapable constraints.

This points towards an approach, which is peculiarly Baudelairian: the extraction of the extraordinary from the commonplace and vice-versa. In 'Les petites vieilles', from observation of everyday life and some of its inhabitants, the poet builds an extraordinarily complex, yet strongly structured and coherent narrative, descriptive and dramatic structure which incorporates a wealth of concrete detail, imagery, a variety of registers and endows the ordinary with depths from which he extracts new and surprising imaginative re-creations. His ability to identify with another's everyday and to re-invent it, brings to the fore the extraordinary dimension both of the poet and of the characters he so sympathetically describes, so that, in Baudelaire's own words, 'tout, même, l'horreur, tourne aux enchantements' ('Les petites vieilles'). Mallarmé follows a similar route in 'Aumône'. But far from identifying with the beggar, he distances himself from him and poetically invests the beggar's actions with a meaning which has both ordinary and extraordinary qualities: the image of the 'métal cher' as 'ardente fanfare', of tobacco as incense, the mention of nymphs on the ceiling of the cafés, the effect of drink on the beggar,

> [...] l'aurore est un lac de vin d'or
> Et tu jures avoir au gosier les étoiles.

are not unlike some of the imagery in Baudelaire's 'Le vin des chiffonniers' (p.127). The blurring of boundary lines between extraordinary and ordinary, between familiar and strange, the merging of grotesque and banal is a Baudelairian trait, which Mallarmé also borrowed. The difference resides in the obliqueness, the diffuseness with which Mallarmé proceeds, away from the direct Baudelaire stance. In 'Les Fenêtres', Mallarmé moves from one dimension into another, from one register into another, from a borrowed diction to a distinctively Mallarmean one. The realistic Baudelairian notation, often prosaic or trivial, is shot through with an imaginative, dream-like and meditative thread. The fifth verb works as a hinge between the realistically descriptive and Baudelairian, between the triviality of everyday living and a metaphysical, contemplative mode which is as distinct from the prosaic quality of the first four verses as it is from the purely sensual imagery of the fifth verse. The various directions in which the poem seems to go eventually rejoin and create a number of relationships, enabling the poet to explore several facets of reality beneath superficially perplexing and contradictory patterns. The boundaries between the phenomenal, the emotional and the metaphysical are crossed and recrossed, with clear indications of the poet's own unique voice present among the borrowed lexical fabric of the poem, a kind of Ariadne's thread which leads eventually to a re-assessment of the everyday in its more negative form of *ici-bas*.

Mallarmé's and Baudelaire's verse display, then, a number of obvious similarities and but also significant differences in their varied complexities. Some syntactical and lexical traits are easily recognisable and have often been commented upon: the abundance of abstract substantives, some archaisms, a proliferation

INTRODUCTION: THE POETICS OF THE PROSAIC

of epithets to lend concrete qualities to prosaic as well as imaginative material, the use of the singular for generalising and universalising purposes. The complexity of Baudelaire's 'Le Cygne', for instance, rests first on the many registers used by the poet, in the numerous *tableaux vivants* which he incorporates into the poem, in the freedom with which he moves between historical, mythological and geographical location, but also on the reworking of the quotidian and its relationship with the past and the far-away. He writes both on the real and the allegorical level, and intertwines the factually descriptive and the imaginatively recreated. 'Tout pour moi devient allégorie', he declares in 'Le Cygne'. The everyday world possesses the powerful ability to resurrect memories ('Un vieux souvenir sonne à plein souffle du cor'), of imparting a sense of value to the past, of bringing to mind other people's quotidian, that of Andromaque, of the *négresse*. But the poem is also about displacement and alienation within time and space, the sense that the ordinary is unfamiliar, *unheimlich* and possesses Heideggerian depths of concealment and refusal. It can only make sense in relation to a mythical image, a past, a far-away, or an experience reworked into allegory. All the threads, levels, changes of direction find cohesion and magnificent equilibrium in the cadence and symmetry of the Baudelairian alexandrine. The majestic and regular rhythm pattern both undermines and brings a sense of unity to the inner tensions and dissensions of the poem. If the message of the poem seems to be about an alien everyday and a quotidian that exists mainly because it feeds on the past, the regular flow of the alexandrine often provides a reassuringly satisfying sense of the uniform passage of time unaffected by emotional responses.

In 'L'Azur' [P, 20-1], Mallarmé develops Baudelairian images of alienation and exile, neither of them seeming to be a comfortable habitat for the poet. But Mallarmé also develops in 'L'Azur' themes which escape a neat comparison with Baudelaire. He is, like Baudelaire's swan, 'exilé', 'Ridicule et sublime, / Et rongé d'un désir sans trêve' but he seeks to escape into the ordinary rather than from the ordinary, and if Baudelaire's 'ciel ironique et cruellement bleu' sounds very much like Mallarmé's 'azur' and its 'sereine ironie', Mallarmé's poem, by turning cloudless sky into a symbol of a different dimension altogether develops and reworks the theme in a direction that departs from Baudelaire's. The support of the descriptive and the narrative in 'Tableaux parisiens' has changed into a much more generalised and vague, partly urban environment which privileges the dull, the unpicturesque and re-invests it with positive potential (*cendres / brumes / brouillards*

/*suies / tristes cheminées*, etc.). But the poet's efforts to reintegrate 'la litière / Où le bétail des hommes est couché', and ultimately to share their unremarkable death are defeated by his own awareness of the existence of another dimension, present behind or beyond the ordinary, in turn hidden and revealed, also manifested in the everyday world in the ordinary sound of church bells. The poem seems to suggest that the ordinary in its untroubled, simple manifestations does not exist, and that it is not possible to escape an awareness of a multi-layered reality shot through with an *unheimlich* and alienating dimension.

Baudelaire has often been praised for his ability to make the trivial and the vulgar moving. This is a typically Baudelairian quality, a way for the poet of poetically revalorising areas of human experience which are usually either rejected or ignored as material for poetic creation. Yet his compassionate portraits of beggars and the elderly, in 'Tableaux parisiens', for instance, make such an unusual use of quite extraordinary verbal resources, and are invested with such emotional vehemence that they leave the reader not with an awareness of the banal but of the extraordinary within the banal. On the other hand, the exotic seems to be treated in the reverse manner. In 'Le voyage', it is exposed as a fallacy, without any of the qualities which are usually attributed to it. The driving force is to escape the everyday at any cost, to

> Plonger au fond du gouffre, Enfer ou Ciel, qu'importe?
> Au fond de l'inconnu pour trouver du nouveau!

But it seems that escape from one earthbound place to another is not enough, that escape needs to be from one dimension into another, from time into eternity, to make a complete break with a quotidian often synonymous with *ennui*. Mallarmé is also suspicious of the superficially exotic; in 'Las de l'amer repos', after the still-Baudelairian opening lines, the poet turns to an oriental ideal, away from the routine of his ordinary environment. However, this is not in order to privilege the exotic and to escape from his own vocation; the goal is to relocate within a more naturally and spiritually fulfilling dimension, that of an art in tune with simple and ordinary life, a poetic project prematurely wilting from the effect of an untimely uprooting from childhood, and in need of a new quotidian away from extreme pressure, even when pressure forms an integral part of the poet's familiar environment: his lamp, his friends. This is a positive answer to poetic *impuissance* and to Baudelairian spleen, a quite different resolution of the tensions engendered by the overlap and merging of poetic and ordinary dimension. The fertile and dynamic mix of dimensions in Baudelaire's poetry has enabled the younger poet to discover his own formula in order to create 'une sorcellerie évocatoire'. Although Mallarmé moves away from a Baudelairian treatment of themes, whilst following the positive indications given by his predecessor, particularly on subjects related to the everyday, he exploits similar material; however, at the same time, he manages to escape a powerful influence on the one level by his use of syntax and versification, and on another level by his constant awareness of relationships between everyday and poetic, familiar and strange. Where he departs from his predecessor and marks his own specificity is by distancing himself from a Baudelairian sense of the ordinary and the extraordinary as two sides of the same coin, and perceiving the everyday as a more complex and potentially destructive interfusion.

We need to acknowledge Mallarmé's debt to his literary fathers, if only to move on and be able to claim an incontrovertible specificity in the way he dealt with the ordinary in his texts, a specificity that becomes more and more marked, and has clearly evolved into a quite unique and innovative strategy by the time he embarks on writing 'L'Après-midi d'un faune' and 'Hérodiade'. As he develops a more demanding, difficult and involved diction, he is also confronted with issues of syntax and lexis that have at their very centre the questions posed by the literary treatment of the ordinary world and the exigencies of the poetic craft. Much of Mallarmé's later poetry reads like an exorcism of the everyday world. The ordinary is under threat from either complex syntax and the types of difficulty listed by Steiner, or a deliberate choice of themes away from the quotidian routine, at least at the superficial level. This conscious cutting away from the everyday, though it does not perform in Mallarmé's poetry the central task of giving the work a *raison d'être* as it does with the Surrealists for instance, paradoxically highlights the importance of the function of the ordinary within Mallarmé's writing. The interest of an approach which lets the texts themselves set the agenda within their own complexities and contradictions, is that it does uncover one facet of Mallarmean writing which the poet has disguised and yet revealed: that it is mostly with ordinary words that one writes poetry, and that the dimension of the ordinary world is also the dimension of the poetic world. It is in the detail of the poet's texts themselves that the dynamic potential of the ordinary as analytical tool is most rewarding. The central challenge of this project will therefore be to track down, first through a close analysis of syntax in the following chapter, and then with a study of Mallarmé's lexis, the textual evidence of engagement with and response to a dimension and a concept that have acted in Mallarmé's *œuvre* as the proverbial thorn in the flesh, only to spur him on to greater textual elaboration and syntactic inventiveness.

CHAPTER II
Syntax

The difficulty of Mallarmé's texts arises not at the level of semantics so much as at the level of pragmatics. The distinctive Mallarmean texture makes heavy demands upon the reader's patience and willingness to engage with the textures both of prose and of verse. Can a style that makes such extraordinary demands upon its readers still claim to be in any sense 'ordinary', or able to sustain links with the everyday world? Does the ordinary reader feel at times, as Mallarmé himself suggests he might in 'Le Mystère dans les lettres' (1896)[66] that he is the victim of 'une plaisanterie immense et médiocre' [OC, 382]? Has Mallarmean difficulty more to do with stylistic pirouetting and syntactic puzzle making than with a real attempt at expression and communication?

Syntax might not be the very first place where one might look for instances of ordinary events. For most native speakers, it simply merges into the everyday and does not involve more than a passing inquiry as to ordinary usage. In the case of Mallarmé, he insists on dramatising what other writers and poets are keen to hide or simply take for granted: the sinews and structural processes of syntactic construction and creation. He constantly draws attention to the syntactic drama, foregrounding a number of features and events that have a significant impact first on the reader's reception of the text, then on the nature of the interface between syntax and the ordinary. The constant spotlight placed upon mere syntactic devices forces the reader into an awareness of the writing and the creative process, which hallmarks the poet's production as eminently modern in its concern to uncover the structuring dynamic at work within the texts. Mallarmé's use of syntax is indeed fascinating in its eagerness to jettison a number of ordinary syntactic features and to test and explode grammatical rule. Even the famously complex Proustian sentence behaves with exemplary propriety when compared to that of Mallarmé's later prose. It is therefore impossible to study the texts without a close analysis of syntax and its effects on textual matter, and Mallarmé's own insistence on highlighting syntactic events

---

[66] All the dates given for Mallarmé's texts, unless otherwise indicated, are the dates of first publication.

imperatively requires from his reader an interest in syntax and an awareness of its magic.

Any inquiry which is concerned with complexity (and in Mallarmé's case, all inquiries have to be) will inevitably have to pay close attention to the stylistic features and syntactic habits of the author. It may include an analysis of the retracing of a route back to or away from the dimension of the ordinary, in a paradoxically inverted trajectory which might lead the reader from the familiar to the unfamiliar and from the unfamiliar to the familiar but may also at any point intertwine the two routes, or choose a circular or reflexive navigatory pattern. This inquiry will be concerned with the ordinary within language, understood as the syntactic arrangement of words on a page. All of these can be defined, documented, listed and illustrated. Having first made an inventory of the most striking Mallarmean syntactic features, and acknowledged the contribution of Scherer and Norman Paxton in particular, I shall, in this chapter, set these features against an account of the ordinary as referent but also as ingredient within Mallarmé's poetic language. In a second part of the chapter, I intend to analyse temporality in conjunction with syntax, and to uncover the role of the ordinary in Mallarmé's use of tenses and time indicators.

In Mallarmé's case, the immediate question is: are the features that stamp a poem or a text in prose as Mallarmean more or less definable than those of other writers? Does the complexity of his style make it more or less difficult to characterise than the style of his contemporaries, for instance? There can exist only a limited number of linguistic patterns, even in a style as innovative as Mallarmé's. That a successful parody of Mallarmé's style was achieved by one 'Adoré Floupette'[67] in 1886 seems to confirm this. The difficulty of Mallarmé's style is more a consequence of structural and stylistic choices, which can be defined, than of any mysterious, indeterminable and original creative principle. Steiner's taxonomy of difficulty[68] is one possible avenue of inquiry. But it is almost entirely reader based, analysing difficulty from the standpoint of the recipient in a legitimate attempt to clarify the concept itself and to formulate an analytical tool. As a critic, one can either examine specific stylistic features and analyse their effect or take the opposite route. I shall start with syntactic devices and authorial stylistic choices and then consider their

---

[67] 'Adoré Floupette' is the pen name of two poets, Gabriel Vicaire and Henri Beauclair, authors of *Les Déliquescences*.

[68] See above, pp.28-35.

effects not so much on the reader as on the concept of the ordinary: on the one hand, the reinforcing of everyday life and on the other, rather paradoxically, the exorcising of the everyday through a very deliberate use of language.

A number of major contributions have been made on the subject of the Mallarmean use of language, and I shall refer the reader to them throughout this chapter. The most striking features of Mallarmé's syntax and vocabulary have of course already been documented in the general studies by Thibaudet[69] and Noulet.[70] The works of Scherer[71] and Paxton[72] are entirely devoted to the analysis of Mallarmé's use of language. The interplay between simple and complex syntax has been touched upon, but this interplay has not been brought into relationship with the question of the ordinary. Kristeva's semiotic analysis does focus on a number of syntactical features, with particular reference and interpretation of a number of striking Mallarmean traits and I shall examine some of her conclusions relating in particular to the perceived destruction of syntactic order and pronominal stability, and the relation of the poet to subject and verb.

In my continuing discussion of the interface between syntax and the ordinary, I shall attend to the following and especially interesting individual features of Mallarmé's writing: his use of simple, predicative syntax, as it appears with reassuring frequency in his verse and his prose and its alternation with more complex self-embedded structures. The use of disjunction, interpolation, suspension, apposition and inversion feature prominently in the poet's *œuvre* and will therefore need careful study in order to isolate the dynamic principle at work within the Mallarmean sentence. The use of different forms of ellipsis, his partiality for adverbs in *-ment*, the use of isolative, dislocatory syntax[73] and adjacency, and the often perverse-seeming use of punctuation can all be interpreted as expressions of his perception and response to the ordinary, and will therefore be the subject of a close analysis.

---

[69] Albert Thibaudet, *La Poésie de Stéphane Mallarmé*.

[70] Emilie Noulet, *L'Œuvre poétique de Stéphane Mallarmé*.

[71] Jacques Scherer, *L'Expression littéraire dans l'œuvre de Mallarmé*.

[72] Norman Paxton, *The Development of Mallarmé's Prose Style* (Geneva: Droz, 1968).

[73] I shall use the expression 'isolative syntax' to refer to a discreet semantic and syntactic event giving unusual status to a word or an expression within a sentence. I shall use the term 'dislocatory' to refer to an unusual and contrived dislocation of semantic and syntactic groups.

But we need first of all to define what we call 'ordinary syntax', and ask whether Mallarmé exploits it at all. To speak of ordinary syntax is to raise a serious linguistic and to some extent philosophical issue: what is the most ordinary 'ordinary syntax'? It could be described as an unqualified proposition without embedding, subordinate clauses or ellipsis, the exemplary 'the cat sat on the mat' subject-predicate form which is the basis on which most European languages work. This zero degree of syntactic complexity promotes a sense of immediate recognition and understanding on the part of the reader. It clearly falls into the Kristevian symbolic category, extending the thetic tradition that demands coherence and logic within language and promotes easy comprehension. It is the language used to make simple points or observations, to describe a common experience in everyday terms; it is predicative even in its interrogative form and concerned with clear and immediate communication.

We may readily isolate within the Mallarmé corpus incidences of such syntax. A close look at the beginning of 'Brise marine' (1866) but also at later works such as the much analysed *Un Coup de dés* (1897) will show a constant and regular return to basic and simple predicativeness often brought in at a culminating point of the poem or essay. In 'Brise marine' we find:

> La chair est triste, hélas! et j'ai lu tous les livres. [P, 22]

The two predicative propositions are connected by the commonest agent of coordination, thus multiplying the effect of their simple straightforwardness. In the lengthy sentences of 'Hérodiade' (1869), the poet intersperses such basic grammatical structures as:

> Depuis longtemps la gorge ancienne est tarie [OC, 43][74]

and further on:

> car tout est présage et mauvais rêve!

In the prose works also we find instances of the same pattern. In 'Crayonné au théâtre' (1887-1898), we find sentences as minimal as 'je comprends' [OC, 315] or 'l'acteur mène ce discours' [OC, 300].

---

[74] In the Gallimard edition of *Poésies est* has been changed to *et* (p. 79). This is also the case for the 1989 Flammarion edition. Both versions are syntactically acceptable.

As we have suggested, it is clear that Mallarmé does make use of the most ordinary of 'ordinary syntax' right through his work. Even his most transgressional text, in Kristevian terms, *Un Coup de dés* [OC, 459-77] still displays examples of simple predicative syntax, as in the sentence half-announced in the title: 'Un Coup de dés [...] jamais [...] n'abolira [...] le hasard', or:

> RIEN
> N'AURA EU LIEU
> QUE LE LIEU [OC, 474-5]

for instance, or in

> jadis il empoignait la barre [OC, 463]

or in the last line of the poem:

> Toute Pensée émet un Coup de Dés [OC, 477].

Ordinary syntax is used as a guideline, a landmark, throughout the corpus, from which syntactical elaboration departs and returns, sometimes in almost rhythmical alternation; in *Un Coup de dés*, it works against the principle of *non-finitude* that Kristeva analyses in her study of the poem. Throughout Mallarmé's work, we encounter the straightforward sentence that is instantly recognisable to the reader as lacking any of Steiner's categories of difficulty and therefore gaining within the corpus an enhanced status as familiar landmark. But it is then subverted by the immediate appearance of a particularly complex proposition, as in 'Le tombeau d'Edgar Poe'[75] [P, 60]:

> Eux, comme un vil sursaut d'hydre oyant jadis l'ange
> Donner un sens plus pur aux mots de la tribu

The formulaic quality of the second line of the second quatrain is set against the complexity of the first line. The ordinary syntactic pattern of the second line gains immediate force as it emerges from the complexity of the first line. Its ordinariness strikes the reader as extraordinary within the structure of the poem, as the full impact of the line seems to explode out of the complex preceding structure. This pattern of alternate syntactic simplicity

---

[75] This sonnet was first published in America in *Edgar Allan Poe: A Memorial Volume* (Baltimore: Turnbull Brothers, 1877).

and complexity is one of the most remarkable features of the Mallarmean use of language. In 'Toast funèbre',[76] [P, 42-3] this rhythm is striking; throughout the poem, simple propositional syntax such as 'Ton apparition ne va pas me suffire' (1.5) alternates with complex syntax replete with subordinate clauses and appositions. The third part of the poem starting with 'Le Maître' (1.32) contains a sentence made of ten lines, for example, challenging grammatical orthodoxy. Yet ordinary syntax in the Mallarmé corpus is not an illusion produced by eager critics intent on imposing on the writing an external normalising and straitening process, but the necessary referent within which Mallarmé exercised his gift as *syntaxier*. He perceived syntax as absolutely essential to communication, a guarantee of intelligibility: 'Quel pivot, j'entends, dans ces contrastes, à l'intelligibilité? il faut une garantie - / La Syntaxe' [OC, 385]. Mallarmé claims a basic intelligibility, a coherence in the relationship between language and logic that corresponds, in Kristevian terms, to an almost thetic tradition. He turns to syntactic laws not to transgress them, but to invoque their qualities of systematised logic and accepted rule in order to protect and reinforce the propositional and straitforward nature of ordinary communication. And yet he is also caught up in the challenge to transform and subvert systems of expression and meaning and linguistic traditions that fail to give him the freedom to explore new syntactic fields and explode accepted boundaries.

In his early verse, Mallarmé's syntax and lexis are mostly a Baudelairian derivative, with strong Hugolian reminiscences. Sentence ordering is well within the limits of grammatical orthodoxy, syntactic links are evident, punctuation has the usual function of clarifying structural ambiguities, and the use of ellipsis is virtually non-existent. But in 'Le Guignon' [P, 4-5] (1862) we find embryonic evidence of characteristic stylistic features of Mallarmé's later writing: the use of a generalising singular ('le pied dans nos chemins'), of substantivised adjectives ('le nu de son glaive'), a typically Mallarmean complement of the adjective ('ces héros excédés de malaises badins'). The prose of 'Symphonie littéraire' [OC, 261-5] (1864) also lacks the syntactic ambiguity and puzzling condensation of some of the later 'Médaillons et portraits' (1896). But it already displays Mallarmé's penchant for adverbs in *-ment (purement, miraculeusement, adorablement, puissamment, violemment,*

---

[76] The poem was published in *Tombeau de Théophile Gautier* (Paris: Lemerre, 1873), 23 October, exactly a year after the death of Gautier.

mystiquement), his love of appositional phrases and enclaves, of a long sentence with various embeddings, as in the opening dedicace of 'Symphonie littéraire' [OC, 261];[77] it also shows a favouring of ellipsis of the orthodox and readily understandable kind ('Maintenant qu'écrire') and a much used complement of the adjective ('une âme dédaigneuse du banal coup d'aile d'un enthousiasme humain') [OC, 262].

The two major syntactic elements responsible for Mallarmé's stylistic complexity are already present: ellipsis and embedding, but their discreet use which could still fall into the category of ordinary literary usage does not have the attention-drawing, insistent and self-aware quality that they will come to acquire in the later works. The syntax performs a task which is understated: connections are fully expressed, the message has a look of completeness and the syntax seems to be subordinate to the expression of this message. The ability of the syntax to structure and mould the very contents of the text is less apparent than in later texts. Mallarmé's syntactic infractions are not dramatised and foregrounded but discreetly interwoven in a mildly subversive pattern, whilst the logical and predicative syntactic aspects, the symbolic in Kristevian terms, dominates.

It is the more complex syntax that requires close examination. Both ordinary and complex syntax can reinforce banal points. The relationship exists therefore in various forms and at different levels. I shall attempt to highlight what is extraordinary, unfamiliar, in strenuous syntax, but also how it can reinforce some very straightforward points and how it gets back to the ordinary in suggesting connections between things and events of the ordinary world. In 'L'Après-midi d'un faune' (1876), for example, quite apart from the reference to a world made of concrete, solid, manipulable things, and of the imagery, it is the syntax which performs the task of a spontaneous, poetic re-endowing of the banal with simple structures. Ordinary syntax is used throughout the poem, and it is rendered striking and extraordinary by its typographical position and its very simplicity: 'Aimai-je un rêve?', 'réfléchissons', 'je vais parler longtemps des déesses', 'O nymphes, regonflons des SOUVENIRS divers', 'j'accours', 'je tiens la reine', etc... These are all strikingly simple propositional sentences, reflecting by their lack of complexity the

---

[77] 'Symphonie littéraire' was written in Tournon in 1864: 'Muse moderne de l'Impuissance, qui m'interdis depuis longtemps le trésor familier des Rythmes, et me condamnes (aimable supplice) à ne faire plus que relire, - jusqu'au jour où tu m'auras enveloppé dans ton irrémédiable filet, l'ennui, et tout sera fini alors, - les maîtres inaccessibles dont la beauté me désespère.'

transparently erotic musings of the faun and the straightforward physical nature of his desire. Kristeva might argue that the erotic pulsion as part of the semiotic has a disruptive effect re-enacted at the level of the language by syntactic disruption. Yet Mallarmé chooses to express what belongs to the semiotic by abiding by syntactic rules and by giving predicative coherence to incoherent impulse. Ordinary syntax punctuates at regular intervals the unfolding of dream and desire, of monologue within monologue, of narrative and drama at once within and outside the spiral of the faun's rêverie. The symbolic is therefore clearly imposed upon the semiotic, giving overall dominance to a logically expressed subjectivity, asserting its unifying control.

However, the active verbs such as *veux, offrais, aimai, coupais, vais, ai sucé, élève, regarde, accours, ravis, adore, tiens*, describing the faun's actions often constructed within a simple ordinary predicative structure alternate with the far more complex self-embedded structure of the faun's imaginings and the intimations of doubt which set up a multiplicity of syntactical, metaphoric and psychological relationships. The faun's conscious and unconscious desires seem to be written into the text by way of this syntactic device of embeddedness, opening up within the poem a labyrinth of interwoven sensations, dreams and desires:

> Autre que ce doux rien par leur lèvre ébruité,
> Le baiser, qui tout bas des perfides assure,
> Mon sein, vierge de preuve, atteste une morsure
> Mystérieuse, due à quelque auguste dent;
> Mais, bast! arcane tel élut pour confident
> Le jonc vaste et jumeau dont sous l'azur on joue:
> Qui, détournant à soi le trouble de la joue,
> Rêve, dans un solo long, que nous amusions
> La beauté d'alentour par des confusions
> Fausses entre elle-même et notre chant crédule;
> Et de faire aussi haut que l'amour se module
> Evanouir du songe ordinaire de dos
> Ou de flanc pur suivis avec mes regards clos,
> Une sonore, vaine et monotone ligne. [P, 35-9]

The whole paragraph is one long, sinuous and convoluted sentence, including several clauses, appositional propositions, coordinated propositions and the use of colons, semi-colons, (although these disguise at times the closural force of simple proposition), commas and exclamation marks. As the faun oscillates between disappointment ('aimai-je un rêve?', 'mon sein, vierge de preuve', 'pour bannir un regret', etc.) and near-gratification, between apprehension of the concrete world and a sensuous revelling in ordinary aspects of reality on the one hand and a striving to turn dream into material reality on the other, the syntax re-enacts the complexity of mental processes. In the following passages, both doubt and desire are reinforced and given full expressive weight by a syntax that alternates between the straightforwardly predicative and the clausal:

>   Aimai-je un rêve?
> Mon doute, amas de nuit ancienne, s'achève
> En maint rameau subtil, qui, demeuré les vrais
> Bois mêmes, prouve, hélas! que bien seul je m'offrais
> Pour triomphe la faute idéale de roses -
> Réfléchissons...
>   ou si les femmes dont tu gloses
> Figurent un souhait de tes sens fabuleux!
> Faune, l'illusion s'échappe des yeux bleus
> Et froids, comme une source en pleurs, de la plus chaste:
> [...]
>   Inerte, tout brûle dans l'heure fauve

and

>   j'élève au ciel d'été la grappe vide

and

> [...] pourpre et déjà mûre,
> Chaque grenade éclate et d'abeilles murmure;

Against the backdrop of a material world that the faun is familiar with, and for which he finds adequate and simple expression, it is his own self, the baffling complexities of his inner world, that provide rich material for involved syntax. His identity as subject is under threat, his apprehension of himself becomes fragmented and diffuse as the semiotic expressed in complex, artfully anarchic syntax reasserts its dominance over the symbolic. The complex syntax of the paragraph starting with 'Autre' previously quoted [P, 36] dilutes the formulaic and closural force of the predicative sentence, thus re-enacting at the syntactic level the faun's own struggle with his hazy perception of reality and his lack of self-knowledge. Yet the sense of confusion in the faun's mind is expressed not by confused syntax but by a carefully orchestrated complexity, a 'dramatised' syntax where words and their relationships are the main characters. In a contrapuntal play of certainty and familiarity, the ordinary, predicative syntax, like the simple melody of the syrinx, reinvests the banal world with a much needed if intermittent sense of security and unity in material and sensual reality.

I. Interpolation and disjunction

The use of disjunction, interpolation, suspension, apposition and inversion in Mallarmé's work have of course already been documented in the detailed studies of Thibaudet, Noulet, Scherer and Paxton. As syntactic features called upon to play alternately both a simplifying and complexifying role, they require particular attention. The splitting of close-knit syntactic groups, often creating ambiguity as to word function, and a sense of artificiality adds to the complexity of the Mallarmean sentence. Examples both from the prose and the poetic works are numerous, starting quite early in Mallarmé's career, although they tend to focus attention on privileged themes rather than to deliberately introduce complexity. In 'Les Fenêtres' [P, 10-1], we find in stanza 8:

> [...] et j'aime
> - Que la vitre soit l'art, soit la mysticité -
> A renaître, portant mon rêve en diadème,

'Hérodiade' is particularly rich in examples of this kind. In 'Scène' [P, 27-34], the infinitive *entrer* which completes the verb group on line 11 appears only three lines later.

> [...] tu m'as vue, ô nourrice d'hiver,
> Sous la lourde prison de pierres et de fer
> Où de mes vieux lions traînent les siècles fauves
> Entrer, et je marchais, fatale, les mains sauves,
> Dans le parfum désert de ces anciens rois;

Does this extraordinary use of one syntactic device rejoin the dimension of the ordinary by being an affective, emotional way of writing, less bound by the rules of grammar, as in the spoken style? Does it uncover an almost chronic need to challenge the unifying function of the symbolic? Does it allow us, as Kristeva might argue, to claim that this points to a breaking through the symbolic surface of the semiotic? Mallarmé himself emphasised the importance of the oral, the conversational, the intuitive and immediate response: 'Le Vers et tout écrit au fond par cela qu'issu de la parole doit se montrer à même de subir l'épreuve orale ou d'affronter la diction comme un mode de présentation extérieur' [OC, 855]. If it might betray a hesitation on the part of the author as to his own stylistic identity, a general anxiety about textuality expressed by a very individual choice of syntactic traits, it also points to his awareness of a number of operations inherent in the act of writing, and to his unwillingness to conceal or suppress the reality of the material and bodily processes involved.

This awareness expressed in the use of disjunction and interpolation greatly increases the demands made on the reader. The need for mental gymnastics on the part of the reader coming across the essay on Berthe Morisot for instance, in 'Médaillons et portraits' (1896) is so unrelenting that he/she can be forgiven for yearning for syntactic simplicity:

> Féerie, oui, quotidienne - sans distance, par l'inspiration, plus que le plein air enflant un glissement, le matin ou après-midi, de cygnes à nous; ni au-delà que ne s'acclimate, des ailes détournée et de tous paradis, l'enthousiaste innéité de la jeunesse dans une profondeur de journée [OC, 537].

Mallarmé's predilection for inversion, cleft-sentence structure, ellipsis of verb and article, deferral and suspension finds adequate expression in this sentence. It avoids vacancy mainly because of the free associative quality acquired by the lack of link words and the striking proximity of imagery. The painterly quality of the sentence is particularly felicitous when depicting the visual delight of moving from one detail to another while looking at the artist's work. The immediacy of the impact made by the picture on the onlooker is translated at the syntactic level by the complexity of the sentence structure, which strives to reproduce the instinctive response evoked in the poet, thus giving pre-eminence to the Kristevian semiotic. By separating the noun 'Féerie' from its qualifying adjective 'quotidienne' with the interjected affirmative adverb 'oui', the poet underlines both the unusualness of the combination and the ambivalence and thought in his own response almost *après coup*. The subsequent dash announces a further exploration of his complex response to the picture, a mixture of pictorial detail (*enflant, les cygnes*) and personal interpretation (*par l'inspiration*). Yet the syntactic complexity of the sentence does not lead to a sense of vacancy or chaos, to anarchic proliferation or complete destruction of syntactic rule, but to an entirely opposite imaginative impact. It is the perfect vehicle for a descriptive as well as intuitive and interpretative response, inviting the reader to participate by his own necessarily active role in the evocation of a world both magical and ordinary.

II. Ellipsis

As one of the syntactic devices featuring most frequently in the Mallarmé corpus, ellipsis needs careful analysis. In *The Development of Mallarmé's Prose Style*, Paxton studies the nature and effect of some of Mallarmé's revisions of his early prose works. He identifies the main procedure as that of deletion, the effect as that of condensation and the syntactic device as ellipsis:

> The practice of ellipsis is very frequent, but only when the words omitted are quite banal and the result readily comprehensible by Mallarmé's bourgeois readers (p.51)

Ellipsis in the Mallarmé's corpus becomes so frequent as to seem an almost obsessive habit in his later years and it is therefore possible to list the different types of ellipses, that, very common, of the verb *être*, of the subject, of *je* as the subject, of possessive adjectives and of personal pronouns. It is present both in prose and poetic works: in 'Las de l'amer repos' (1866), we read:

> - Que dire à cette Aurore, ô Rêves, visité
> Par les roses, quand, peur de ses roses livides,
> Le vaste cimetière unira les trous vides? [P, 16-7]

In 'La Chevelure' (1887), we also find an ellipsis of the verb:

> [...] (je dirais mourir un diadème) [P, 40]

In the 'Poèmes en prose', we find examples of ellipsis of *Je*: 'j'obéis et fis arrêter' [OC, 280], or in 'Le nénuphar blanc' (1885): '[...] j'accomplis selon les règles la manœuvre: me dégageai, virai et je contournais déjà une ondulation du ruisseau' [...] [OC, 286]. In Mallarmé's prose essays, we find almost stenographic sentences, as in the essay 'Le Genre ou des Modernes' (1887), which starts: 'Ici, succincte, une parenthèse' [OC, 312], or in 'Notes sur le théâtre' (1887): 'Vu le crocodile' [OC, 337].

Why have all elements such as *je*, the verb *être*, possessive adjectives, personal pronouns, which seem in ordinary syntax to have an important role, been perceived by Mallarmé as syntactical superfluities? Why do they seem more expendable than other elements of syntax? Scherer would attribute it to une forme d'écriture qui vise à la réussite émotionnelle, à être une incantation plutôt qu'à être comprise. Il arrive même que la musique de la phrase soit si expressive qu'elle dispense d'énoncer les mots banals (p.203).

But there is no evidence that Mallarmé deliberately sacrificed intelligibility for the sake of musicality, and that the reader is then absolved from further trying to unravel the Mallarmean sentence. Kristeva's domain of the semiotic, characterised by indifference to coherence in language, by enigma, by what is feminine in nature, might well be invoked to explain this supremely Mallarmean syntactic trait. I would like to argue that it has everything to do with Mallarmé's engagement or fear of engagement with the ordinary world, translated at the level of language by the systematic disappearance of the banal term needed to make sense of a sentence. This term is missing, yet absolutely essential and ordinary, fulfilling a necessary function. By its absence, the rules of orthodox grammar are violated. The term is therefore not absent in the ordinary sense (its absence is too noticeable) but seems to hover in a kind of meaningful proximity, having been present in the first place but having been purposefully removed, deliberately suppressed. It falls to the reader to re-introduce the banal term in order to restore meaning to the extremely condensed sentences. This process of the re-introduction of the ordinary absent term which is nevertheless tacitly understood as present gives it prominence by the simple fact of our having to think it out and of necessitating a deliberate process of re-introduction after deliberate authorial suppression. Kristeva argues that the suppressed term becomes so ambiguous that it cannot be replaced within the text.[78] Yet the syntactic imperative does clearly guide the reader who is then able to replace within the sentence the suppressed but necessary term. The ordinary cannot be taken for granted, but in Cavellian terms, needs to undergo a process of recovery, of restoration. The reading process which often demands a backward movement, a retracing of steps, as well as a

---

[78] '[...] dans le texte de Mallarmé, plusieurs éléments sont supprimés qui ne sont ni des pro-formes ni des éléments identiques à d'autres. Si les règles de la suppression exigent que l'élément supprimé dans la suite terminale ait été représenté en tant que catégorie dans la suite sous-jacente aux transformations, on constate que ce représentant catégoriel n'existe pas ou bien que, quand on peut le reconstituer, il est plus qu'ambigu, au sens qu'il peut être reconstitué à plusieurs endroits. On peut appeler ce type de suppressions des suppressions non récupérables (non recoverable deletion)' p.281, *La Révolution du langage poétique*.

forwards movement, also needs to involve a similar process of restoration.

The different kinds of ellipses all tend to augment obliquity and complexity. We find in 'Variations sur un sujet', for instance, a typically Mallarmean sentence combining ellipsis and superabundant punctuation with the metaphoric expression of the poet's deeply felt belief in *le Livre*:

> Chimère, y avoir pensé atteste, au reflet de ses squames, combien le cycle présent, ou quart dernier de siècle, subit quelque éclair absolu - dont l'échevèlement d'ondée à mes carreaux essuie le trouble ruisselant, jusqu'à illuminer ceci - que, plus ou moins, tous les livres, contiennent la fusion de quelques redites comptées: même il n'en serait qu'un - au monde, sa loi - bible comme la simulent des nations [OC, 367].

There seem in fact to be several processes unfolding here simultaneously: as the banal term is systematically removed (article, verb *être*, link preposition, coordination) the syntax in general also becomes more removed from the banal as complexity is introduced by absence. This can be seen in the absence of agent for the subject-phrase 'y avoir pensé', the absence of connective phrase between 'au monde, sa loi'. Yet the tacit presence of the unexpressed banal term brings back more forcefully and noticeably the absent term and thus reintroduces the dimension of the banal into syntax. Far from removing the sentence from the realm of the everyday, the complexity of the syntax allows the coming together in fruitful proximity and sometimes stimulating overlapping of the ordinary manifestation of a rainy and stormy day on the poet's window ('échevèlement d'ondée à mes carreaux') with an all embracing view of the world in its present and immediate past. The ordinary is therefore present at every level, particularly at the syntactic level, invested with metaphoric power but also investing the thought processes of the poet with a forceful and constant reminder of its inescapability.

By transgressing the laws of syntax in a passive absence of the banal term, a new discourse *en-dessous* is engendered. The repression or removal of the subject is of particular interest for a Kristevian interpretation, and would point towards a possible manifestation of the death instinct within the body of the texts as the identity of the subject disappears. Yet absence of the subject leads to a number of important conclusions that might not support a Kristevian view: the uncertainty about the identity of the agent, the dispersal, almost vaporisation of this particular function which results in a new illegal dominance of the verb or the complement results in a changed status for the various syntactic members of the sentence. The subject as banal term therefore loses its dominance, but by its notable absence regains a different enhanced status as it is dispersed throughout the sentence and therefore potentially present at different levels and at different chronological points.

On the other hand, we can also find instances where the banal term is not removed, and yet the syntax is far from ordinary: *La Dernière Mode* displays a wealth of complex syntax, yet well within orthodox grammar and without extensive use of ellipsis. The following sentence taken from the eighth issue (December 1874) shows a use of syntax which without recourse to ellipsis, has a complex construction whilst engaging with an everyday subject in a rich and complex yet still relatively ordinary way:

> Somme toute, jamais ne régnèrent plus superbement les tissus opulents et même lourds, le velours et presque les brocarts d'argent ou d'or, non moins que, léger, moelleux, clair, le nouveau cachemire qui se porte le soir; mais parmi cette enveloppe, somptueuse ou simple, plus qu'à aucune époque va transparaître la Femme, visible, dessinée, elle-même, avec la grâce entière de son contour ou les principales lignes de sa personne (alors que, par derrière, la magnificence vaste de la traîne attire tous les plis et l'ampleur massive de l'étoffe) [OC, 833].

The text displays a wealth of incidental propositions, an abundance of qualifying adjectives, and the desire by the poet to catch in one syntactic entity, one sentence, the fashion traits of the time. The switches in tenses, from the *passé-simple* of the first verb to the present of the verb of the qualifying clause and the immediate future of the second main verb, enact in their time-layering the physical and literal layering of fashionable materials, the detail of their textures and colours. It is this attempt at simultaneity and completeness in one sentence that makes for syntactic complexity. In the opening expression, 'Somme toute', Mallarmé gives us a clue to his syntactic and literary project in the sentence. As 'Woman' appears more clearly in her essence envelopped in fashionable materials, so ordinary syntax is made more apparent under the weight of adjectives and the length of the sentence afforded by a superabundant use of punctuation. The two main clauses are simply constructed, lacking in any ambiguity. The function of each word is not in doubt. The richness of the textual material is underlined by the ordinariness of the syntax, which gathers in its folds a shimmer of descriptive and sensuous words, and they in turn lend the sentence a dazzling pseudo-complexity.

The process of removing syntax from the ordinary and that of removing the ordinary from syntax are quite separate, and their effects provide rich matter for analysis. The latter affirms the functional importance of absence, of a nothingness that still keeps the imprint of something. The impression given is one of incompleteness, yet with a promise of the possibility of completeness, or a hint at an anterior state of completeness. In 'La musique et les Lettres' (1895), we find: 'Audace, cette désaffectation, l'unique; dont rabattre...' [OC, 644]. The absence of conjugated verbs and the tacitly understood presence of the verb *être* contribute towards a sense of depth and brevity. This makes for a kind of literary shorthand, a deliberate focusing on word and meaning, concentrating the reader's attention whilst at the same time restoring a sense of the alien within the familiar by relativising syntactic function and status within the sentence. We perceive the noun devoid of its article differently, aware of its notable absence, sensing in the consequent incompleteness a desire to make use of absence as an innovative form not of rejection but of a subtle attention-drawing device.

III. Apposition and adjacency

In *L'Expression littéraire dans l'œuvre de Mallarmé*, Scherer has illustrated the various types of ellipsis that Mallarmé favours - of subjects, the verb *être*, and pronouns - but without drawing any conclusion other than that there is consequently added condensation of textual matter. He does not explore the effect of such extensive use of what would seem to be a 'negative' syntactical device. He does not comment on or draw attention to the fact that it is often the tools of syntactic connection which are eliminated. Instead of subordination, even coordination, we have adjacency in the forms of appositions and enclaves. In 'Le Pitre châtié' (1887), we find:

Yeux, lacs avec ma simple ivresse de renaître [P, 9]

or in 'Las de l'amer repos':

[...] trois grands cils d'émeraude, roseaux [P, 17]

These appositions are still easily understood. In the later prose style, they become more demanding, innovative and experimental.

In 'Médaillons et portraits', on Laurent Tailhade (1894), Mallarmé writes:

> [...] cuirassée de fragilité à l'épreuve par le préalable bris plombant sa diaprure, dont pas un enflammé morceau d'avance comme la passion le colore, gemme, manteau, sourire, lis, ne manque à votre éblouissante Rosace, attendu et par cela qu'elle-même d'abord simule dans un suspens ou défi, l'éclat, unique, en quoi par profession irradie l'indemne esprit du Poète [OC, 527].

This has two opposite effects, almost irresolvable: it isolates words or syntactic structures, as in 'gemme, manteau, sourire, lis', but it also brings words closer together than they normally would be. Apposition therefore allows for unusual *rapprochements*. The absence of articles often removes a familiar syntactic element, the obvious and yet unnoticed indicator of common categories, remarkable mainly by its absence, thus bringing a new relationship to words usually separated or linked by their presence. This syntactic closeness can either enrich meaning and expression or sometimes lead to the very edge of vacancy. If we remember Mallarmé's words,

> Tout l'acte disponible, à jamais et seulement, reste de saisir les rapports, entre temps, rares ou multipliés; d'après quelque état intérieur et que l'on veuille à son gré étendre, simplifier le monde [OC, 647],

we realise that what is attempted is in fact a greater fostering of links. Indeed there is a sense both of simplification because of loss of matter, but also of greater complexification because of unexpressed connections. Once the limitations of syntactical connection are removed, the possibilities of *rapports* are infinitely multiplied, but so also is the risk of vacancy and disruption and of fatal and total removal from the familiar. Yet by pushing back syntactic boundaries and imposing new and illegal proximities to words, the potential for re-endowing the banal with lively and unusual meaning has the added and paradoxical attraction that in this case, less is more.

The tension between striving for meaningful connections and the possibility of losing connections is heightened in Mallarmé's poetry by metre, rhythm and rhyme seen as sense-making elements. The interaction of these elements is not always one of fusion but of alternating dominance of one or the other elements. This has the effect of a highly dramatised syntax leading to a dramatising of the content and rhythm of the sentence in prose as well as poetry. In 'Hérodiade', we are alternately aware of the length and complexity of the sentences, of the rhythm created by an emphatic use of repetitions and of the insistent presence of rich rhymes. Not only in poetry, but also in prose texts, the typography chosen by Mallarmé, with great attention given to *blanc* and type-face, contributes to a sense of dramatic fragmentation of the ordinary text, a sense that the *blancs* might well represent the deletion of what is a banal connecting sentence between paragraphs or single sentences. A text such as 'Crise de vers' or 'L'Action restreinte' has an immediate visual impact on the reader. The banal white space is too strikingly self-conscious to be ignored, a referent within which the more extraordinary syntactical events can take place. Mallarmé exploits this banal white space to such a degree that its very ordinariness becomes the focus of extraordinary attention from the reader and forces its banality into the writing.

IV. Omission of finite verbs, extensive use of infinites

Within a list of typically Mallarmean syntactic features, the frequent omission of finite verbs must also figure. In 'Las de l'amer repos', we find

- Que dire à cette Aurore [...] [P, 16]

in 'L'après-midi d'un faune':

Et de faire aussi haut que l'amour se module
Evanouir du songe ordinaire de dos [P, 37]

in 'La chevelure':

Mais sans or soupirer que cette vive nue [P, 40],

'M'introduire dans ton histoire' (1887) has an infinitive in the very first line. In the prose texts also, we find the frequent omission of finite verbs and a propensity to use infinitives. In 'Crise de vers', we read: 'Ouïr l'indiscutable rayon' [OC, 365] and further on 'Parler n'a trait à la réalité des choses que commercialement' [OC, 366], 'Narrer, enseigner, même décrire' [...] [OC, 368], 'A quoi bon la merveille de transposer un fait de nature en sa presque disparition vibratoire' [...] [OC, 368]. Is Mallarmé trying to escape time, to avoid syntactically engaging with the process of time-flow and to transfer even language on to a timeless, static plane? Time, as the general condition within which our ordinary world evolves is one of the first grammatical concepts to be inculcated. No child escapes the tedious learning of *conjugaisons*. The deliberate avoidance of the conjugated verb, if it gives Mallarmé's sentence a superficial look of simplicity, seems an artificial removal from an unavoidable fact of life and from the ordinary world governed by time. One could argue against Kristeva's qualification of the Mallarmean predilection for infinitives that it is not a symptom of *sur*-grammaticalité but of 'sous-grammaticalité'. And yet the banal avoidance of objective reality can have positive creative consequences. The opting out of time is also an opting into new, richer and more diverse possibilities at the syntactic level, into a simplification which has nothing to do with impoverishment but has an exploratory quality with a strange sense of residual impenetrability, 'Avec le rien de mystère, indispensable, qui demeure, exprimé, quelque peu' [OC, 370].

The second consequence of the use of infinitives is the disappearance not only of time markers, but also in a number of cases of the subject. Thus Mallarmé manages to escape on the one hand the constraints of time, and on the other the clear identification and identity of a named agent. The resulting dispersal, absence or rejection of a single unified entity functioning within the sentence as motivating and acting force further highlights a systematised hesitancy at the symbolic level. The poet calls into question the fixed boundaries between subject and object, between noun and verb, not by open destruction of the syntactic order, but by a productive subversion of the principle that assigns clear functions to syntactic elements and expects logical links and expressed relations between grammatical units. The principle at work has both to do with Lefèbvrian ambiguity or Heideggerian refusal and concealment. In its amalgamation of both models, it operates within the texts a dispersal that conceals an ambiguous presence whilst it refuses to acknowledge the supremacy of a time bound 'being' and unified subject.

V. Use of adverbs in -*ment*

The stylistic features that we have identified within the Mallarmé corpus are present, as we have seen, both in the poetry and in the prose works, and although much more evident in the later works, are discreetly displayed in the early works also. We need to include in this inventory Mallarmé's partiality for adverbs in -*ment*. Although a study of adverbs might well belong to another area of inquiry, that of lexis, the use of adverbs such as *ordinairement, quotidiennement* and *probablement* is a significant feature of Mallarmé's use of language and can also be studied from a syntactic angle. In 'Prose' (1885), the position and over-emphasised importance of *ordinairement* underlines not its ordinariness but its extraordinariness. In *La Dernière Mode*, where it also features in the sentence 'et les grandes amitiés inoubliables de la vie naissent ordinairement de ce fait' [OC, 716-7] it has a less emphatic force but in 'Variations sur un sujet' it is set with some grandeur between two commas: 'Quelque fidélité suppléant ce qu'on appela, ordinairement, le public' [OC, 416]. The adverb *quotidiennement* is also used in 'Médaillons et portraits', for instance, again placed before the verb: '[...] juste de quoi autoriser la discrétion dont toujours il voila son intimité, même aux siens, celui qui quotidiennement y tendait l'étoffe de fastueux pensers' [OC, 483]. In the essay: 'Sur l'idéal à vingt ans' (1898), where it also precedes the verb, it has the effect of strongly emphasising the labour involved in literary creation: 'Le moyen, je le publie, consiste quotidiennement à épousseter, de ma native illumination, l'apport hasardeux extérieur, qu'on recueille, plutôt, sous le nom d'expérience' [OC, 883].

In the prose poem 'Le démon de l'analogie' (1891), we find a wealth of adverbs in *-ment*, all ordinary in themselves; but their very length and syntactic isolation within the sentence make them extraordinary. The use of the six adverbs mentioned above shows a typically oscillatory pattern between certainty and uncertainty, between glimpses of near-understanding and confusion, between language as tool of the poet's trade and language as an unfamiliar and unnerving medium with a life of its own. The poet's mastery and control of language (as described in his quotidian labours) suddenly proves to be less of a certainty and possibly guided by forces outside his control. A reality that has no rational explanation intrudes into the poet's own subjective world in a way that gives his ordinary world an extraordinary dimension. Where the adverb *quotidiennement* precedes the verb, it introduces within the strangeness of the familiar the sheer relentless difficulty of working with language, but also the boredom of the linguistic task imposed by the poet's teaching profession, 'le reste mal abjuré d'un labeur de linguistique par lequel quotidiennement sanglote de s'interrompre ma noble faculté poétique' [OC, 273].

Why is there such a strong adverbialising of the quotidian world? The banal seems to be deliberately introduced as an inescapable referent within which less ordinary syntactic events happen. The function of the adverb is to accompany a syntactically essential verb. But the sheer weight and length of the adverb overshadowing the verb it accompanies make it not so much a secondary modifying term as the principal, highlighted element of the sentence. In 'Le Démon de l'analogie', it has the task of setting the whole unsettling, *unheimlich* episode within an ordinary day in the routine of the poet's life. These adverbs also suggest continuity, a backcloth and by their very presence, the ordinary as background to more extraordinary events is taken into account. In the essay on 'Berthe Morisot', it is the adverb *ordinairement* itself which has an unfamiliar effect, as it does not accompany a verb but is teamed with a noun: 'les expositions ordinairement de Monet et Renoir' [OC, 533]. The ellipsis of the verb it accompanies clearly shows the supremacy of the adverb over the verb which might seem syntactically more important. The naming of the ordinary as qualifier in this insistent manner, teamed in extraordinary fashion with an unexpressed verb and adjacent to artistic events out of the ordinary (*les expositions*) seems to bring together two worlds, the quotidian and art, two realms which endow each other with new meaning by their very proximity.

VI. Isolative and Dislocatory Syntax

Proximity in terms of Mallarmean syntax does not always mean harmony or a satisfying bringing together of complementary terms. Leo Bersani writes in *The Death of Stéphane Mallarmé*:

> [...] the opposition between chance and necessity seems irrelevant to a view of words 'par le heurt de leur inégalité mobilisés' that is, to a view of the disruptive effect of verbal juxtapositions on structural stability. The peculiarities of Mallarmé's syntax, far from reinforcing structural coherence, set words free from their relational 'necessities'. Mallarmé frequently begins his poems, and even his prose pieces, with de-stabilising, anti-structural lines in which the principal relations among words are merely relations of shock or collision. (p.75)

If necessity seems to govern orthodox syntax, what is it that governs a style 'in which the principal relations [...] are merely relations of shock and collision'? One could argue that it is a self-conscious and persistent determination to establish new and unusual, even extraordinary relations, not by including syntactic links, but by removing them all. It is the removal of links, arising out of a new and violent vision of syntax, a forced proximity, that promotes an overlapping of different qualities and orders of experience, of different categories of images. Adjacency and isolation are sometimes conflicting in their effects, sequences of syntactic elements are often more important as time indicators than the verb endings and the interaction of elements is left to the elements themselves rather than to a pattern of syntactic links.

The effect is one of self-generated energy, of a re-energising of the ordinary, of a re-endowing of it with a sense of contained violence and of uncertain and precarious balance where apparent unresolvedness masks extreme manipulation and control. The parsing of 'A la nue accablante tu' [P, 71], for instance, is at the very least an exercise in interpretation and choice rather than a straightforward application of grammatical rules. The ambiguous *tu* of the first line seems in itself a monosyllabic outrage to orthodox syntax, a forceful reminder that the most familiar looking words can be exploited in the most unfamiliar ways. The extensive use of interpolation has the effect of controlled aggression, of tearing apart of words that belong together syntactically and semantically.

Alongside the sense of control and manipulation the reader often gets an overall impression of confusion, fragmentation and hesitancy rather than control. We are reminded that under the ordered and unifying surface of ordinary terms grammatical revolution and syntactic anarchy may lurk. Syntax is a means both of applying laws and of subverting them, of being subject to them and of using them, of control and of dispersal; that which disperses also retrieves. In the essay on Edouard Manet, we read:

> Cet œil - Manet - d'une enfance de lignée vieille citadine, neuf, sur un objet, les personnes posé, vierge et abstrait, gardait naguères l'immédiate fraîcheur de la rencontre, aux griffes d'un rire du regard, à narguer, dans la pose, ensuite, les fatigues de vingtième séance [OC, 532].

The constant truncation, as in the first part of the sentence, the deferrals, particularly of the main verb 'gardait', the interpolations and grammatical ambiguities, (the adjectives 'posé, vierge et abstrait' could qualify both 'œil' and 'objet', for instance) make this sentence difficult to read and require a mental exercise in re-uniting the dislocated elements. The movement of the sentence is not one of uniform, linear unfurling, but one of self-referral backwards and forwards in a way that gives syntax absolute control over time: the reading time and the more general time-pattern ultimately fused with past and future, an experience more akin to *temps vécu* than to scientific or objective time. Time is therefore re-invested with that arbitrary, subjective quality which is part of the ordinary experience of life. Extraordinary and complex syntax here is making a simple, banal statement on the nature and quality of an everyday experience of time.

The more complex Mallarmean syntax will therefore always gain from an analysis that will on the one hand place it within the general referent of ordinary experience, and on the other hand rediscover in the process of reading the ordinary hidden within the text. Thibaudet and Virginia LaCharité advocate a reading of Mallarmé in reverse, and detect in his writings 'a pattern of inverse association and meaning'.[79] This for LaCharité is the key to an understanding of Mallarmé's more complex and puzzling works. But it is too simplistic and might well be misleading when studying a poem as difficult as 'Prose' or *Un Coup de Dés*. The texts have to be read not just backwards but also of course forwards, diagonally, laterally, looking for alternation, pulsation and gradation. The time experience for the reader of Mallarmé, intimately linked to the spatial dimension of the disordering on the page of the syntactic elements is one that will reproduce the ordinary processes of memory and dream, of projection into past and future, but in such rapid sequence that the ultimate effect may be one of simultaneity and timelessness.

The use of a syntax of violence, where dislocation and interpolation are a main stylistic feature, where isolative devices are frequent, paradoxically promotes within the larger unit of the sentence and beyond the superficial fragmented look, a new kaleidoscopic creation of *rapports*. Alongside the destruction of what seems familiar via, in syntactic terms, an unfamiliar and extraordinary route, we discover that our experience of reading Mallarmé can lead us back to a re-energised perception of the everyday. Mallarmé's refusal 'd'exhiber les choses à un imperturbable premier plan' [OC, 384] accounts for the sometimes disorientating focus of his syntax and its consequent effect of complexity. The violent breaking up of the sentence and the substitution of isolation and adjacency for syntactical links have opened up the possibility of multi-connectability, or of a synchronic network of meanings.

VII. Punctuation

The visible syntactic signs of truncation and dislocation are often represented on the page by punctuation. Mallarmé's use of punctuation is often extraordinary in its effects and deserves analysis. Malcolm Parkes, in *Pause and Effect: an Introduction to*

---

[79] See Virginia LaCharité, *Un Coup de Dés: the Dynamics of Space* (Lexington, Kentucky: French Forum, 1987), p.172.

the History of Punctuation in the West describes the ordinary function of punctuation:

> Its primary function is to resolve structural uncertainties in a text, and to signal nuances of semantic significance which might otherwise not be conveyed at all, or would at best be much more difficult for a reader to figure out. (p.1)

So what does Mallarmé's punctuation do? It is rather difficult to ascertain as it is not always clear where editorial changes have been made, particularly by Mondor on the prose texts. The reader of Mallarmé has therefore to take into account an editing process, which might not always reflect Mallarmé's own choices. Nevertheless, the punctuation in his verse is open to fewer uncertainties. As a typographic and rhythmic element of verse, it is extremely sparse, and might indicate that Mallarmé does not seek to 'resolve structural uncertainties' but rather attempts to conserve them, or to remove a conventional use of sign that is barely necessary in a poem such as 'Petit air' [P, 54], for instance, where the three octosyllabic quatrains and the last two lines have a clear structure and a strong rhythmic pattern. If it is by its absence that punctuation might give rise to ambiguity in poetry, it is by its insistent superabundant presence that it actively creates and encourages ambiguity in Mallarmé's prose. It rarely has the clear role of elucidating, but rather that of lending the text a curiously porous texture, full of pauses that interrupt the natural flow and act as silent links where expressed links have been deleted. The text is cut up into a jigsaw puzzle of sections, shaped by commas, full stops and semi-colons. Mallarmé effectively, both in poetry and prose, subverts the common purpose of punctuation, which is to remove ambiguity.

Present or absent, the role of punctuation is not to clarify, then, but is either to protect ambiguity or to create possible new meaning. Judy Kravis notes in *The Prose of Stéphane Mallarmé: the Evolution of a Literary Language*: 'in 'Variations', Mallarmé even goes so far as to use punctuation and layout as virtual and sparse part of speech' (p.82). Indeed where one might expect coordination, or subordination, one often finds the silent pause of a comma. The following sentence from the essay on Villiers de L'Isle-Adam, by making extraordinary use of commas, seems to be subjected to a kind of infiltration by silence and a dimension other than that of language:

> Le même partout, ou le seul, sur l'asphalte et dans sa nuée, ce personnage, énonciateur de merveilleux discours tout à l'heure répercutés, à tout le moins jouissait de sa situation, étranger presque avec les mêmes mots, mieux employés - on restait, lui parti, certes étonné comme par la grandiloquence d'un texte en suspens, sauf à n'apercevoir, en réalité, maintenant, dans l'espace, d'autres majuscules que d'étalages ou d'annonces. [OC, 484]

The punctuation here seems to help to reproduce a sense of spoken, conversational rhythm, and of emerging thoughts as the writer remembers his friend, with all the usual pauses involved in the process. The painful, hesitant work of memory, the attempt to express a sense of loss, its effect on the everyday world of those left behind all find their expression in the over-use of punctuation. In this way, we are part of the *labeur de linguistique*, of the physical labour involved in writing and of the emotional travail of memory and grief. Thibaudet writes in *La Poésie de Stéphane Mallarmé*:

> Mallarmé, pour sa prose, veut créer une ponctuation qui ne soit pas du dehors et de la grammaire, appliquée au discours, mais qui s'exhale du dedans, conscience et sueur visible de l'effort par lequel la pensée développe sa plénitude de vie. (p.334)

Punctuation here is almost seen as the 'breathing' of the text, a pacing and pulsating that is not one of easy flow but one of difficult and arduous labouring.

The very unfamiliarity of Mallarmé's use of punctuation seems to produce simultaneously two contrasting effects: on the one hand, it protects and creates ambiguity, truncates the sentence in an unusual and disorientating manner, introduces uncomfortable silences into what would seem to be the natural flow of syntax, on the other hand its strangeness as written text might feel quite familiar in the course of ordinary conversation, where silences instead of expressed links are more acceptable, as is a less obviously structured and more appositional style. The insistent rhythmic pattern has also some of the characteristics, almost distractingly so at times, of a most ordinary experience, that of breathing. The text is therefore caught in a tension between familiar and unfamiliar, a tension which in some ways remains quite unresolvable by the reader trapped in the intriguing effects of a punctuation which is subversive but also possesses the almost tangible quality of a physical manifestation.

VIII. Syntax and time

Temporal assumptions and language are an integral part both of everyday life as experienced in its most banal manifestations and of artistic and literary representations. Time is indeed a major thematic and structural principle, and the poetry and prose of Mallarmé exploit this dimension as subject matter, at the metaphorical level and within the verbal fabric of his work. In the second part of this chapter, it is more specifically with its syntactic and occasionally lexical manifestations - where they overlap - that this study is concerned. The questions that arise centre on the relationship between syntactic time in Mallarmé's work and the dimension of the banal. The banal world not only has its own temporal dimension inseparable from its particular qualities of uniformity, ordinariness and routine, but it is often seen in terms of time, and expressed, measured and assessed within a lexis related to the temporal. Routine and boredom are evaluated in time, time rendered empty and unproductive. Syntactic time in Mallarmé's work is one expression of the temporal dimension which can be measured against the time of the banal. What type of constraints does it bring to the time axis that makes it of particular interest? What is the nature of the relationship and how is it possible to highlight particular points of overlap and interaction, and to offer an interpretative conclusion derived from a close syntactic analysis?

Time in language is most explicitly expressed in the use of syntax, and it seems therefore most helpful to devote the introductory part of this study to an anthology of time markers in Mallarmé's *œuvre*. It will comprise a section on nouns and lexis, on adverbs, on verbs and tenses, on the structure and chronology of sentences, on punctuation and the way it affects reading time. The second part of the study will isolate special moments of interest within the Mallarmé corpus which display the interaction between banal and temporal in particularly fascinating, original and unusual syntactic terms: a predilection for the substantive rather than the verb, an extremely understated and discreet use of tenses, a liberal use of the infinitive, a tendency to favour long sentences with many incidentals. I shall also attempt to highlight and interpret the use of ellipsis, deferral and embedding in temporal terms, and try to determine whether the clear linguistic choices of temporal indexicals and time markers are in fact motivated by the poet's attitude towards ordinary life. In the third and final part of this analysis, I shall compare Mallarmé's treatment of the banal and of the temporal dimensions, and draw conclusions as to the possibility of dealing with the two dimensions separately. I shall also underline the new ways in which a close syntactic analysis centred on two specific areas, time and the world of the ordinary, enables the reader of Mallarmé to discover a rich exegetical potential.

In the Mallarmé corpus, as in most literary works, the dynamic representation of time seems to rest mainly in the use of verb and tense.[80] Although linguistic utterances are subject to the linearity of chronological reading time, and therefore may be thought to exist in a permanent present, properties such as non-linearity, non-circularity and duration are expressed by the various time markers within the sentence. Mallarmé is particularly adept at manipulating tenses, displaying a restlessness which betrays a certain *nervosité* where time is concerned. This unease is reflected in the way time is rendered more complex, expressed not so much as a succession of moments, but also as past, present and future experienced conjointly, or as an eternal present of varying value. Time in its everyday manifestations is both sustaining and destructive, the locus of hope and fulfilment, and that of death. It is this very awareness of the banality and the complexity of time that Mallarmé attempts to express, both acknowledging and trying to escape from the constraints of the ordinariness and the extraordinariness of time. The complexities and the essentially ambiguous nature of time are represented by a complex system of tenses, aspect, mode and temporal modifiers. It is possible to distinguish explicit and implicit ways of speaking about time. Obviously, both are present in the Mallarmé corpus. 'Hérodiade' [P, 77-9], for instance makes numerous references to the past by specific designation: 'le neigeux jadis', 'un passé de ramages', 'du passé longue évocation', etc. The use of a variety of tenses

---

[80] The area of interpretation of tenses and of time in syntax has been much disputed territory. There are obvious tensions and disagreements amongst grammarians about approaches and interpretations. My reader is referred to the following: W.Wolfgang Holdheim, *The Hermeneutic Mode* (London: Cornell University Press, 1984), Cesare Segre, *Structures and Time, Narration, Poetry, Models* (Chicago and London: University of Chicago Press, 1979), *The Voices of Time*, ed. J.T.Fraser (London: Penguin, 1968), Norbert Hornstein, *As Time Goes by: Tense and Universal Grammar* (Cambridge and London: MIT Press, 1993), *Time, Tense and Quantifiers: Proceeding of the Stuttgart Conference on the Logic of Tense and Quantification*, ed. Christian Rohrer (Tübingen: Max Niemeyer Verlag, 1980), Quentin Smith, *Language and Time* (New York and Oxford: Oxford University Press, 1993).

implies some temporal movement within the poem: the present to describe the surroundings

> Ah! des pays déchus et tristes le manoir!
> Pas de clapotement! L'eau morne se résigne,
> Que ne visite plus la plume ni le cygne
> Inoubliable: l'eau reflète l'abandon
> De l'automne éteignant en elle son brandon [P, 77]

the *passé composé* to situate a specific event in the past

> Une Aurore a, plumage héraldique, choisi
> Notre tour cinéraire et sacrificatrice,

the *passé simple* as alternative to the *passé composé* and an extra dimension of finality and desolation

> Du cygne quand parmi le pâle mausolée
> Ou la plume plongea la tête, désolée
> Par le diamant pur de quelque étoile, mais
> Antérieure, qui ne scintilla jamais.

and the future to express potential accomplishment of prophecy or foreboding:

> Reviendra-t-il un jour des pays cisalpins! [P, 79]

The tense variations are particularly noticeable in 'Hérodiade'[81] because of the dominant use of the present tense, imparting to the poem a sense of immobility, a freezing of temporal movement within the frame both of a suspended, almost unreal pseudo-mythological time, and, at the metaphoric level, within the frame of a mirror or frozen water. All the events of importance to the narrative within the poem have either already happened, or will possibly happen in the future. The sense of stasis relates both to time and to space, and the claustrophobia of circularity is reflected at the structural level by repetition whilst the stasis is expressed at the syntactic level by a dominant use of the present tense.

---

[81] For a very stimulating analysis of 'Hérodiade', see Leo Bersani"s *The Death of Stéphane Mallarmé* (Cambridge: Cambridge University Press, 1982), pp.7-17.

In 'Le vierge, le vivace et le bel aujourd'hui' [P, 57], we find a more complex pattern and sequence of tenses: the immediate future of the second line

>Va-t-il nous déchirer avec un coup d'aile ivre,

the present, then a *passé composé* that reframes the poem within a new temporal dimension. In the second quatrain, past and present are brought together in a typically Mallarmean anachronistic treatment of time as the adverb of time *autrefois* is placed next to the verb *se souvient* in the present tense:

>Un cygne d'autrefois se souvient que c'est lui
>Magnifique mais qui sans espoir se délivre
>Pour n'avoir pas chanté la région où vivre
>Quand du stérile hiver a resplendi l'ennui.

The first tercet opens with a surprising future which underlines the poet's imaginative investment in a new time plane:

>Tout son col secouera cette blanche agonie
>Par l'espace infligée à l'oiseau qui le nie,
>Mais non l'horreur du sol où le plumage est pris.

The horror of space is also the horror of time. Both are impossible to escape. No facet of temporal dimension is missed out. Within the *temps logique* of the poem, we are aware that the *temps vécu* moves backwards, from a concrete picture of a present experience into a lost paradise, and then forwards as it springs into a future that extends into eternity. It seems that the only time dimension that is truly uninhabitable for the swan is the present with its contingencies and its ultimate and inevitable promise of death.

But the present for Mallarmé is also the time of the banal. It brings all events into a uniform, flat and dull light:

>D'exhiber les choses à un imperturbable premier plan, en camelots, activés par la pression de l'instant, d'accord - écrire, dans le cas, pourquoi, indûment, sauf pour étaler la banalité [OC, 384];

Therefore the retrospective and anticipatory modes are ways of escaping banality. Heidegger also identifies the domain of the banal as that of an average present, a kind of levelled uniform time, a succession of present moments devoid of the depth and richness of the past and of the potential of the future.[82] The past is a present that is no more, the future is also a present, but that is not yet. The essential, subjective differentiations that are invested in the concepts of past and future have altogether disappeared to be replaced by the horror of the monotonous. And yet it is obvious that the dimension of the ordinary is also located in the past and the future, and that an awareness and experience of boredom, for instance, as in Beckett's *En attendant Godot,* is possible only because of an awareness of the passing of time and of the continuation of time in the future without the relief or expectation of change. The present possesses a heterogeneous quality, made up from a compacted mixture of other time levels. Inversely, the present as expressed syntactically by the present tense can quite obviously describe extraordinary events, and is referred to by George Wright in a statistical study he has compiled on verb forms in the lyric as 'the lyric tense'.[83] It is therefore possible to say that syntax expressing a temporal dimension, particularly in verb tenses, does not characterise the ordinary, or the extraordinary, by any specific markers. Futurity and pastness as well as presentness are part of everyday experience, and syntax has the complexity and flexibility to express both the objectivity of clock time and the subjective nuances of a lyrical and personal discourse.[84]

How do the dimensions of the banal and of time interrelate within Mallarmé's corpus? Is it possible that within the temporal Mallarmé's work is coerced back into a relationship with the world of the ordinary? Mallarmé seems to be particularly interested in describing micro-movements, gradations, subtle transitions, and *glissements* so discreet as to be almost imperceptible. I have already referred to the almost immobile world of 'Hérodiade',[85] both in time and space. In 'Sainte' [P, 41] the present tense is used throughout to express a temporal

---

[82] For an application of the Heideggerian concept of time to a literary work, see W.Wolfgang Holdheim's *The Hermeneutic Mode*, and particularly chapter 3, 'A Re-evaluation of Gide's *Paludes*'. Heidegger characterises this everyday as *jetzt-Zeit*, a mere sequence of consecutive 'nows', a pure position of the clock hand. The past is simply a 'now' that is no more, the future one that is not yet (p.90).

[83] George Wright, 'The Lyric Present: Simple Present Verbs in English Poems', *PMLA*, May 1974.

[84] In *Lyric Time: Dickinson and the Limits of the Genre*, Sharon Cameron explores the effects of a very subjective and personal perception of time on one poet's writings.

[85] See above, pp.89-90.

movement that both extends into eternity and yet has the static quality of a representation on a stained glass window. 'Sainte', written in 1865, has a superficial syntactic unity provided by the use of the present tense, which is subtly undermined throughout the poem by other syntactic markers in the guise of adverbs and adjectives. Yet the amplitude of the time span it embraces extends from one single movement, the time it takes for one evening ray of sunshine to touch a stained glass window, to eternity, symbolised by the reference to angels and to silence:

> A ce vitrage d'ostensoir
> Que frôle une harpe par l'Ange
> Formée avec son vol du soir
> Pour la délicate phalange
>
> Du doigt, que, sans le vieux santal
> Ni le vieux livre, elle balance
> Sur le plumage instrumental,
> Musicienne du silence.

In 'Le vierge, le vivace et le bel aujourd'hui' [P, 57], which has already been discussed in this chapter, within the frame of one frozen moment, *aujourd'hui*, this present is re-interpreted in the light of the past and of an immediate as well as of a hypothetical future:

> Le vierge, le vivace et le bel aujourd'hui
> Va-t-il nous déchirer avec un coup d'aile ivre
> Ce lac dur oublié que hante sous le givre
> Le transparent glacier des vols qui n'ont pas fui!

A close analysis of the syntactic verbal markers enables the reader to follow the rather erratic temporal movements that structure the poem, and form the narrative and dramatic skeleton on which the poem rests. Where the poem rejoins the ordinary world is indeed in the perception of temporality. It oscillates between interior and exterior, between objective and subjective, between physical time and psychological time in a backward and forwards movement, which mirrors the pendulum swing of everyday experience of time. It recognises that the Heracleitian flux of time is rarely perceived in real experience of time, that memory, expectation, anticipation, hope and nostalgia alter our perception and have a direct bearing on our apprehension as well as our representation of our temporal environment.

Having established the interest of a study of syntax, temporality and the dimension of the banal within the Mallarmé corpus, and having highlighted the relationships and overlap between the various terms, it will be useful to compile a limited anthology of time markers in the Mallarmé works. I shall start with a short study of lexis as relevant background to a syntactic analysis. Mallarmé favours substantives, and it is therefore useful to look at nouns used repeatedly and specifically to describe time. Seasons, times of the day, nouns describing the past, either distant or immediate, are legion: *le jour, le soir, la nuit, le matin, l'éternité, l'été, l'hiver, le passé, la fin, le siècle*, etc. Mallarmé does indeed refer to quite ordinary temporal realities by using ordinary substantives prolifically. 'Renouveau' [P, 14] contains references both to seasons and times of the day, and also to a mode of perception of time, *ennui* and *attente*, both seen almost as a pathological experience of temporality.[86] In 'Hérodiade' [P, 77-9], Mallarmé makes liberal use of *jadis* both as adverb and substantive.[87] 'Remémoration d'amis belges' [P, 50] could be interpreted as being temporally situated in the less concrete 'jamais banal', again an adverb used as a noun in one possible reading of the line. 'Sur les bois oubliés' [P, 158-9] also has a precise season and time of day as its framework.

Mallarmé also uses a number of adjectives explicitly linked to time. They act as intensifiers or as modifiers within the sentence, occasionally taking over from the substantive: a variety of forms of *vieux, ancien, séculaire, aboli, antique, éternel* are common in the verse in particular.[88] If the nouns are mainly of time measurements, the adjectives usually qualify the substantives within the framework of the past rather than the present. The various components of the sentence are therefore bringing together different time planes, the present tense of the verb, for

---

[86] The vocabulary used in 'Renouveau' does suggest a very negative experience of time: *maladif, sang morne, impuissance, bâillement, énervé* are terms which express a sense of the insidious and debilitating effects of empty, banal, everyday time.

[87] The repetition of words such as *le passé, le souvenir, jadis* (used both as adverb and as substantive in 'le neigeux jadis'), *l'heure, l'horloge* give 'Ouverture ancienne' in particular an obsessive and claustrophobic quality. Time, and the past have become an inescapable prison where the present just withers and dies, and the future is as alien as a contemporary teenage lifestyle would be to Hérodiade.

[88] The repetition of *vieux, vieil, antique, ancien* in 'Ouverture ancienne' underline the youth of Hérodiade, condemned to live, or attempt to live, in the stifling atmosphere of a rich yet petrifying past.

instance, teamed with a substantive and adjective referring quite clearly and explicitly to the past. In 'Hérodiade', we find:

> La chambre, singulière en un cadre, attirail
> De siècles belliqueux, orfèvrerie éteinte,
> A le neigeux jadis pour ancienne teinte [P, 77-9].

Adverbs of time are also very frequent: *jadis, toujours, jamais, cependant, maintenant, après, encore*, etc. form a list of ordinary words in common usage except perhaps for *jadis*. They refer to a specific moment, *maintenant*, to a distant and undefined past, *jadis*, to an unalterable temporal state, *toujours, jamais*, or to a temporal sequence, *après, encore*. In *Un Coup de Dés* [OC, 459], 'JAMAIS' at the beginning of the poem refers the reader to an extratemporal dimension, that of the impossible. And yet the rest of the poem is replete with a multiplicity of time markers, among them *jadis* [OC, 463] which reflect at the syntactic level the complexity of the relationship between the different time planes.

But the most interesting time marker is the verb and its conjugation. I have already remarked on the frequency of the present tense,[89] which, although it does seem a common feature of lyric poetry in general, is nevertheless in the Mallarmé corpus a stylistic phenomenon deserving of comment and interpretation. The simplicity of the tense hides in fact a varied usage, which endows it with past and future properties. Its apparent straightforwardness is belied by the fact that it is called upon to perform the task of giving a false impression of temporal simplicity and stability whilst allowing under the almost motionless surface of the verbal fabric the subtle play of micro-movements as in 'Sainte'. It implies duration, but also transition, near-stasis but also gradation. The moment it describes is the moment of change rather than a firmly placed past or future dimension. It represents a process rather than an event, or an event in the process of metamorphosis. Its pastness and futurity are too interfused to be readily distinguishable into clear past or future. In 'Toast funèbre' [P, 42-3], the past tenses are reserved for external reality:

> Car je t'ai mis, moi-même, en un lieu de porphyre [P, 42]

and further on

---

[89] See above, p.90-3.

> J'ai méprisé l'horreur lucide d'une larme,
> Quand, sourd même à mon vers sacré qui ne l'alarme,
> Quelqu'un de ces passants, fier, aveugle et muet,
> Hôte de son linceul vague, se transmuait
> En le vierge héros de l'attente posthume.

The immediate future of 'Ton apparition ne va pas me suffire' suggests that, even though the dominant tense is the present, the future as well as the past are an integral part of the present. The crucial temporal question is asked in the third part of the poem:

> Est-il de ce destin rien qui demeure, non?

The answer lies to a great extent in the use of a present tense that actualises the past and already creates the future by its evocation in the present tense.

Among the syntactic devices used by Mallarmé and studied in the first part of this chapter,[90] a few are particularly significant in terms of chronology of the sentence and of the reading time, and need to be mentioned within an analysis of temporality: ellipsis, embedding and the Mallarmean use of punctuation in particular affect the time dimension. Devices of deferral and inversion affect the chronological development of the sentence, thus creating a kind of syntactic anachronism. Examples of this syntactic anachronism abound, especially in the prose works:

> Au traitement, si intéressant, par la versification subi, de repos et d'interrègne, gît, moins que dans nos circonstances mentales vierges, la crise. [OC, 365]

The length of the sentences and the multiplicity of clauses inevitably influence the movement of the sentences and produce a slowing down, often emphasised by the abundant punctuation in the prose works. The reading time is therefore affected, the reader being subject to the slow development, the frequent pauses, and possibly needing to re-read the sentences. Mallarmé himself explained the temporal effect of his choice of punctuation:

---

[90] See above, pp.74-8 for ellipsis, pp.72-3 for embedding, pp.85-8 for punctuation.

> L'avantage, si j'ai droit à le dire, littéraire, de cette distance copiée qui mentalement sépare des groupes de mots ou les mots entre eux, semble d'accélérer tantôt et de ralentir le mouvement, le scandant, l'intimant même selon la vision simultanée de la Page...[91]

I intend now to analyse and interpret some moments of special interest within the Mallarmé corpus, both because of their link with the banal world and because of their relationship with the temporal dimension. Mallarmé's predilection for substantives as opposed to verbs has already been noted by commentators.[92] But this feature is of particular interest when it is examined within a study of temporality. The verb is indeed the word that bears the dynamic mark of time, the word that describes action in time. Why does Mallarmé so consistently avoid it, or use it in weakened and discreet forms such as present tense and infinitives? Does Mallarmé use these features in order to escape time, to avoid the effects of time, and to become immune to a dimension that is an integral part of ordinary life? Georges Poulet, in *La distance intérieure,* argues that 'le temps mallarméen [...], comme le temps normal, est fait de passé et de futur bien plus que de présent' (pp.346-7). Yet this is a past and a future that are only very discreetly indicated.

The number of infinitives, both in verse and in prose, is particularly striking. In 'Eventail', for instance, we find:

> De frigides roses pour vivre
> Toutes la même interrompront
> Avec un blanc calice prompt
> Votre souffle devenu givre
>
> Mais que mon battement délivre
> La touffe par un choc profond
> Cette frigidité se fond
> En du rire de fleurir ivre
> A jeter le ciel en détail
> Voilà comme bon éventail
> Tu conviens mieux qu'une fiole [P, 162]

---

[91] 'Souvenirs sur Mallarmé', *La Nouvelle Revue*, 1 December 1898, p.452, quoted by Jacques Scherer in *L'Expression littéraire dans l'œuvre de Mallarmé*, p.63.
[92] For example, see Scherer's *L'Expression littéraire dans l'œuvre de Mallarmé*.

The text oscillates between infinitives and present tense, with one future tense in the second line. The syntax seems to have caught the very *battement* of the fan, the movement to and fro, always present yet always past and future, leaving to the infinitives the task of marking the fleeting and transitory, almost simultaneous past, present and future quality of the moment. In the sonnet 'Surgi de la croupe et du bond' [P, 67], a similar oscillation between present tense and infinitive finds a precarious resolution in the intimation of a future that has the hallmark of death and the end of any future:

> Le pur vase d'aucun breuvage
> Que l'inexhaustible veuvage
> Agonise mais ne consent,
>
> Naïf baiser des plus funèbres!
> A rien expirer annonçant
> Une rose dans les ténèbres.

The time dimension virtually disappears in the annihilation of a future potential of an emotional, spiritual and sensual nature. The reality of the rose is immediately lost in deep darkness and the denial of any form of action inevitably leads to dark night and vacancy. The imprint of what could have been, or what exists but invisibly so, lends to the agony the dimension of eternity. Time is synonymous with uncertainty, translated at the syntactic level by the use of the infinitive in *expirer*.

In 'Prose' [P, 44-6], the temporal markers are shared between adverbs, substantives, adjectives and verb tenses. The instability of the time location is indicated by the unusual variety in tenses in the fourteen quatrains. The *je* of the narrator within the poem situates himself both within and without a number of time frameworks, and ocasionally leaves the reader with the feeling that the narrator is poised precariously between time planes. Ordinary time is referred to in a variety of ways: with adverbs, *aujourd'hui* (l.3, first quatrain), *déjà*, (l.2, thirteenth quatrain), *avant* (l.1, last quatrain); with substantives: *mémoire* (l.1, first quatrain), *patience* (l.3, second quatrain), *ère* (l.1, fourth quatrain), *Eté* (l.4, fifth quatrain), *aïeul* (l.2, fourteenth quatrain); with adjectives, *antique* (l.4, ninth quatrain), *éternels* (l.4, thirteenth quatrain), and with phrases, *A cette heure* (l.2, tenth quatrain) and *Sans fin* (l.2, twelfth quatrain). It is the interplay between the syntactic and semantic elements that produces the temporal uncertainty, and the time movements, unlike the micro-movements of 'Sainte', span huge areas, from a very distant past to a hazy future and eventually to eternity.

In the first quatrain, the combination of *mémoire* and *aujourd'hui* immediately sets up an antithetical relationship, a connection that will rest on different time planes: is the narrator speaking from the framework of *aujourd'hui* or from that of *mémoire*? The present tense of the second quatrain in 'j'installe' seems to refer not to a specific point in time but to an ongoing process that is able to embrace both *mémoire* and *aujourd'hui*. From the frame of reference of a present stretching back into past time but also firmly grounding the narrator in today, he is able to open up the Pandora's box of memory; the switch to the *imparfait* and *passé-simple* ambiguously presenting events as history, which could also be a dream-past, is constantly re-evaluated and redefined by the intermingled use of the present tense. The existence of an island or a country is perceived as confirmed or discarded largely because of the tenses used: the present tense that characterises the island, 'Oui, dans une île que l'air charge/ De vue et non de visions' has the effect of lending it a solidity that is confirmed by a semantic as well as syntactic element. On the other hand, the *passé-simple* in the last line of the twelfth quatrain, 'Que ce pays n'exista pas', expresses not only the unreality of the country, but its lack of existence in a past that itself is no more. This double absence, almost at the end of the poem, framed in a crescendo of negations and denials, eventually gains the strength and presence of an established fact. The poem is built on a double postulate: on the one hand, ordinary time exists and no one can escape it. Both past and future are part of it, and it is therefore sensible and necessary to acknowledge the fact. On the other hand, ordinary time exists in order to escape it, to re-invent a different time plane, to measure one's imagination and memory against it, and ultimately to defeat its hold, first by taking a leap into a dream-like past, secondly by an insistent denial of its destructive properties, and finally by the use of magic incantatory names, *Anastase* and *Pulchérie*, in order to jump straight from life to eternity, bypassing at the same time the gaping laugh of the sepulchre.

In the poem, the discreet use of infinitives, interspersed with past and present tenses, usually completes a verbal phrase: '[...] ne sais-tu/ Te lever' [...] in the first quatrain, or 'Tout en moi s'exaltait de voir'/ La famille des iridées/ Surgir à ce nouveau devoir', in the eighth quatrain, or '[...] comme à l'entendre/ J'occupe mon antique soin' in the ninth quatrain, or 'Quand son jeu monotone ment/ A vouloir que l'ampleur arrive' in the eleventh quatrain, or 'D'ouïr tout le ciel et la carte' in the twelfth quatrain, and finally in the last quatrain 'Avant qu'un sépulcre ne rie /[...]/ De porter ce nom: Pulchérie!'. The infinitives in the poem are not so much a mark of hesitancy and of the need to escape the constraints of time by keeping all the temporal choices open, as an important complement to an active verb; this means adopting the time characteristics of the verb it accompanies, and being subject to agency. Time is re-asserting its power, even on the temporally unmarked, and the escape from it only allows one into yet another time frame.

In the prose works we find, similarly, that the verbal patterns linked to temporality tend to have a separate status:

> Voter, même pour soi, ne contente pas, en tant qu'expansion d'hymne avec trompettes intimant l'allégresse de n'émettre aucun nom; ni l'émeute, suffisamment, n'enveloppe de la tourmente nécessaire à ruisseler, se confondre, et renaître, héros [OC, 654].

Most of the verbs in this passage have no personal or temporal markers: *voter, émettre, ruisseler, se confondre, renaître*. There is no human agency - the subject of *contente* is an infinitive verb *voter* - and no time agency; the verbs of action seem to hover in a mist of potential unspecified temporal possibilities: *ruisseler, se confondre, renaître*. Detached, untouched by the process of time, the verb becomes more solid and tangible, acquires substance, the quality of a substantive. It becomes syntactically interchangeable within the sentence, as it is not bound to a subject. And yet, inescapably, temporality by the very absence of a marker, is not only suggested but also potentially present in all its forms and aspects. As in ordinary life, where it forms not only the backdrop to ordinary events but also the very fabric of the banal, it just is, it exists at a basic, first degree, unreflective level.

But Mallarmé, if he shies away from temporal verbal markers, makes abundant use of temporal indexicals such as temporal adverbs (*maintenant*, for example), or temporal pronouns. He frequently refers directly to moments in time which are generally part of ordinary experience, such as various times of day, or seasons. In the sonnet 'O si chère de loin et proche et blanche', the time dimension is clearly given by the nouns rather than by the verbs:

> Le sais-tu, oui! pour moi voici des ans, voici
> Toujours que ton sourire éblouissant prolonge
> La même rose avec son bel été qui plonge
> Dans autrefois et puis dans le futur aussi [P, 159-60].

Within one quatrain, Mallarmé both banalises and de-banalises ordinary notions of time. Time is experienced first in its ordinary, measurable dimension, that of years, but is then perceived again from within that dimension as an everlasting summer, as a subjective and almost indestructible plane fed by 'ton sourire éblouissant', joining together past and future. This is one instance where time is seen as enriching, nurturing and sustaining a positive experience. However, the poet does not refer explicitly to the present; the present tense is used, but the temporal dimensions mentioned are the past, future and a static *toujours*. Mallarmé writes in 'L'Action restreinte': 'il n'est pas de Présent, non - un présent n'existe pas ...' [OC, 372]. Bergson[93] also believes that the present is not, that the present is pure becoming, whereas the past has been and does not cease to be. It exists at the very heart of the present. Mallarmé, in his sonnet, goes even further. Not only does the past live at the very heart of the present, it also lives at the heart of the future, in an interfusedness which cannot be separated neatly into a succession of moments but in which past, present and future exist almost simultaneously.

In 'Eventail (de Madame Mallarmé)' [P, 47], we find a combination of time markers both syntactic and lexical. The first quatrain immediately sets up a temporal tension between the present tense of *se dégage* and the adjective *futur*:

> Avec comme pour langage
> Rien qu'un battement aux cieux
> Le futur vers se dégage
> Du logis très précieux.

The present moment of the movement of the fan, a very ordinary event, holds already within its very fleetingness the promise of future creativity and production: *le vers*. But the poet in order to be able to envisage the possibility of future work, has also to ascertain its link to the past, expressed in the *passé-composé* 'a lui' in the second quatrain:

> Aile tout bas la courrière
> Cet éventail si c'est lui
> Le même par qui derrière

---

[93] For a critique of the Bergsonian concept of time, see Geneviève Lloyd's *Being in Time: Selves and Narrators in Philosophy and Literature* (London and New York: Routledge, 1993).

Toi quelque miroir a lui

The future and past find their locus in a transitory present, symbolised by the *va-et-vient* of the fan, a continuous and yet oscillatory movement to and fro between times planes and time perceptions. The future is the place of creation, the past that of inspiration and the present that of the awareness of the existence both of inspiration and creation.

In the third quatrain, the immediate future of *va redescendre* and the infinitive *rendre* intimate the potential of failure, and its continuing effect on the poet:

> Limpide (où va redescendre
> Pourchassée en chaque grain
> Un peu d'invisible cendre
> Seule à me rendre chagrin).

The poet acknowledges the possibility of loss and defeat, and the infinitive of *rendre* devoid of time marker indicates that fear of banal failure as opposed to extraordinary creativity is habitual for the poet. The final lines of the poem, with the adverb *toujours*, both indicating time, and yet denying its finiteness, re-situates the whole poem on yet another temporal plane: that of eternity, or that of routine and boredom:

> Toujours tel il apparaisse
> Entre tes mains sans paresse.

The tension and the ambiguity resurface here, between *toujours*, which can be interpreted either as banal routine and repetition of a banal event - the movement of the fan - or as potential for ongoing inspiration and creativity. The unorthodox subjunctive *apparaisse*, whilst obviously serving a rhythmic purpose, has an unfamiliar ring which awakes new and unusual resonances in *toujours*. It echoes with a strange sense of longing and wistfulness in the temporally unending adverb. Mallarmé carefully avoids giving us a clue. The banal event contains embryonically both routine and excitement; the monotonous *battement* spans the short distance between vision and reality, vacancy and fulfilment, without ever defining it by settling for one or the other.

The immediate present is for Mallarmé the time he finds least congenial, to the point, as we have seen, of denying its existence. In 'Mimique', he speaks of 'une apparence fausse de présent'[94] [OC, 310]. Immediacy and banality are almost synonymous. But in denying that the present exists at all, Mallarmé implies that the banal is either unlocatable or itself does not exist:

> Hors des premier-Paris chargés de divulguer une foi en le quotidien néant et inexperts si le fléau mesure sa période à un fragment, important ou pas, de siècle [OC, 372].

It is within the *quotidien néant* that the banal exists, with its threatening power of vacancy within vacancy. Time, both in its nurturing aspect and its destructive aspect, is represented in Mallarmé's work. It is as the paradox of time is re-enacted at the level of syntax that we are given the most interesting features of Mallarmé's restless engagement both with the temporal and with the banal as they interact.

It is therefore possible to conclude that Mallarmé's manipulation of time within syntax is not so much an attempt to circumscribe and define time as a concern to keep the whole gamut of temporal possibilities uncurtailed. This is the most positive interpretation of his extensive use of the infinitive, of his choice of the present tense and of weak or unspecific verbs. It is also possible to argue that those choices are a way of escaping the contingencies of time, the constraints of a dimension that ultimately is the locus of destruction, decay and death. Mallarmé's perception of time is not the simple flux described by Apollinaire in 'Sous le pont Mirabeau', nor is it the often overconscious and empty experience of Benjamin Constant's Adolphe. Rather than continuity, we have a restless moving from present to past to future as in 'Le vierge, le vivace et le bel aujourd'hui'. Mallarmé is trying to assert a type of performance as opposed to a sequential stream of time. But this surface, illusionary form of performance has the quality of a palimpsest, as one temporal layer hides another, possibly only to reveal a terminal vacancy. As with the dimension of the everyday, Mallarmé's treatment of the temporal is characterised by fear and fascination, by a desire to explore it, know it and own it, and also by a need to exorcise it and to squeeze it out of his work. At one level, the two categories are so totally interrelated that it is not possible to distinguish them and to treat them separately. Everyday life takes place in time, and time affects ordinary life. But both the banal and the temporal are characterised by paradoxical qualities. It is by the use of a

---

94 In italics in the text.

particularly flexible and rich syntax that Mallarmé attempted both to escape and to reconcile himself to the inevitable contingencies and constraints of temporality and of the banal world in their necessary interweaving.

Syntax in Mallarmé's texts has more than a highly performative task; it has mastery over a number of crucial elements of language which are also part of the dimension of the ordinary: time, space, the balancing of tensions and the posing of basic problems which are found to be either insoluble or to need a different order of experience in order to be answered. 'La direction personnelle enthousiaste de la phrase' [OC, 366] does indeed fall to syntax. By a strong reworking of ordinary syntax, by a productive subversion of its laws and an exploding of its limits, structures are made strange, are dramatised and made visible that would otherwise be taken for granted. One such structure, the contours of which are made apparent by Mallarmé's use of syntax, is that of the ordinary. In a twofold process which, on the one hand removes syntax from the ordinary by systematic transgression, and on the other removes the ordinary in the form of banal terms from syntax, we can distinguish the two conflicting elements which also characterise Mallarmé's attitude to time: fascination and fear, exploration and exorcism. In its mimetic function, as in the description of the faun's desire and imaginative apprehension of reality, or in the reworking of time as experienced in all its contradictions and unlinearity, syntax exploits the main characteristics of ordinary experience and re-creates the dimension of the banal. Syntax effectively provides a way of re-inventing the ordinary scene, of readily catching up into the stylistic texture syntactical accidents, incidents and tensions. Different orders of experience are brought close to each other to make unofficial connections, and it is this opening up inside the structure of the text of the possibility of infinite re-connectability, which gives syntax its immense power to create and innovate. It is when connections are not literally expressed, when syntactic links are implied, that connections are actually more abundant, unusual and able to re-introduce an everyday world from which the complex syntax seems to have been removed. But the systematic violation of banal alliances, the refusal to bow to ordinary usage, particularly in the late prose, the determination to violate the Kristevian law of the father as expressed in orthodox syntax will inevitably lead to the treading of a fine line between stimulating innovation and almost destructive vacancy. The banal ordering of a sentence and the use of essential banal terms can be seen either as an unimaginative use of language, or as a reassuringly familiar, almost civilising influence, the oil that keeps the wheels of ordinary communication turning. Mallarmé's syntax, in its more unfamiliar and disorientating effects, skirts the abyss of vacancy as it seeks to exorcise the ordinary and has to deal with the risks as well as the creative potential involved in such a process.

CHAPTER III
Vocabulary: 'Les aptes mots'

In this chapter, I shall analyse Mallarmé's vocabulary, paying particular attention to lexical categories and the way in which these overlap in poetry and prose. Departures from the use of everyday vocabulary have often been commented upon by Mallarmé critics, but a lengthier comparative study of Mallarmé's lexis in its very 'everydayness', spanning the corpus, has not been attempted. Scherer, in his *L'Expression littéraire dans l'œuvre de Mallarmé*,[95] devotes fewer than ten pages to the subject of Mallarmé's use of vocabulary, commenting mainly on the limited use of rare and archaic terms, and deeming Mallarmé's lexis, because of its very commonness, unworthy of further attention. In the context of a study of Mallarmé and the ordinary, however, the analysis of a vocabulary qualified as ordinary is of particular interest. Not only has it generally been dismissed by critics as unworthy of specific comment, but also his lexis itself has appeared insignificant when compared with his hugely innovative syntax. The ordinariness but also the diversity of Mallarmé's vocabulary, particularly in his prose, suggests that accusations in early Mallarmé criticism of extreme forms of eclecticism and of removal from the everyday are often unfounded.

After a brief survey of the use of everyday vocabulary in Baudelaire, Hugo and Coppée, I shall analyse Mallarmé's lexicon in its deliberately limited and often ordinary form in the poetic works, and in its extended form in the prose works. I shall isolate patterns of prominence, conflict in registers, the tendency of Mallarmé's vocabulary to avoid the specific and the specialised in the verse, and, inversely, to include words from a number of terminologies in the prose works.

Mallarmé writes in 'Proses diverses':

> Un vocabulaire appartient en commun, cela seul!
> au poète et à tous, de qui l'œuvre, je m'incline, est
> de le ramener perpétuellement à la signification

---

[95] Jacques Scherer, *L'Expression littéraire dans l'œuvre de Mallarmé*, pp. 64-71.

courante, comme se conserve un sol national [OC, 854].

The poet claims not only a surprisingly democratic use of vocabulary but also the guardianship of a national heritage. Even in poetic endeavour, words do not become detached or alienated from their use or original meaning. The expression of such difficult concepts as 'l'Infini', for instance, abstract and removed from everyday reality as it may seem, according to Mallarmé in 'La Musique et les lettres', 'se rend, comme sous l'interrogation d'un doigté, à l'emploi des mots, aptes, quotidiens' [OC, 648]. Poetry makes use of, and is subject to, the same everyday words as prose or conversation. Mallarmé, in his lecture, expresses a strong awareness of the rootedness of verse within everyday vocabulary:

> - que l'interprète, par gageure, ni même en virtuose, mais charitablement, aille comme matériaux pour rendre l'illusion, choisir les mots, les aptes mots, de l'école, du logis et du marché. Le vers va s'émouvoir de quelque balancement, terrible et suave, comme l'orchestre, aile tendue; mais avec des serres enracinées à vous. Là-bas, où que se soit, nier l'indicible, qui ment [OC, 653].

It is with the very use of everyday words that the poet is able to defy the inexpressible, thereby exposing both the reality of the ordinary and the unreality of a silence that contains not truth but a lie. The rootedness of verse in the words of the everyday does not preclude movement, music or flight, but allows it to communicate with the reader while at the same time serving to 'rendre l'illusion'; the words of the everyday have therefore a double role: to anchor the verse in the reality of the everyday world and thus to communicate with the reader, but also, by allowing artistic expression to take place, to challenge the silence of 'l'indicible' whilst at the same time recreating an imaginary poetic world with ordinary material.

The opposition between poetic diction and ordinary terms had become less and less rigorous and clear-cut in nineteenth-century French literature, and one of the characteristics of modern poetry is the mixtures of styles and registers that is so striking in the poems of Laforgue,[96] for instance. Earlier, Sainte-Beuve[97] and

---

[96] Jules Laforgue (1860-1887), *Derniers vers*, 'L'Hiver qui vient'. See also in *Poésies complètes* (Gallimard, 1970), 'Complaintes sur certains ennuis', p.86, with the well-known line: 'Ah! que la Vie est quotidienne...'

Desbordes-Valmore[98] introduced everyday life into their verse, mainly with the use of familiar or 'intimiste' discourse, and a vocabulary largely drawn from ordinary usage. Coppée[99] followed in their wake, and his talent for incorporating the banal in his poems was readily acknowledged by Mallarmé in 1869: 'Je songe alors à vos poèmes, parfaits avec rien, dont la lumière est si exacte, mêlée à son indispensable élément de banalité; il y a un dosage dont vous gardez le secret...'(*Propos sur la poésie*, p.103).[100] And in 1887, he writes: 'Votre vers au timbre grave et fondu comme un trait de violoncelle garde cette musique supérieure quels que soient les mots et les tours très courants que vous employez comme par un étrange défi' (p.151).[101] Hugo made an impassionned plea for the use of familiar language in poetry, and for the inclusion within poetic diction of words describing ordinary life and everyday circumstances and realities.[102] Being literal became a quality. Baudelaire also extended his vocabulary to include everyday terms, as Gautier noted in his article published as 'Notice' to the 1868 edition of *Les Fleurs du mal*, '[...] reculant toujours les bornes de la langue, empruntant à tous les vocabulaires techniques, prenant des couleurs à toutes les palettes, des notes à tous les claviers...'. In 'Tableaux parisiens', the predominance of everyday terms might almost lead one to conclude that the poetic and the prosaic are interchangeable. Mallarmé's own use of vocabulary is therefore part of a rich and ongoing literary *débat* on the legitimacy of incorporating, on the one hand, a number of words from the traditional poetic lexicon, and also, on the other hand, a significant number of terms drawn from the everyday, including the colloquial and the vulgar.

---

[97] Charles Augustin Sainte-Beuve, (1804-1869), see 'Les rayons jaunes' in 'Vie, poésies et pensées de Joseph Delorme', in *Poésies complètes*, vol.1 (Paris: Lemerre, 1929), pp.95-9.

[98] Marceline Desbordes-Valmore (1786-1859). The titles of poems published in *Poésies* (Paris: Gallimard, 1983) give an idea of the subject matter as the events of everyday life: 'Dors-tu?', 'L'attente', 'Ma fille', 'Coucher d'un petit garçon', 'J'avais froid', 'Ma chambre' etc...

[99] François Coppée, (1842-1908), *Les Intimités, Promenades intérieures*. See *Œuvres complètes*, vol.1 (Paris: Hébert, 1885).

[100] Letter from Avignon, 26 October 1869, addressed to François Coppée.

[101] Stéphane Mallarmé, *Propos sur la poésie* recueillis et présentés par Henri Mondor (Monaco: Editions du Rocher, 1953).

[102] Victor Hugo, 'Réponse à un acte d'accusation', *Les Contemplations* (Paris: Gallimard-Poésie, 1973), pp.42-8.

An examination of Mallarmé's lexicon will reveal a quantitatively modest vocabulary, particularly in the poetry, with fewer than three thousand words used. 'Je n'ai créé mon œuvre que par élimination', he writes to Eugène Lefébure on 17 May 1867 from Besançon.[103] This does indeed apply to the vocabulary used in his poetry. The lexis of the prose is of course more extensive, with a cross-section of terms taken from physiology and anatomy in 'Les Mots anglais' [OC, 889][104] for instance, from the language of trade and commerce in 'Or' [OC, 398][105] or law in 'Magie' [OC, 399].[106] Liturgical and political terminology also figure prominently in texts that are not primarily and ostensibly about religious observance or politics.[107] This points not only to Mallarmé's engagement with contemporary issues and concerns, but also to the fertility of a literary imagination always ready to experiment and innovate not only in syntactic matters but also in lexical ones.

I shall first divide Mallarmé's vocabulary into two broad lexical categories, with subdivisions: first of all the small category of words that emphatically do not belong to ordinary vocabulary, that is to say a vocabulary commonly used by a majority of readers; this will include a mention of archaisms, rare words and neologisms. Against this notable but quantitatively limited category, I shall then set the poet's extensive and sometimes startling use of everyday vocabulary, that is the use of terms that are not specifically marked as belonging to poetic diction, and the use of words borrowed from non-literary terminologies and from

---

[103] *Propos sur la Poésie*, p.91.

[104] See OC, 901: 'A toute la nature apparenté et se rapprochant ainsi de l'organisme dépositaire de la vie, le Mot présente, dans ses voyelles et ses diphtongues, comme une chair; et, dans ses consonnes, comme une ossature délicate à disséquer'.

[105] See OC, 398: '[...] j'y ai la notion de ce que peuvent être des sommes, par cent et au-delà, égales à celles dont l'énoncé, dans le réquisitoire, pendant un procès financier, laisse, quant à leurs existences, froid. L'incapacité des chiffres, grandiloquents, à traduire, ici relève d'un cas; on cherche, avec cet indice que, si un nombre se majore et recule, vers l'improbable, il inscrit plus de zéros: signifiant que son total équivaut spirituellement à rien, presque'.

[106] See OC, 399: 'la législation pétrifiée romaine', for instance or 'Un public, soustrait au recensement, éprouve du goût pour des pratiques, ici, que le maintien, à la cour papale, d'une charge en vue de les confondre, désigne comme vivaces'.

[107] For a list of terms and examples from Mallarmé's lexis, please see pp.145-50 under 'Appendices to Chapter 3' at the end of this chapter.

lexical domains belonging to the colloquial, the familiar or the vulgar. I shall also look at the contexts within which such words appear, and study the way in which ordinary words lose their ordinariness in a given textual environment. Paradoxically, the less common terms can sometimes undergo a process of 'banalisation' whilst ordinary vocabulary gains added depths within a variety of literary contexts.

Scherer gives a fairly extensive glossary of rare words in Mallarmé's *œuvre*,[108] and comments, as I have already mentioned, on their surprisingly small numbers. They are drawn from a variety of sources, from botany (*iridées*, P, 45), to astronomy (*septuor*, P, 59), or physics (*ignition*, P, 40). Their startlingly extraordinary quality is particularly noticeable within the context of a generally ordinary use of vocabulary. Their dramatic appearance within the texts is carefully orchestrated by the writer/*metteur en scène*. As in the case of unusual syntactic events, the rare word has the role of underlining the creative process and potential within language, drawing attention away from, and back to, the more ordinary lexical elements. It might therefore be possible to argue that the etymologically simple yet unusual *lampadophore* of 'Ses purs ongles' [P, 59] splendidly highlights the ordinariness of the remaining words in the line - *angoisse, minuit, soutient* - and functions not so much as an alien term startling the reader out of complacency but as setting up the tensions of everyday versus unfamiliar, presence versus absence, reality versus dream. Rare words tend to be dramatically isolated within ordinary diction, and sometimes teamed with concrete, almost trivial words in an attempt to set up new and rich connections: in the sonnet 'Mes bouquins refermés', the first line of the second tercet 'Le pied sur quelque guivre où notre amour tisonne' [P, 72], the comfortable domestic picture is subtly undermined by the rare word which presents the reader with a number of difficulties. If we refer back to Steiner's taxonomy,[109] this is clearly an instance of 'contingent' difficulty, but by no means only that. Because the reader is induced to feel that he has some understanding of the line, due to the juxtaposing of difficult words with ordinary terms, we also have an instance of 'modal' difficulty, in which the sensibilities of the reader come into play. This is also an example of 'tactical' difficulty in the sense that Mallarmé strives to 'make new' his text by alternating rare and ordinary lexis, setting up new relationships between words.

---

[108] *L'Expression littéraire dans l'œuvre de Mallarmé*, pp. 69-70.

[109] See above, pp.28-35.

Archaisms in the Mallarmean lexis constitute a restricted category, used extremely discreetly. However, their usage is intriguing if only because Mallarmé makes so few and such precise choices. The *nonchaloir* of 'Les fenêtres' [P, 10] referring back to the time dimension of the *souvenirs* appropriately characterises a never actualised past, present only in its unrealised potential, and set next to the graphic details of an unappealing world of human suffering, cast in Baudelairian terms: 'chauffer sa pourriture', 'les poils blancs et les os de la maigre figure' [P, 10]. Again, *oyant* in 'Le Tombeau d'Edgar Poe' [P, 60] is placed next to the word *jadis*, and thus is justified by the reference to the past. The poet's choices seem to be less a deliberate distancing from everyday vocabulary than an entering into an ordinary that is now past and authenticated by archaic diction.

Neologisms in the Mallarmé corpus are a rare but significant occurrence. Their restricted use crucially underlines the tension between an unproblematised ordinary lexis and an altogether liberated and liberating process of word creation. Their more frequent appearance in the prose works hints at the fact that Mallarmé was less conservative and more permissive in his use of terms in prose where the restrictions of rhyme and metre are absent. Neologisms appear in his letters, a symptom of the poet's need to place the stamp of his own creative genius on the commonplace of correspondence with terms such as *flûtise*,[110] and *exquisités*.[111] They also appear in his articles, mostly in the form of lengthy adverbs: *élyséennement* [OC, 535], for instance, in the article on Berthe Morisot, not only lengthy but also weighed down by mythological reference, strikingly yoked with the adjective *savoureux*, encapsulating in the unusual formulation the expectation of uncomprehending art critics. Mallarmé's predilection for adverbs in *-ment*, which has been commented on in the chapter on syntax,[112] reflected in his neologisms or near-neologisms reinforces his general tendency to qualify even the qualifiers, and to add not so much width as depth to his semantic field whilst at the same time mirroring in the lengthy term, syllable after syllable, 'pli selon pli', the unfolding of a fan, or a poem. If one might argue that it is in the domain of syntax that Mallarmé's creative genius is most clearly at work, one could also argue that

---

[110] Letter of 29 October 1888 to Ernest Raynaud from Paris, quoted in *Propos sur la Poésie*, p.163.

[111] Letter of 16 November 1884 to Paul Margueritte from Paris, in *Propos sur la Poésie*, p.136.

[112] See above, pp.81-3.

his sometimes outrageous production of illegal terms is yet another facet of his literary inventiveness.

Mallarmé's lexicon borrows from a vast range of non-literary terminologies, giving his writings a sense of rootedness in the life and the issues of his time. Much of his vocabulary is borrowed from the world of commerce and banking, as in 'Or'.[113] The vocabulary in *Un Coup de Dés* displays a variety of mathematical terms, together with nautical references, intriguingly mapping an impossible and extraordinary journey across the pages in tantalisingly ordinary words [OC, 459]. In 'Sauvegarde', Mallarmé incorporates a range of political and social terms, which clearly show his interest in, and knowledge of, a variety of contemporary issues. They are found next to more traditionally literary and poetic terms such as *lumière, mort, rêve, idéalement, trépas, ombre, mystère, transparence*, thus setting up a constant jostling for pre-eminence between lexicons. The juxtaposition, combination and overlap of the traditionally poetic and the non-literary in Mallarmé's prose produce a pattern of oscillation between a specialised vocabulary related to an aspect of everyday life, and a more general poetic and literary terminology which lends the topic discussed a depth beyond its specific field. Woven together within the text, the double strand constantly removes and reintroduces the theme of the ordinary as the terminologies invest and divest each other of supremacy whilst neither eclipses the potent effect of the other.

Mallarmé's lexis, if it does quite clearly in some instances[114] borrow from the Symbolist vocabulary, is at the same time much broader and much narrower than *fin-de-siècle* taste dictated. Unlike Gautier, who writes in his preface to *Les Fleurs du mal*: 'pour les poètes, les mots ont, en eux-mêmes et en dehors du sens qu'ils expriment, une beauté et une valeur propre comme des pierres précieuses qui ne sont pas encore taillées et montées en

---

[113] 'Or' is based on a comparison between the disappearance of the evening sun and the disappearance of a bank, and concludes with a final comparison between words and money. The comparison is clearly expressed in the various lexical fields drawn upon: the world of banking, that of nature and also that of the writer. The greyness of the banking world is expressed in the terminology the poet uses as a striking contrast to the world of nature and of writing. The moral of the tale is summed up in the poet's evaluation of sums of money: '[...] si un nombre se majore et recule, vers l'improbable, il inscrit plus de zéros: signifiant que son total équivaut spirituellement à rien, presque', in sharp contrast to the writer's task of '[...] amonceler la clarté radieuse avec des mots qu'il profère comme ceux de Vérité et de Beauté'.

[114] See 'Les Fleurs' [P, 12-3] and 'Hérodiade-Ouverture ancienne' [P, 77-9].

bracelets, en collier ou en bagues', Mallarmé's conception of the word is always within a context, 'les mots [...] se reflètent les uns sur les autres jusqu'à paraître ne plus avoir leur couleur propre, mais n'être que les transitions d'une gamme'.[115] The musical metaphor reflects Mallarmé's own concern: to establish relationships of harmony or dissonance between words, altering mood and atmosphere by subtle proximities in the same way as minor or major chords will impart to the same melody an entirely different harmonic and emotional background. In 'Crise de vers', he mentions '[les mots qui s'allument] de reflets réciproques comme une virtuelle traînée de feux sur des pierreries' [OC, 366]. The visual comparison, as it focuses again on the effect of proximity, underlines the infinite creative potential in word combination and its endlessly enhancing effect.

Mallarmé's verbal preferences and valorisations of certain terms need therefore to be framed contextually and also chronologically in order to distinguish the different levels at which the use of ordinary vocabulary takes on particular significance. Indeed, in many instances, it is the position of words within the Mallarmean sentence that determines their semantic value, and not their semantic value that determines their position. Ordinary words will be deliberately valorised by their unusual placing within the line or sentence, as is the case for a number of adverbs, for instance, with the effect of either adding new value to what is commonly held as ordinary, or transforming this ordinariness into something quite unfamiliar.

Mallarmé's verbal preferences in his poetry can be easily established. The fact that Valéry has chosen to use an almost identical lexis gives some indication of its modernity and flexibility. Indeed, two studies devoted to Valéry's use of vocabulary, Albert Henry's *Langage et poésie chez Paul Valéry*,[116] and Pierre Guiraud's *Langage et versification d'après l'œuvre de Paul Valéry*[117] seem to spend as much time in drawing up a catalogue of *mots-thèmes*[118] and *mots-clés*[119] in Mallarmé's

---

[115] Letter of 5 December 1866 to François Coppée, in *Propos sur la Poésie*, p.85.

[116] Albert Henry, *Langage et poésie chez Paul Valéry* (Paris: Mercure de France, 1952).

[117] Pierre Guiraud, *Langage et versification d'après l'œuvre de Paul Valéry* (Paris: Klincksieck, 1953).

[118] Pierre Guiraud's definition in *Langage et versification d'après l'œuvre de Paul Valéry*: 'mots les plus fréquents d'un texte' (p.155).

[119] Pierre Guiraud's definition: 'mot qui ne se distingue pas par sa fréquence

poetic *œuvre* as they do in defining a specifically Valéryan lexis. In *Poésies*, Mallarmé uses a number of terms marked as poetic diction. This is relatively restricted compared to the greater part of his vocabulary, which is made up of simple and general terms derived from a vocabulary used in everyday life. His predilection for words such as *azur* and *aboli* have been much commented upon, and I shall refer the reader to the studies of Marchal, Thibaudet and Richard[120] for an account of their usage in the Mallarmé corpus.

Mallarmé's extensive use of adverbs in *-ment*, which has already been studied from a syntactic point of view in chapter 2,[121] will need further comment from a lexical angle. The adverbs appear throughout the corpus, drawing the reader's eye by their very length and position within the sentence. They seem to anchor the original substantive into the sentence by the length and substance of their very notable presence. In *Poésies*, they tend to be semantically ordinary, but to occupy unusual positions within the lines.[122] The unusual factor therefore is not only their frequency but also their position within line or sentence. The use of adverbs in *-ment* becomes more frequent in the chronology of the corpus. In the 'Poèmes en prose' [OC, 270-89], besides the common adverbs, we find a number of more unusual ones which

---

absolue mais par sa fréquence relative, par l'emploi que l'auteur en fait par rapport à l'usage courant' (p.155).

[120] Bertrand Marchal, *Lecture de Mallarmé* (Paris: Corti, 1985).
Albert Thibaudet, *La Poésie de Stéphane Mallarmé* (Paris: Gallimard, 1926).
Jean-Pierre Richard, *L'Univers imaginaire de Mallarmé* (Paris: Seuil, 1961).

[121] See above, pp.81-3.

[122] See in 'L'Azur' [P, 20-1], 2nd line of the 1st strophe:
    Accable, belle indolemment comme les fleurs,
or in 'La Chevelure' [P, 40], 3rd line of the 2nd strophe:
    Originellement la seule continue
where it is placed and emphasised at the beginning of the line, or in 'Prose', where we find two adverbs in *-ment* at the beginning of the 2nd lines of the first and the 7th quatrains:
    Triomphalement ne sais-tu [P, 44]
    Ordinairement se para [P, 45]
In 'Petit air II', it figures at the beginning of the poem:
    Indomptablement a dû [P, 55]
somehow initially unconnected syntactically to verb or noun, but strongly marking the mood of the poem by its semantic and lexical reference, emphasising by the fact that it makes up the greatest part of the first line the dominance of qualifier over qualified, giving substance to the less tangible over the obviously material.

act as a powerful catalyst for emotive material, trailing in their very length dramatic potential and expanding the poetic charge. The prose works display an even greater use of the adverbs, with prosaic terms rendered extraordinary by this adverbialising. In one of the later essays on Berthe Morisot, it might be possible to argue that a study of the adverbs would suffice to explore the semantic fields and the main themes of the text, as they function as creators of atmosphere and provide a continuum of themes and visual patterning within the text. The near-neologisms of *éblouissamment* and *exquisément* reveal epiphanic moments within the ordinary tenor of life.[123] In 'Conflit' [OC, 355], they punctuate with great regularity the pivotal moments of Mallarmé's essay, whilst at the same time providing a reassuringly ordinary commentary on an ordinary event formulated in complex language.[124]

The lexical sets and patterning within the poetic works are far more restricted than in the prose, but with greater connotative potential. Thus an ordinary word such as *fenêtres*, *vitre*, or *trou* in *Poésies* will have a far wider connotative field than the same term used in some of the essays on contemporary issues, or in *La Dernière Mode*. There does seem to exist a hierarchy of vocabulary within the Mallarmé corpus, and it is not always the more literary or poetic term which is favoured. The extensive use of terms drawn from a variety of terminologies which Mallarmé has carefully woven into the language of the prose works calls for comment.

The vocabulary of *La Dernière Mode*,[125] the fashion magazine ostensibly dedicated to the description of contemporary everyday life, displays an extraordinary proliferation of terms

---

[123] 'Médaillons et portraits' [OC, 533-7]. Mallarmé uses a number of adverbs in *-ment* in this essay, some unusual, underlining the extraordinary side of Morisot's talent (*précieusement, éblouissamment, suprêmement, élyséennement, exquisement*) and more common ones to describe the more ordinary background of her everyday life (*ordinairement, autrement, superficiellement, inopportunément*), and it is also with adverbs in *-ment* that he paints the characteristics of her personality (*passionnément, tendrement, indépendamment*).

[124] The adverbs in *-ment* seem to undergird the whole essay, providing both structure, rhythm and *points de repère*. Mallarmé's own reaction to the invasion of the solitary retreat by a team of workers is expressed in adverbs (*invraisemblablement, librement*), and the workers themselves are characterised by a number of adverbs (*couramment, gratuitement, violemment, interminablement, journellement*).

[125] *La Dernière Mode* was published from September 1874 to December 1874.

drawn from the poetic and the literary on the one hand, and the prosaic and the trivial on the other. The two lexicons jostle fascinatingly for supremacy, invaded by a significant number of terms from the ethical and the liturgical worlds, and even from the domain of anthropology, as is demonstrated in this extract from the *première livraison:*

> Cherchons le Bijou, isolé, en lui-même. Où? partout: c'est-à-dire *un peu* sur la surface du globe, et *beaucoup* à Paris: car Paris fournit le monde de bijoux. Quoi! toute contrée, comme, par sa nature, une flore, ne présente-t-elle pas, issu des mains de l'homme, un écrin complet? L'instinct de beauté et de relation avec les climats divers, qui règle, sous chaque ciel, la production des roses, des tulipes et des oeillets, est-il étranger à celle des pendants d'oreilles, des bagues, des bracelets? Fleurs et joyaux: chaque espèce n'a-t-elle pas comme qui dirait son sol? Tel éclat de soleil convient à cette fleur, tel type de femme à ce joyau. Cette harmonie naturelle régna dans le passé, mais elle semble abolie dans le présent; si l'on en excepte les peuples aux yeux de tous demeurés barbares, ou encore certains paysans qui, chez nous, passent pour rebelles à la civilisation. La Civilisation! lisez "l'époque où a disparu presque toute puissance créatrice... dans la Bijouterie comme dans le Mobilier"; et, dans l'un comme dans l'autre, nous sommes forcés ou d'exhumer ou d'importer. Importer quoi? les bracelets de verre filé de l'Inde et les pendants d'oreilles en papier découpé de la Chine? non; mais, souvent, le goût naïf qui préside à leur confection. [OC, 711-2].

Botany, anthropology and philosophy mix in this characteristic passage of *La Dernière Mode*, whilst the register throughout remains conversational, almost casual and intimate, with friendly interjections (*Quoi!, lisez, importer quoi?, non*), and perfectly appropriate for a woman's magazine dealing with such everyday matters as the preparation of food and remedies for minor ailments. The references to exotic civilisations and faraway lands, which might imply a distancing from everyday life, are vividly stamped as being part of it. The anthropological strand that runs through the text subverts and reassesses what could be interpreted as ordinary prejudices. Paris, capital of fashion and creation in fashion, needs to find inspiration in the 'barbare' world. The familiar environment needs to find enrichment in the unfamiliar. Both as theme of the text and as lexical principle, ordinary and extraordinary, familiar and exotic combine to enhance the philosophical and textual matter of the article. By his use of terms drawn from a variety of terminologies, Mallarmé plays on subtly subversive and destabilising perceptions of contemporary society. Stereotypes and preconceptions are turned on their heads, images and comparisons gently lead the unsuspecting *lectrices* from the familiar world of self-adornment to the strange shores of barbaric lands. The dynamic principle, both in the philosophical content and in the lexical choices of the author, is summarised in a pivotal expression which is also its central message, 'puissance créatrice'.

Subversion and provocation in the choice of lexis are apparent throughout *La Dernière Mode*. In an article on children's clothes, the language of law is used with ironic effect: 'Lois, décrets, projets, arrêtés, comme disent les messieurs, tout est maintenant promulgué, pour ce qui est de la mode: et nul Message nouveau de cette souveraine (qui, elle, est tout le monde!)' [OC, 812].[126] The metaphor of fashion as a dictator of laws is not in itself particularly original. It is the (almost illegal) accumulation of legal terms combined with the humorous tone and ironic undermining of the metaphor in parentheses that places special emphasis on the terminology. The comic and the subversive potential of mixing terminologies is exploited with skill and a grain of perversity by a poet impersonating a female fashion editor. The principle of extravagance as an essential ingredient of fashion is re-enacted at the level of lexis by an extravagant use of terminologies that do not necessarily belong to the area of fashion. This is indeed linguistic comedy of a high order, a source of prime creativity which produces memorable forms of outrageous mixing, matching, re-shaping and intertwining of unlikely vocabularies.

Yet in the following extract, Mallarmé seeks to encourage a practical and economical approach to fashion by attempting to link two different domains, both often seen as peculiarly female:

> Toilettes et aumônes, il y a entre ces deux choses un mystérieux point de contact, et notamment dans ce cas. La mousseline d'un soir, la Robe merveilleuse de Bal peut également se tailler en de blancs rideaux propres [OC, 777].

---

[126] Mallarmé's sense of humour is often seen in his use of vocabulary drawn from terminologies that seem far removed from the subject treated. This is particularly noticeable in *La Dernière Mode*, where the general tone is *enjoué*, sometimes with a sarcastic edge, as in the example above. Both 'les messieurs' and their linguistic choices, and 'la mode' are satirised.

The two strands announced in the first words seek to combine, together with their respective lexes, dream and luxury on the one hand, and compassion and economy on the other. Perhaps 'les blancs rideaux propres' could provide a metaphor in their ordinariness and inexpensiveness, for the basic material of the poet: '[...] les mots, les aptes mots, de l'école, du logis et du marché [OC, 653]. The feature that is notable in *La Dernière Mode* is that, although Mallarmé does write on the subject of *l'école*, as in his articles entitled 'Conseils sur l'éducation', of the *logis*, as in his reports on interior decoration, and of the *marché*, with advice on food and recipes, he does not generally choose a literal and simply descriptive vocabulary, but a rich combination of terminologies that produces by its complexity a poeticising of the trivial and the banal,[127] a subverting of ordinary perception and of stereotypes, and a perverse and at times comic destabilisation of ordinary expectations.

The variety of registers in the Mallarmé corpus, created not only by his use of syntax but also by his use of lexis, can be divided into several categories. We have already listed the specifically poetic terms that the writer privileges, and studied his use of words belonging to everyday vocabulary. Although Mallarmé's language is generally seen as extremely literary, he does make extensive use of conversational, casual, trivial and even vulgar terms. He enters into the imaginative potential and inventiveness of language by enlarging his own lexical domain, parading with notable humour and enjoyment a number of casual terms. These instances of usage of quite different registers need to be studied within their textual context, as quite different conclusions will be drawn from the use of colloquialisms in

---

[127] Mallarmé was particularly extravagant in his description of *toilettes*; he describes here the addition of a butterfly to a ball dress: 'ce cachet, il lui sera donné surtout par une nouvelle complétant les informations qui précèdent: c'est, quoi? l'annonce d'un emblématique Papillon qui, vaste, superbe, taillé dans les tissus légers et délicieux, élèvera son vol immobile à hauteur, Mesdames, de l'une ou de l'autre de vos joues [...]. Vos frisures feront tomber leurs anneaux dans l'intervalle des deux ailes. Brillante imagination, n'est-ce pas? qui rappelle les métamorphoses mêlant à des gazes d'insectes un visage de femme dans les albums anciens de Grandville' [OC, 764]. But Mallarmé is equally lyrical in his description of gas lamps: 'filant dans des verres, il apporte aux séjours d'intimité les réminiscences de lieux publics, évitables malgré tout le bénéfice à tirer de cet agent actuel d'éclairage. Si la lampe, qui verse le calme doré de l'huile est studieuse, comme la bougie, où voltige une lueur ardente, est mondaine, le gaz, lui, a des caractères très-spéciaux: celui, principalement, d'un esprit toujours à nos ordres, invisible et présent' [OC, 736].

poetry, where it will be perceived as marked diction and as extraordinary, and the use of casual terminology in the *Vers de circonstance*.

Baudelaire's treatment of the everyday in all its unpleasantness and horror had not only extended his own vocabulary to include prosaic, traditionally unacceptable words in poetry, it had also introduced a new tolerance towards a wider lexis by his successors. Mallarmé's early and more derivative verse[128] displays much Baudelairean use of terms drawn from anatomy and physiology. But his later work too incorporates a few surprisingly 'unpoetic' or casual terms; if the mention of *poux* in 'La Marchande d'Herbes Aromatiques' in 'Chansons bas' [P, 52] is but a realistically piquant detail, the last line of the third quatrain in 'Billet' [P, 53] for instance, goes well beyond the piquant into the colloquial and strangely straightforward, set in a rather complex syntactic structure:

> [...]
> Tourbillon de mousseline ou
> Fureur éparses en écumes
> Que soulève par son genou
> Celle même dont nous vécûmes
>
> Pour tout, hormis lui, rebattu
> Spirituelle, ivre, immobile
> Foudroyer avec le tutu,
> Sans se faire autrement de bile
>
> Sinon rieur que puisse l'air
> De sa jupe éventer Whistler.

Mallarmé again displays his sense of humour, which is expressed as in *La Dernière Mode* in the mixing of registers. This poem belongs to some extent to the *Vers de circonstance*, written as it was for a special edition of an English review, *The Whirlwind*, and destined to accompany some of Whistler's lithographs in November 1890. Although it is generally referred to as a sonnet, the form of the poem is not strictly that of the sonnet, and its subversion both of prosodic rules and of the traditional register of lyric poetry reveals Mallarmé's comic ability, his eye for the amusing detail and formulation and his delight in the

---

[128] See above, pp.46-62 on the influence of Baudelaire's concept of the everyday on Mallarmé.

juxtaposition of different lexical domains. The vocabulary of the poem curiously mixes terms, which are found in 'Salut' or *Un Coup de dés*, but also in *La Dernière Mode* and in *Vers de circonstance*. It combines both the description of the acrobatic movements of a dancer and the immobility of a drawing, opening within the poem different potential realities: that of a live dancer in movement ('tourbillon de mousseline etc.'), that of a pictorial representation of a dancer ('spirituelle, ivre, immobile ') and that of the artist, Whistler himself, contemplating his work or possibly his model ('De sa jupe éventer Whistler'). The reader is therefore placed before a choice, which is expressed in the mixing of registers, from the colloquial 'Sans se faire autrement de bile' to the slightly archaic 'hormis'. The vivid description of the dancer's movements as 'tourbillon', 'fureur' and 'foudroyer' powerfully sketch the scene for the reader who will himself paint the image in his mind. Therefore, it is possible to say that the poem itself is the picture, and functions at a number of different levels, thus inventing and reinventing new modes of being and investing a familiar scene with a wide range of enriching possible interpretative models. This is again an instance of Mallarmé's literary imagination expressing itself in high comedy, revelling in the sheer wildness and provocative potential of words let loose and exploding on the page in all their specific, conflicting and creative potential.

The later sonnet 'Le Tombeau de Charles Baudelaire' [P, 61], in its effort to pay *le peintre de la vie moderne* a compliment by imitating his own contrast-laden style, displays a high level of conflict between registers. The modern urban landscape of *cités*, *réverbères* and *gaz* is set against references to *temple*, *idole Anubis* and *poison tutélaire*, bringing together on the one hand the unpleasant realities of city life in *fin-de-siècle* Paris characterised by *la bouche sépulcrale d'égout*, and on the other *le temple enseveli* of a strange and foreign religion:

> Le temple enseveli divulgue par la bouche
> Sépulcrale d'égout bavant boue et rubis
> Abominablement quelque idole Anubis
> Tout le museau flambé comme un aboi farouche

The carefully constructed alexandrines and the highly literary sonnet form itself, contrast uneasily with the use of the familiar terms *louche* and *découche*:

> Ou que le gaz récent torde la mèche louche

> Essuyeuse on le sait des opprobres subis
> Il allume hagard un immortel pubis
> Dont le vol selon le réverbère découche

Colloquial language in this context is clearly not ordinary, although it refers to everyday urban life. Its artificial placing within a more literary vocabulary has the effect of defamiliarising the words, setting them apart from what is ordinarily poetic. The prosaic details of the *bouche d'égout*, the *réverbère* and *gaz* become charged not with the positive potential of recognisable Parisian sights, but with a menacing otherness emphasized by the alien presence of colloquial terms. However much Mallarmé wanted to create a pastiche of Baudelairian diction and subject matter, the fundamental unease and tension created by the use of various registers tend to leave the reader with a sense of lexical disorientation only rarely encountered in the Baudelaire corpus.

One instance of the use of familiar terms must be commented upon before we turn to the *Vers de circonstance* and the prose works. The sonnet 'Mes bouquins refermés' [P, 72] intriguingly opens on a familiar noun:

> Mes bouquins refermés sur le nom de Paphos,
> Il m'amuse d'élire avec le seul génie
> Une ruine, par mille écumes bénie
> Sous l'hyacinthe, au loin, de ses jours triomphaux.

The remainder of the sonnet includes some of the more literary vocabulary, and also some rare words such as *nénie* and *guivre*. The second word of the poem seems to be set ironically against the rest of the lexis of the poem, except perhaps for the unusual use of *tisonner* which conjures up pictures of a familiar, 'intimiste' surrounding. The poet's love for and familiarity with his books might have suggested the affectionate use of the term, the very materiality of his books and their ordinary and constant presence a reassuring reality expressed in the use of the familiar term and, although to some degree responsible for the poet's excursion into the dream world suggested by the name Paphos, also a means of returning to the ordinary world of work.

Familiar terms and colloquialisms are relatively rare in the *Vers de circonstance*. Paraphonisms and *jeux de mots*, particularly on the rhyme, are the main features of this poeticisation of the prosaic and the ordinary. Mallarmé makes use of a number of

VOCABULARY: 'LES APTES MOTS'

English or pseudo-English terms[129], among them *club* and *sporting*, thereby adding to the verses a pleasantly cosmopolitan touch, and enriching the lexical background with foregrounded foreign elements. We also find incidences of 'baby talk' as well as the use of the occasional word or expression borrowed from slang. But the greater part of the vocabulary includes and extends beyond the lexis of *Poésies*, and although the verses celebrate ordinary events of life, such as birthdays or the sending of gifts, they borrow from poetic diction a range of terms which throw a

---

[129] They appear in a quatrain entitled 'Amis':

> Ce mot, veuillez le porter à
> Monsieur le Marquis de Trévise
> Au 6 place de l'Opéra.
> *Club* où du *Sporting* on devise [OC,93].

The expression *very select* appears in a quatrain named 'Amies':

> Paris, chez Madame Méry
> Laurent, qui vit loin des profanes
> Dans sa maisonnette *very*
> *Select* du 9 Boulevard Lannes [OC, 98].

The quatrain in which we find the expression *cold cream* has almost a Laforguian quality:

> Comme la lune l'en prie
> Un blanc nuage pour *cold*
> *Cream* étend la rêverie
> De Mademoiselle Hérold [OC, 108].

We also read *Liberty*, ('chapeau Liberty') [OC,135], *Christmas*, ('J'écoute la bonne aventure/ Que vous chuchote ce Christmas') [OC, 156], *Bird'seye* (sic) in a quatrain addressed to Madame Whistler:

> N'allez pas, je le dis en vers,
> Eva, rose qu'on ne cueille
> Regarder la vie à travers
> La fumée âcre du Bird'seye [OC, 156].

The expression *old staff* is found in a quatrain which also includes slang:

> Pleureur moins que chantant victoire
> Ce toast venu d'un du *old staff*
> Exprime que j'aimerais boire
> Avec tous et même être paf [OC, 157].

metaphoric veil over the prosaic world of *mouchoirs, fruits confits,* and *œufs de Pâques*.[130]

In contrast to the poetic works, the prose writings display an extraordinary range of vocabulary and the proliferation of terms taken from a great variety of terminologies seems to be linked to the ordinariness of the subject matter. The more ordinary the subject, the more extraordinary the language. The more extraordinary the themes, the simpler and more ordinary the lexis, as if Mallarmé were incapable of linking ordinary subject or content and ordinary diction. Yet he cannot do without the language of the everyday, 'les aptes mots de l'école, du logis et du marché', as he has himself written on several occasions. The tensions that are created by this inverse pattern inevitably leave the reader torn between recognition of the rootedness of language in the everyday world, and an alienation from the ordinary world. This reflects Mallarmé's own unease with ordinary life, but also his recognition of his need for, and his attraction towards it. The difficulties that arise from an occasionally inconsistent use of registers,[131] from an oscillation between marked poetic diction and general or common lexis, from juxtapositions of slang and literary terms, of ethical and fashionable, result in the fact that the reader is indeed subjected to words 'par le heurt de leur inégalité mobilisés' [OC, 366]. Mallarmé has indeed exploited this inherent *inégalité* of words, exploiting its comic, subversive and

---

[130] There are a great number of amusing examples of poetic lexis applied to very ordinary events, as with the following quatrain accompanying a gift of handkerchiefs:

> Lisa
>   que votre nez répète
> Le salut dans chaque mouchoir
> D'une impartiale trompette
> A l'an qui se lève ou va choir. [OC, 133]

'Verre d'eau' is dedicated to Méry Laurent, and close to the lexis of 'Rondels' II [P, 160-1]

> Ta lèvre contre le cristal
> Gorgée à gorgée y compose
> Le souvenir pourpre et vital
> De la moins éphémère rose [OC, 131].

[131] The inconsistencies in the use of registers can of course also be exploited for ironic or comic purposes, as I have already pointed out.

VOCABULARY: 'LES APTES MOTS' 125

creative potential. One could argue that he has also at times been its victim.

Not only does Mallarmé use a range of terms relating to everyday life, as we have seen at the beginning of this chapter, he also names the ordinary by using a variety of words explicitly referring to the everyday world: *ordinaire, ordinairement, banal, banalité, quotidien, quotidiennement, journalier, journellement, commun* and *vulgaire*, are all part of the same broad semantic field.[132] This amounts to the use of a metalanguage that reinforces Mallarmé's syntactical and lexical engagement with the ordinary. Although the theme is the same, this is a major departure in the way it is handled, and in the nature of the engagement. On the one hand, the ordinary is present throughout the corpus at the level of a lexis drawn from ordinary terminology. On the other, the use of a metalanguage explicitly naming the ordinary by frequently employing the word *ordinaire* and its cognates and synonyms superimposed on ordinary terminology draws attention to thematic concerns and philosophical investigation. The resulting dramatic, exponential multiplication of levels and connections highlights a new anxiety at the heart of Mallarmé's inquiry and response. The specular sense of re-enactment at several levels of a constant, almost obsessive naming of the ordinary, creates at the level of the text on the page an extraordinary effect, an improbable new poetic layering which eventually underlines not the lexical ordirariness but the almost spooky investment in a dimension that is transformed into a new and alien one. The heightened drama that unfolds within the texts is infinitely reinforced by a metalanguage that is, to say the least, *insolite*, if not altogether obsessive in its relentless underlining of a dimension avowedly shunned by the poet. Examples of the use of terms belonging to this metalanguage abound, especially in the prose works, but they are also to be found in the prose poems, and make four striking appearances in *Poésies*. The fact that the only part of the corpus in which they are not used is the *Vers de circonstance* deserves comment. Although these occasional verses are written specifically to celebrate or accompany the events of ordinary life, such as birthdays or New Year wishes, they never

---

[132] I have compiled a table of the usage of nominal and adjectival forms of the terms in Mallarmé's verse, his prose and in *La Dernière Mode*, and a separate table of the usage of the adverbs *ordinairement, quotidiennement, d'ordinaire* in verse, prose and *La Dernière Mode* (see p.145). The tables are largely self-explanatory, stressing the wide usage of the terms, particularly in the prose works.

explicitly name the everyday and are often convoluted and occasionally *précieux* in their form and language.

Paradoxically, the most ordinary circumstances of life are not characterised as such in lexical terms. Can we derive from this observation the notion that the naming of the ordinary so abundant in other parts of the corpus is really the naming not so much of 'le menu jeu de l'existence' [OC, 389] as the inventing of a critical category with wide-ranging philosophical and aesthetic consequences within Mallarmé's writings and his imaginary universe? At the level of stylistic observation, verbal mannerisms such as the persistent use of *ordinairement* arouse the suspicion that they reveal nodal points within Mallarmé's poetic world particularly invested with emotional and conceptual tensions and paradoxes.

A detailed study of Mallarmé's use of terms such as *ordinaire,* and the effects of this unrelenting and pervasive naming of the ordinary throws up a number of fascinating points. The dynamics of labelling and categorising are of particular interest when they relate to the ordinary because they clearly point to rich patterns of tensions and clusters of paradoxes in Mallarmé's emotional, psychological and imaginary world which are reflected at the level of lexis. The most obvious effect of naming the ordinary is the abstracting of its reality in the very naming, the transforming of tangible and specific life situation and circumstances into a concept or a model.[133]

In 'Conflit' [OC, 358], when Mallarmé describes 'toutes les bouches *ordinaires* tues au ras du sol', the reader is left not with the reality of the life and conversation of working men, but with a curiously disembodied and abstracted picture of mouths 'comme y dégorgeant leur vanité de parole' [OC, 358]. When he writes in 'Le Mystère dans les lettres' [OC, 383] '[...] je crois décidément à quelque chose d'abscons, signifiant fermé et caché, qui habite le *commun*', a vague indeterminate and neutral term in this instance, it has the effect not of characterising but of redefining in abstract terms a substantive singularly lacking in substance.

But Mallarmé's naming of the ordinary is also used as a censoring device, a way of ensuring that its explicit appearances within the corpus exorcise a more implicit and less controllable presence. The more insidious and all-pervasive quality of the

---

[133] Inevitably, one is reminded of Mallarmé's 'Crise de vers': ' Je dis: une fleur! et, hors de l'oubli où ma voix relègue aucun contour, en tant que quelque chose d'autre que les calices sus, musicalement se lève, idée même et suave, l'absente de tous bouquets' [OC, 368].

everyday is therefore denied by an explicit naming that categorises without characterising and that labels without specifying. The striking start of one of the pieces of 'Diptyque', 'La littérature' [OC, 850], with the exclamatory 'Banalité!' sets the tone for the rest of the essay; with one resounding word Mallarmé both exorcises and reclaims, excludes and includes. 'Banalité' both includes 'la masse et la majorité' and excludes those unable to grasp 'des notions [...] à un degré de raréfaction au-delà de l'*ordinaire* atteinte'.[134] The censoring process exists both within and without the ordinary, named both to ward off the evils of 'le vulgaire' and to condemn the 'confrères' capable only of 'l'ordinaire atteinte'.

As well as a censoring device, Mallarmé's use of words such as *ordinaire, banal,* or *quotidien* works as a safety mechanism, keeping powerful affective energies in check. Categories and labels are a helpful means of keeping material from becoming over-intense, and naming is a way of controlling and imposing on puzzling or possibly frightening circumstances and experiences a measure of order, understanding and interpretation. In 'Autobiographie' [OC, 664)][135] Mallarmé reveals very little of the tenor of his own everyday life, and explicitly refers to it only once: 'Voilà toute ma vie denuée d'anecdotes, à l'envers de ce qu'ont depuis si longtemps ressassé les grands journaux où j'ai toujours passé pour très étrange: je scrute et ne vois rien d'autre que les ennuis *quotidiens* [...]'. The naming of his own personal circumstances using a general plural

---

[134] This 'Fragment d'un objet d'article' as it is subtitled, the second part of 'Diptyque', has a further title: 'Doctrine', and was written in 1893. The comparison between writers and 'kabbalistes' further develops the theme of magic and occultism within 'banalité', the need to recognise within what is only too familiar, the twenty-four letters of the alphabet, the unlimited potential for true art and creativity.

[135] Written on 16 November in Paris in answer to Verlaine's request for biographical details of Mallarmé's life, *Autobiographie* has a curiously unfinished feel. The poet skims over what would ordinarily be considered important events in life, such as marriage, and chooses to write about his own production and his perception of contemporary literary events rather than the events of ordinary life. Written in pencil 'pour laisser l'air d'une de ces bonnes conversations d'amis à l'écart et sans éclat de voix', *Autobiographie* points to a very Mallarmean concept of the everyday, created to suit his own imaginary universe rather than to accommodate stereotypes of ordinary life. His perception of his world and himself is stimulated by a set of criteria uniquely his, invented and reinvented to encompass an ordinary which is often far removed from a superficial understanding of *the* ordinary.

and an adjective that hides more than it reveals enables Mallarmé to stay safely at a distance, away from the affective energies and disturbing dynamics at work in the quotidian.

But it can also be at times a way of making contact with the world of ordinary human engagements by moving from the concept of the everyday towards an acknowledged reality. The framework of the concept allows for a process of recognition which, if guarded, nevertheless takes in both negative and positive aspects of the quotidian. Time and again the words *ordinaire* or *banal* are teamed with the vicissitudes or objects of daily living, from the description of the 'Exposition internationale de Londres' and the 'décor familier de notre existence *quotidienne*'[136] [OC, 679)] to the painful attempt to remember his friend Villiers de l'Isle-Adam not only in his unique and unusual capacity as a writer but also in his everyday life: 'Sa vie - je cherche rien qui réponde à ce terme: véritablement et dans le sens *ordinaire*, vécut-il?' [OC, 482][137]. Mallarmé earnestly seeks to define what the ordinary means in the life of a fellow writer whom he clearly thinks and labels as extraordinary, a man from whom he would like to ' [...] écarter toute trace *journalière*' [OC, 502], and yet at the time of Villiers' disappearance, it is the ordinary man that Mallarmé tries to glimpse behind 'la discrétion dont toujours il voila son intimité, mêmes aux siens, celui qui *quotidiennement* y tendait l'étoffe de fastueux pensers' [OC,

---

[136] This article was initially written as a conference paper in 1889-90 in Paris, and formed the basis for several published articles. Villiers symbolises for Mallarmé the extraordinary, only occasionally visiting the ordinary world, barely aware of its existence: 'Il habita, à Paris, une haute ruine inexistant, avec l'œil sur le coucher héraldique du soleil (nul ne le visita); et en descendait à ses moments, pour aller, venir, et s'y différencier de l'agitation [...]'. For Mallarmé, Villiers also represents the anti-ordinary, despising 'le sens commun', as Mallarmé makes clear in the quoted extract from *Tribulat Bonhommet*. And yet even Villiers, in all his ivory-towerness and strangeness, can only be defined within the category of the ordinary, or within the limits of a questioning of the ordinary as lived experience, as Mallarmé clearly indicates in the opening question on p. 482.

[137] The answer to Mallarmé's question is both given and withheld in the essay; the difficulty that Mallarmé encounters is one that has far reaching consequences for his perception of the everyday: is it possible to define anything at all, let alone an individual's life, outside of the ordinary as conceptual framework and as lived reality and experience? Mallarmé almost acknowledges defeat when he answers, or does not answer, his own question in terms of complete simplicity, yet complete evasion too: 'Simplement, on le rencontra, ce fut tout' [OC, 483].

483]. He acknowledges that it is easier to pay tribute to the artist than to recall the man in the circumstances of his everyday life.

From the concept to the reality, naming the ordinary is also a way of building bridges between the observation of empirical raw material and philosophical explanation. With great versatility, Mallarmé moves between the concept of the ordinary as a critical category against which to measure interesting departures, and the listing of ordinary components of life: objects, feelings, relationships characterised as ordinary or banal. The reasons for Mallarmé's need to build a conceptual framework have already been discussed. And yet at no point does Mallarmé give a clear definition of what he understands by *le quotidien, le banal, l'ordinaire*. He never consciously queries his own understanding of the words. His image seems intriguingly non-problematised. We are left with a range of ambiguous responses on the part of the poet, which have to be deciphered almost between the lines, and in the larger context of the writing.

There is certainly no lack of empirical raw material characterising objects or situations as *ordinaires* at a superficial and unproblematic level, either in the 'Proses diverses' or in the eight issues of *La Dernière Mode*. Concept and observation interact uneasily as Mallarmé switches from the specific to the vague, from category to quality and from referend to detail of everyday life. The various planes at times confirm each other, but also jostle for precedence in texts which explicitly name the ordinary as conceptual framework only to establish a distance and then focus on the ordinary circumstances or objects of life. The very focusing on a microcosmic manifestation of the quotidian often forces the reader to ask the question: what kind of ordinary is Mallarmé writing about? There are several possibilities: it could just reveal itself to be a rhetorical trick which will enable the poet to conduct speculative thought on the subject without getting swamped by the inescapable presence of the quotidian, or Mallarmé could be adroitly avoiding any real engagement with the world of the ordinary by naming it and its manifestations and accessories only to cover his literary tracks and disguise his fear and repugnance at being drawn into the quotidian at any level. A close look at the variety of expressions and lexical items that cluster around the word *ordinaire* will enable the reader to appreciate the complexity of Mallarmé's response and treatment of the ordinary. In order to demonstrate the dense encrustation at the level of usage it will be helpful to list a number of examples, which appear at the end of this chapter.[138]

The listing of the examples of uses that Mallarmé makes of substantives, adjectives and adverbs naming the ordinary is the necessary preliminary to a study of the different levels of meaning within the various contexts, and to the changes that the same words undergo when used in poetry or prose. Mallarmé makes both ordinary and extraordinary uses of *ordinaire, ordinairement, banal, banalité,* and other terms semantically related.[139] They can either be employed for their very ordinariness, for the simple way in which they designate a whole area of human engagement which is inescapably part of everyone's experience, 'le menu jeu de l'existence' [OC, 389][140] or they can be used in a way that has strong negative or positive connotations, laden with affective energies and personal meaning and interpretations. Most of the examples listed below fit into one or the other of these broad categories.

Mallarmé's use of the substantives *l'ordinaire, le banal, la banalité, le quotidien, le commun, le vulgaire* is relatively restricted when compared with his extensive use of the terms in their adjectival or adverbial forms. Yet they are present even in the 'Poèmes en prose'. In 'Un spectacle interrompu', Mallarmé uses the word *banalité* 'Jouir comme la foule du mythe inclus dans toute banalité [...]' [OC, 276].[141] We find for the first time an

---

[138] I shall refer my reader to the appendices on pp.145-50.

[139] Mallarmé also uses the words *commun, vulgaire, quotidien, journalier*.

[140] This expression appears in 'Plaisir sacré', published in *Journal* on 5 December 1893. Mallarmé observes and analyses the reaction of a crowd during a Sunday concert, and comments: 'Cette multitude satisfaite par le menu jeu de l'existence, agrandi jusqu'à la politique, tel que journellement le désigne la presse; comment se fait-il - est-ce vrai - cela repose-t-il sur un instinct que, franchissant les intervalles littéraires, elle ait besoin tout à coup de se trouver face à face avec l'Indicible ou le Pur, la poésie sans les mots!' Mallarmé acknowledges the important role of the quotidian routine, 'le menu jeu de l'existence', as a motivation for the crowd of ordinary people to want to meet with a form of art. It is because of the very ordinariness of their lives that ordinary people are drawn to the extraordinary in the guise of music.

[141] Mallarmé insistently describes the ordinary backdrop to a gruesome anecdote, underlining the potential and the realised extraordinary, unfamiliar and fatal capacity of the quotidian to hide the unexpected. The introduction to the prose poem gives the aim of the writer: 'Je veux, en vue de moi seul, écrire comment elle frappa mon regard de poète, telle Anecdote, avant que la divulguent des *reporters* par la foule dressés à assigner à chaque chose son caractère commun'. And yet, despite the poetic diction and the complex syntax,

important link between the concept of the crowd, which appears again and again in the prose works, and that of banality, one the lowest forms of collective life, the other the lowest form of everyday life. Yet it can be invested with imaginative power and pleasure, as the crowd is able to discern, and is therefore able to be transformed and enriched by a new perception of the unexcitingly familiar.

In 'Réminiscence', the term appears in the plural, hinting at a more concrete manifestation, teamed with the tangible expression of circus performers: '[...] des tours de force et banalités alliables au jour' [OC, 279].[142] 'Banalités' has to be interpreted according to the perception of the narrator and the main character. The reader is expected to integrate the everyday life of the circus performer, for whom 'tours de force' are part of a day's routine, rehearsals lacking the magic of the evening performance. We see through the envious eyes of the narrator the 'désinvolture' of 'quelque aîné fameux', eager to impress the orphan. We are made aware both of the strangeness of the circus world seen by the young narrator, and of its ordinariness through the eyes of the performer. Yet again, the world of the ordinary is defined not as a one dimensional and absolute reality, but as a perception dependent on standpoint and a willingness to engage imaginatively with what could be described as different and other. One of the most fascinating uses of *banalité* is found in 'Variations sur un sujet', in 'Etalages':

> Or je n'interromprai un dessein, de discerner, en le volume, dont la consommation s'impose au public, le motif de son usage. Qui est (sans le souci que la littérature vaille à cet effet, mais pour l'opposé) incontinent de réduire l'horizon et le spectacle à une moyenne bouffée de *banalité*, scripturale, essentielle: proportionnée au bâillement humain incapable, seul, d'en puiser le principe, pour l'émettre. Le vague ou le commun et le fruste, plutôt que les bannir, occupation! se les appliquer en tant qu'un état: du

---

Mallarmé makes a careful note of the common detail, the ordinary touch, unable to squeeze out altogether from his own poetic perception the ordinariness of the circumstances and of the occasion.

[142] This follows a metaphor of the ordinary, 'une tartine de fromage mou', but transformed by the poet into further metaphors moving the tangible image of humble food into poetic images which are part of the poet's ordinary poetic universe: [...] la neige des cimes, le lys ou autre blancheur constitutive d'ailes au-dedans'.

> moment que la très simple chose appelée âme ne consent pas fidèlement à scander son vol d'après un ébat inné ou selon la récitation de quelques vers, nouveaux ou toujours les mêmes, sus. [OC, 375].

The horizon seen as the faraway locus of dreams, the infinite, the unknown, a line never reached on which desire is hung, desirable because of its unreachability, is reduced to a transient and inconsequential 'moyenne bouffée de banalité', itself vividly represented as 'proportionnée au baîllement humain'. And yet the physiological manifestation of banality is paradoxically preceded by a characterising of *banalité* in philosophical terms: 'scripturale, essentielle'. On the one hand, Mallarmé names and analyses the principle or concept of banality, its essences and its potential. On the other, he describes it as a yawn, the most ordinary human signal of boredom and lack of interest. It is between these two planes, that of the philosophical and that of the trivial, that Mallarmé situates *banalité*, both as concept and as a precise ordinary human experience. In 'Le Mystère dans les lettres' the word occurs again in association with the act of writing, but of an unliterary type of writing: 'écrire, dans le cas, pourquoi, indûment, sauf pour étaler la *banalité* [OC, 384]. In 'Plaisir sacré', Mallarmé, describing a Sunday concert and the response of the crowd, writes: 'Une intitiation en dessous illumine, ainsi que le lavage dominical de la *banalité*' [OC, 390]. The break in the week's routine is perceived as a cleansing from the trivial day to day, but also in a sense as a polishing up and highlighting of its banality. The contrast between art and the everyday is both effaced and underlined as both dimensions merge and clash. In the essay entitled 'Richard Wagner - rêverie d'un poète français', the metaphor in which the term appears has the unstoppable quality of a force of nature: 'Un poète français contemporain [...] aime [...] à réfléchir aux pompes souveraines de la Poésie, comme elles ne sauraient exister concurremment au flux de *banalité* charrié par les arts dans le faux semblant de civilisation'. [OC, 541]. In 'Crayonné au théâtre - Autre étude de danse', *banalité* has a light ephemeral yet constant quality: 'Toujours une *banalité* flotte entre le spectacle dansé et vous' [OC, 308]. In the seventh issue of *La Dernière Mode*, banality is seen as a necessity, which is not necessarily negative. The vagueness associated with dreams, the fuzziness and lack of focus which sometimes accompanies them turns the image of banality as yawn or current into an indistinct halo floating around maternal musings: 'Car nous n'entreprendrons pas de traiter un sujet aussi vaste que l'est l'horizon des rêves maternels; en suivre une fois pour toutes les traits généraux, un peu vagues par cela même et nécessairement accompagnées de quelque *banalité*' [OC, 812-3]. We have already commented on the use of *banalité* as a single word sentence and exclamation at the beginning of the 'Diptyque', setting a tone which is unusually emotional in its exclamatory effect, echoed half-way through the text by a forceful rejoinder in a further exclamation 'Si!' as if Mallarmé himself had taken on single-handed the battle against the tide of contemporary banality on the *fin-de-siècle* literary scene.

The use of the adjective *banal* in its substantive form of *le banal* is far less frequent, but its appearances introduce a quite different facet of Mallarmé's attitude towards ordinary life. In 'Crayonné au théâtre', the poet creates an interestingly paradoxical metaphor of the banal: '[...] il a fallu formidablement, pour l'infatuation contemporaine, ériger, entre le gouffre de vaine faim et les générations, un simulacre approprié au besoin immédiat, ou l'art officiel qu'on peut aussi appeler vulgaire; indiscutable, prêt à contenir par le voile basaltique du *banal* la poussée de cohue jubilant si peu qu'elle aperçoive une imagerie brute de sa divinité' [OC, 298]. In 'L'Action restreinte', the writer is seen as 'le spirituel histrion' [OC, 370] as well as present anonymously in his hero, and Mallarmé tellingly places him both within the banal and yet clearly visible and distinct from it: 'Le reconnaîtra-t-on dans ces immeubles suspects se détachant, par une surcharge en *le banal,* du commun alignement, avec prétention à synthétiser les faits divers d'un quartier' [OC, 371]. In both extracts, the banal, as opposed to the transience and vagueness of *banalité,* possesses a solidity and a substance immovable in its rock-like quality. *La banalité* for Mallarmé exists almost solely at the conceptual level, defined only by its lack of definition, or in contrast to other characteristics; *le banal* is used as the tangible backdrop against which and within which unusual events happen, an ordinary street for instance, or the routine of daily life.

The occurrence of *l'ordinaire, le quotidien* and *le commun* are far less common in the Mallarmé corpus. In his third letter on the International London Exhibition, Mallarmé associates ugliness and ordinariness: 'Ceux-là seuls qui ont le goût inné du laid ou de l'ordinaire ont, depuis ces quelques années, le droit de s'entourer d'autre chose que d'objets aimables et de goût certain' [OC, 676-7]. *L'ordinaire* in this instance refers to the object of everyday life devoid of aesthetic qualities. Mallarmé uses the substantive *le quotidien* quite often as referring to daily newspapers as in 'Le Livre, instrument spirituel': 'Ainsi, strictement, un *"quotidien"* avant qu'à la vision, peu à peu, mais de qui? paraisse un sens, dans l'ordonnance, voire un charme, je dirai de féerie populaire' [OC, 379]. The quotation marks in the text draw particular attention to the word, emphasising its meaning of everydayness, its literal rather than accepted commercial sense. In 'Etalages', Mallarmé discusses the negative and positive value of the *feuilleton* in the daily papers, the closest the ordinary working-class man at the end of the nineteenth century would get to a literary text: 'Mieux, la fiction proprement dite ou le récit, imaginatif, s'ébat au travers de "quotidiens" achalandés, triomphant à des lieux principaux, jusqu'au sommet; en déloge l'article de fond, ou d'actualité, apparu secondaire' [OC, 376]. In 'Hamlet', Mallarmé uses the term in its less specific meaning of quotidian, in describing the experience of the actress playing Ophelia: 'elle a du naturel, comme l'entendent les ingénues, préférant à s'abandonner aux ballades introduire tout *le quotidien* acquis d'une savante entre les comédiennes' [OC, 301].

Mallarmé also uses the substantive *le commun*, often associated with other terms derived from a similar semantic field. In 'Le "Ten o'clock" de Mr Whistler', Mallarmé argues against the popularising of art, whilst nevertheless underlining the ability of the artist-artisan to discover beauty in the ordinary, and deploring the contemporary trend that valorises the good and the useful above the beautiful. The result is that 'alors jaillirent à l'existence le clinquant, *le commun*, la camelote' [OC, 573].[143] The use of *le commun* is evidently derogatory in this instance, as it is in the rest of the essay where Mallarmé also uses the term *Vulgarité* (with a capital emphasising its supremely negative quality) as the mark of the *amateur* in art: 'il est condamné à rester dehors - et à continuer avec *le commun*' [OC, 579].

Examples of the use of adjectives relating to the ordinary abound throughout the corpus. The most frequently employed is *ordinaire*, which is liberally distributed throughout the prose texts, and also used in the poems. In 'La déclaration foraine', Mallarmé describes the 'rire strident ordinaire des chose et de leur cuivrerie triomphale' [OC, 279]. The ordinary is inhabited by trivial objects, which seem to be screaming out their ordinariness. The quality is here characterised in terms of sound of an unpleasant, menacing and overwhelming nature. The examples of the use of the adjective are too numerous to list, appearing in a wide range of

---

[143] In contrast to the past, 'pas d'article d'usage quotidien, de luxe ou de nécessité qui ne fût point sorti du dessin du maître, et fait par ses ouvriers', Mallarmé describes his time as the point at which [...] se leva une classe nouvelle qui découvrit le bon marché et prévit la fortune dans la fabrication du faux'. What is common and ordinary is also seen as inauthentic.

contexts, from the literary discussion to the anecdotal and the fashion items in *La Dernière Mode*. Again we are led to suspect that the quality of being ordinary relates almost uniquely to the poet himself, and therefore loses its claim to ordinariness in a wide general sense. In 'La cour', Mallarmé writes of 'les décors *ordinaires* de tomes et de parchemins' [OC, 418], yet the beginning of the sentence subverts the ordinary meaning of the term, and creates a new meaning almost unique to Mallarmé:

> Essuyer la poussière, aux chefs-d'oeuvre, sauf en se les rappelant, reste fonction oiseuse, leur vol idéalement lui-même la secoue: il exclut jusqu'au plumeau hiératique de l'ibis à côté de crocodiles et d'ichneumons momifiés dans les décors *ordinaires* de tomes et de parchemins'.

And in 'Igitur ou la folie d'Elbehnon', '[...] la pâleur d'un livre ouvert que présente la table; page et décor *ordinaires* de la Nuit' [OC, 435]. The dust that accumulates on the ancient masterpieces is a reminder of the everyday world common to humankind and underlines the passage of time as well as the static environment of the poet. The contrast between the extraordinary list of unusual momified objects with the ordinary background of ancient books is due not to a simple opposition in nature and quality but to a perception of his environment, which presents not what is ordinary but what is ordinary in a specific context.

Mallarmé also uses the term as a substitute for *habituel:* 'convoquer le peuple des liseurs, l'intéresser, le séduire! et si, une heure accueilli en raison de l'avidité *ordinaire* d'émotions même spirituelles, l'objet de nouveau tombait dans l'oubli cette fois conscient irréparable, sûr' [OC, 563]. The use of the adjective *banal* is almost as widespread and occurs in the poetry and in the prose texts, as does the adjective *quotidien*. It tends to be far more neutral in its usage than *banal* or *ordinaire*, confined either to natural manifestations which form the backdrop to all human activities, or the orderly and necessary framework to life in contemporary society. We also find the word *journalier* as a substitute for *quotidien,* as in the second letter from the Exhibition.

Mallarmé's predilection for long adverbs in *-ment* has already been studied in the chapters on syntax and general vocabulary.[144] But adverbs such as *ordinairement, quotidiennement,* and the adverbial phrase *d'ordinaire* need

---

[144] See above, pp.81-3, p.112 and pp.115-6.

further comment in a chapter devoted to the naming of the ordinary. The fact that *ordinairement* and *quotidiennement*, although qualifying a situation or relationship as ordinary, are not a particularly ordinary usage, and are at times strikingly extraordinary, only makes the tensions created by naming the ordinary more apparent. *Ordinairement* has of course a striking place in 'Prose', but can also be found in the rest of the corpus, in 'Offices', - 'les messieurs qu'*ordinairement* nous paraissons' - [OC, 395], in 'La Cour', - 'Quelque fidélité suppléant ce qu'on appela, *ordinairement*, le public' - [OC, 416], in the preface to *Un Coup de Dés*, - 'les "blancs" en effet, assument l'importance, frappent d'abord; la versification en exigea, comme silence alentour, *ordinairement*, au point qu'un morceau, lyrique ou de peu de pieds, occupe, au milieu, le tiers environ du feuillet' - [OC, 455]. *Ordinairement* lends stability and substance to diverse and varied circumstances, its very length giving the propositions an almost immovable quality. The ordinary is very much present, even in mythology and fairy tales and it is here to stay.

The adverbial phrase *d'ordinaire*, which is in fact a more generally employed synonym for *habituellement* or *d'habitude*, seems to be less favoured by Mallarmé, who makes quite a sparing and unremarkable use of it. The adverb *quotidiennement*, and more rarely, *journellement*, feature also in the Mallarmé corpus, in 'Le Démon de l'analogie', for instance, where the adverb is particularly emphasised and carries the weight of the poet's agony at having to interrupt his poetic pursuits: '[...] le reste mal abjuré d'un labeur de linguistique par lequel *quotidiennement* sanglote de s'interrompre ma noble faculté poétique' [OC, 273]. The routine of teaching, interfering as it does with the poet's literary work, is set in stark contrast to the noble poetic task.

In 'Sur l'idéal à vingt ans', ordinary routine is given positive weight and importance in the use of the adverb: '[...] suffisamment, je me fus fidèle, pour que mon humble vie gardât un sens. Le moyen, je le publie, consiste *quotidiennement* à épousseter, de ma native illumination, l'apport hasardeux extérieur, qu'on recueille, plutôt, sous le nom d'experience' [OC, 883]. Routine examination of one's experience is not seen as an inescapable and almost unbearable punishment, but as a necessary condition for a life consonant with one's ideals. Ordinary life for the poet involves the regular self-analysis that enables him to sift and sort his own experiences in order to avoid any compromise with 'l'apport hasardeux extérieur'.

There are rather fewer examples of low-level, casual use of the words clustering around *ordinaire* than the 'ordinary' use of the terms and their widespread use in everyday conversation would suggest. Their appearance in the poetic works can never be described as casual, and will be commented upon in the course of this chapter. In the prose works, there are occasional instances of simple, straightforward usage, with a view to quick and convenient communication using lexical items recognisable by the majority of readers and needing little redefining because of the generality of the terms. In the 'Contes indiens', where the aim is the communication of a sequence of events, the use of *ordinaire,* and *quotidien* is not problematic, but is a way of characterising time or place, which is undemanding both for the writer and the reader.

In *La Dernière Mode,* Mallarmé is writing for a female public who will interpret the terms within their own experience of the everyday, and the use of the words has therefore to stay within recognisable boundaries for a majority of the reading public. The terms are hardly invested with any affective energy, and seem to be used in a neutral way, with a general meaning of everyday or routine which is neither positive nor negative, but completely accepted and acceptable as part of the tenor of life. Indeed the adjective *ordinaire* can be perceived as mildly positive when it refers to the place where the fashion magazine can normally be found, or when it describes common plants which can nevertheless look innovatively interesting massed together. There is a mildly wistful note in 'L'existence *ordinaire* suit déjà son cours', but the adjective *ordinaire* is used chiefly to distinguish everyday life from holiday time. The terms relate not so much to the ordinary as to the quality of specific situations and objects, which are categorised as ordinary not in terms of positive and negative value, but purely as a convenient way of referring to the most superficial and external layer of our common experience of everyday life.

But there are also a number of occasions within the poetry and the prose when Mallarmé uses the whole semantic field of the ordinary in ways that can only be described as extraordinary, invested with a range of negative but also at times positive connotations which vary in degree and in explicitness according to theme and context. Some of the terms within the broad semantic field of the ordinary are never used in a positive way: *vulgaire, vulgarité,* for instance, whereas *ordinaire,* and even *commun,* can sometimes be found to carry either an ambiguous or positive connotation. The most remarkable departures from common usage appear in the poems and the prose poems, but some of the most ambiguous and revealing ones are also to be found in the prose works.

The striking use of *ordinairement* in the line from the 'Prose' [P, 44-6], in its over-emphasised position, embodies in its very length and weight firstly the importance of the ordinary, and secondly the potential for transcendence of the ordinary; this is achieved without denial of the reality of the world of the ordinary but rather with a reinforcing of its continuing presence. In order to transcend everyday life, one has to acknowledge it, and to keep acknowledging it in order to validate the transcendental *démarche* itself. The celestial sphere evoked in the 'Prose' could not have meaning without *ordinairement*. Ordinary life can be transcended, but the quality of ordinariness itself has in a sense to be displayed and acknowledged (*'Ordinairement* se para'), to be worn as a garment which will in turn let through the light of transcendental experience ('D'un lucide contour') and bestow on it its value. The connotation of *ordinairement* is perhaps the most positive in the whole Mallarmé corpus; the adverb is indispensable to the thought structure of the poem, holding up almost literally by its weight and solidity the fragile edifice of aesthetic creation and philosophical speculation.

In 'L'après-midi d'un faune', the poet uses the adjective *ordinaire* as a qualifier for *songe*:

> Et de faire aussi haut que l'amour se module
> Evanouir du songe *ordinaire* de dos
> Ou de flanc pur suivis avec mes regards clos,
> Une sonore, vaine et monotone ligne. [P, 37]

It would seem at first that the world of ordinary pursuits is far removed from the pastoral world of the faun. And yet the question must be asked: whose ordinary are we referring to? The poem is indeed describing the ordinary world of the faun, a world devoted mainly to lustful dreams of nymphs and shapely bathers. The 'songe ordinaire' is a Verlainian 'rêve familier', the dream with which he habitually charms away his solitude and feeds his delusion. He lives in and for his 'songe ordinaire', easily comforted from disappointment by the promise of more sleep and more dreams. The adjective *ordinaire* in this context has the positive effect of underlining the fact that the reality of life for the faun is contained in a dream, and that dream itself is ordinary life. Everyday life and dream find in 'songe ordinaire' an interfusedness which cannot be qualified as positive or negative, but is an attempt to merge two planes, creating the kind of tension which the poem does not ultimately resolve.

In the *Poésies,* the adjective *banal* is used twice. In 'Les Fenêtres', with its Baudelairian atmosphere and lexis, it is used for its alliteration with *blancheur* and to emphasise the anonymity of the ordinary world of the hospital. The connotation is negative, evoking the boredom and feeling of abandonment experienced by the patient:

> Las du triste hôpital, et de l'encens fétide
> Qui monte en la blancheur *banale* des rideaux
> Vers le grand crucifix ennuyé du mur vide,
> Le moribond sournois y redresse un vieux dos, [P, 10]

The use of *banal* in the sonnet 'Remémoration d'amis belges' [P, 50], has an almost oxymoronic effect:

> O très chers rencontrés en le jamais *banal*
> Bruges multipliant l'aube au défunt canal
> Avec la promenade éparse de maint cygne.

Although the more immediate reading of *banal* is as the adjective accompanying Bruges, and this might well be the more obvious interpretation, it might also be possible to interpret it as accompanying a substantivised *jamais*, particularly if the gender of Bruges is feminine as in Georges Rodenbach's famous title *Bruges la morte*. The linkage of *le jamais* and *banal* at the end of the line draws the reader's eye to a new possibility, besides that of an extraordinary city. The potential substantivisation of the adverb *jamais* as an identifiable time plane already raises a philosophical point: can something which has been objectivised by turning it into a substantive, and therefore by giving it a substance which it does not possess in its ordinary adverbial form, something which not only does not exist but will never exist, be qualified at all? Can it be qualified in terms of the ordinary, the banal? Is non-existence not only part of the ordinary, but its most important quality? A difficult concept, that of the timeless and yet only understandable in terms of time, *jamais,* has either shockingly been called banal, in Mallarmé's lexis a generally intensely negatively invested word, describing what is so routinely present in everyday life as to become almost invisible, certainly not worthy of notice, or the city of Bruges itself has been given the supreme accolade of never being banal. If one opts for the less obvious interpretation, the paradox takes on an extra edge: how can what will never happen (*le jamais*) be described in terms of what routinely happens (*banal*)? Maybe we hear a faint echo of the dilemma in *Un Coup de Dés*: 'RIEN N'AURA EU LIEU QUE LE LIEU' [OC, 474-5], or even in 'Autobiographie' [OC, 664]:

travailler avec mystère en vue de plus tard ou de jamais et de temps en temps à envoyer aux vivants sa carte de visite, stances ou sonnet, pour n'être point lapidé d'eux, s'ils le [le poète] soupçonnaient de savoir qu'ils n'ont pas lieu.

If the words referring to the ordinary tend to be used to make a philosophical point in the poems, they are invested in the prose poems with a powerful emotional charge. In 'Plainte d'automne' [OC, 270-1], the barrel organ is the voice of the everyday, but of an everyday that has lost its banality because of the time distance. This is an ordinary that once was but is no more, the banal melody that expresses its essence redeemed by its belonging to another age: 'Maintenant qu'il [l'orgue de Barbarie] murmurait un air joyeusement vulgaire et qui mit la gaîté au coeur des faubourgs, un air suranné, *banal*: d'où vient que sa ritournelle m'allait à l'âme et me faisait pleurer comme une ballade romantique?' The adjective *banal* is perceived potentially both as positive and negative: the banality of the melody that is able to touch people across time. The poet clearly did not expect to experience the strong emotion he describes on hearing the melody. An adjective that has been perceived by the writer as potentially negatively charged has in fact turned into a positively presented event, and the 'air suranné, banal', is not in effect any different to the 'ballade romantique'.

In 'L'Ecclésiastique', the adjective is again teamed rather strikingly with *mystère*: '[...] or c'est de leur mystère presque *banal* que j'exhiberai un exemple saisissable et frappant des inspirations printanières' [OC, 287]. The intriguing use of *presque* invalidates the power of the adjective whilst reinforcing the noun it qualifies. Is it possible to conceive of an object or situation that is almost banal? Has not the ordinary in order to be banal to be completely so? And is an example that is both mysterious and not quite banal still entitled to claim any links with the ordinary, other than by a token lexical reference? In 'Un spectacle interrompu', Mallarmé writes: 'Jouir comme la foule du mythe inclus dans toute *banalité*' [OC, 276], another instance of Mallarmé's awareness of the potential contained in the banal. In 'Réminiscence', the 'tours de force et *banalités* alliables au jour' [OC, 279] bring together both the extraordinary life of the fairground, removed from most people's experience of the ordinary, and the banal pursuits of everyday life, such as eating and relating to others, an integral part of everyone's quotidian.

In 'La déclaration foraine', Mallarmé describes with a wealth of sensory detail a perception of the ordinary piercingly laughing out of everyday objects, and the overwhelming effect of the senseless noise which is the expression of the ordinary:

> Ainsi ne consent la réalité; car ce fut impitoyablement, hors du rayon qu'on sentait avec luxe expirer aux vernis du landau, comme une vocifération, parmi trop de tacite félicité pour une tombée de jour sur la banlieue, avec orage, dans tous sens à la fois et sans motif, du *rire strident ordinaire des choses* et de leur cuivrerie triomphale: au fait, la cacophonie à l'ouïe de quiconque, un instant écarté, plutôt qu'il ne s'y fond, auprès de son idée, reste à vif devant la hantise de l'existence. [OC, 279].

The fairground music with its relentless cacophonic pounding becomes the voice of ordinary things. Unlike the banal melody of 'Plainte d'automne', the 'rire strident ordinaire des choses' inspires fear and a need to escape from the 'hantise de l'existence'. The adjective is in this instance powerfully charged with negative emotions of subjection to an alien quotidian too cacophonic to allow for order or melody. The 'cuivrerie triomphale' seems to imply a victory on the part of the ordinary, a victory which serves only to exacerbate the rawness of the poet's feeling in the face of 'la hantise de l'existence'.

Mallarmé also uses the adjective *ordinaire* in his essays on writing and versification. It qualifies a negative critical category against which art and literary achievement are measured. In 'Solennité', Mallarmé advocates a process which consists of 'posséder et établir une notion du concept à traiter, mais indéniablement pour l'oublier dans sa façon *ordinaire* et se livrer ensuite à la seule dialectique du Vers' [OC, 332]. The 'façon ordinaire' is but a step on the way, whereas in 'Crise de vers', the 'fragment *ordinaire* d'élocution' [OC, 368] is acceptable only because of the transformation it has undergone.

It is, surprisingly perhaps, in the pages of *La Dernière Mode* that Mallarmé most explicitly acknowledges the difficulty inherent in any attempt to define what is ordinary: 'C'est qu'il faut peut-être ne pas jouer avec les choses *ordinaires*, parce que chacun ne sait pas bien où va le jeu ni où cela finit d'être *ordinaire*' [OC, 751]. Not only are the boundaries almost impossible to establish between what is and what is not ordinary, but the responsibility to deal with the ordinary rests on the individual, 'chacun'. There does not seem to exist an absolute form of the ordinary, only an individual and uncertain perception for which each person is responsible. This relativism in

Mallarmé's concept of the ordinary accounts for the great variation in levels of meaning, and in connotations. The frequent shifts from neutral to negative to positive testify to Mallarmé's own difficulty in determining what is ordinary, and in responding to it. What is Mallarmé achieving when he names not the ordinary, but perhaps more accurately, *an* ordinary? On the one hand, the process of naming is one of distancing oneself, of turning what is perceived as the ordinary into an 'ideal ordinary', in a similar approach to the one he describes in naming 'l'absente de tous les bouquets'. We rejoin here the Platonic world of the cave, where perception is not of reality, but of a perceived reality reinvented and idealised according to the inner world of the individual. We are therefore dealing not with the world of the everyday, but with Mallarmé's own, sometimes unsure and frequently shifting, concept of the ordinary. On the other hand, Mallarmé also uses the concept of the ordinary as a critical category against or within which to measure his and others' achievements. Moreover, Mallarmé also handles and plays with a wealth of ordinary data, and names it as such, without shying away from acknowledging its presence and its necessity, and he displays personal and literary enjoyment in the description of its many facets. The advantage of explicitly naming the ordinary is the sense of manipulation and control that the process affords the poet. What is named as *ordinaire* exercises a powerful fascination on Mallarmé's imagination, but the very process of expression transforms *the* ordinary into *an* ordinary and again into an ordinary re-invented, idealised and owned by the poet himself.

As Mallarmé himself has noted, it is not possible to eliminate the ordinary from one's use of language. The image of the poet as a labourer working with the material and tools of his trade, words, is a familiar Mallarmean one.[145] At the level of lexis,

---

[145] Both in poetry and prose, Mallarmé exploits this metaphor. In 'Las de l'amer repos' [P, 16], he mentions the

> [...] pacte dur
> De creuser par veillée une fosse nouvelle
> Dans le terrain avare et froid de ma cervelle

and in 'Conflit' [OC, 355-60], where Mallarmé observes and interprets the work of labourers in a derelict property: 'Tout à l'heure, dévot ennemi, pénétrant dans une crypte ou cellier en commun, devant la rangée de l'outil double, cette pelle et cette pioche, sexuels - dont le métal, résumant la force pure du travailleur, féconde les terrains sans culture, je fus pris de religion, outre que de mécontentement, émue à m'agenouiller'.

the words are indeed the point of contact with the everyday both of the writer as labourer and the reader as consumer. Mallarmé's restricted and relatively simple poetic vocabulary tended over the years to become even more general as the syntax becomes more complex. The need to anchor the language within the ordinary, more than at any other level, is expressed and demonstrated in Mallarmé's use of vocabulary. The richness and complexity of the lexis in his prose works is the consequence of his interest and knowledge of areas of everyday life outside the strictly poetic and literary. Its extraordinary comprehensiveness derives precisely from the writer's acquaintance with the large number of specialised areas, such as commerce, banking, fashion, law, botany and biology that go to make a many faceted everyday world. But the most intriguing point is Mallarmé's use of a metalanguage specifically naming the ordinary to reinforce his thematic engagement and his philosophical concerns. It hugely dramatises the function of the ordinary as concept, theme and dynamic principle within the corpus; it also insistently and almost obsessively draws attention to the inescapability and all-pervasiveness of a dimension that forces both the writer and the reader into an *insolite* and intense relationship with the words on the page and their paradoxical connections with the ordinary. We are left not with a satisfying sense of comfortable and easy inhabitation of a known dimension, but with a reflexive and specular engagement as one level of the ordinary. This is expressed in terminologies drawn from ordinary life and is not only squared but exponentially multiplied by the insistent and notable use of a metalanguage that both acknowledges and rejects its own textual and philosophical material.

Appendices to Chapter 3

Tables

Table 1	La banalité	le banal	banal	l'ordinaire	ordinaire
Poetry	2	0	4	0	1
Prose	6	2	12	1	4
La Dernière Mode	1	0	6	0	7

Table 2	Le quotidien	Quotidien	Le commun	commun
Poetry	0	1	0	0
Prose	3	36	2	4
La Dernière Mode	0	5	0	0

Table 3	ordinairement	quotidiennement	d'ordinaire
Poetry	2	1	0
Prose	7	5	6
La Dernière Mode	3	0	2

List of examples of Mallarmé's lexis in his verse and prose

I. Poetry:

1) Ordinary high-frequency vocabulary:
Verbs: *aimer, attendre, chercher, dormir, entendre, jeter, mourir.*
Adjectives: *blanc, bleu, froid, seul, triste, vieux.*
Substantives: *chambre, feu, fleur, lèvre, œil, or, plafond, soir, soleil.*

2) Marked poetic diction: *âme, antienne, astre, aurore, azur, chimère, clepsydre, croisée, cueillaison, froidure, glaive, histrion, hyacinthe, limbes, myrrhe, nymphe, onde, parvis, sépulcre, séraphin, songe, sylphe, trépas, viole.*

3) Use of mathematical vocabulary in *Un Coup de Dés*: *nombre, calculs, division, l'infini, se chiffrât-il, évidance de la somme, résultat nul, obliquité, déclivite, successif, compte* [OC, 459].

4) Adverbs in *-ment* commonly used: *abominablement, apparemment, autrement, avarement, certainement, délicieusement, doucement, gentiment, immédiatement, indifféremment, indomptablement, inutilement, joyeusement, lentement, lugubrement, méchamment, monotonement, naïvement, nonchalamment, ordinairement, originellement, probablement, rêveusement, ridiculement, savamment, simplement, solanellement, subitement, tristement, triomphalement.*

5) Adverbs in *-ment* rarely used: *authentiquement, candidement, humidement, inespérément, languissamment, mélancoliquement, prosaïquement, quotidiennement, rythmiquement, subséquemment, tacitement.*

6) Baudelarian derivative vocabulary related to anatomy and physiology: *cul, poils, vers, carcasse, os, crache* [P, 4-6], *rance* [P,9], *ventre, tétine* [P, 157], *fétide, pourriture, toux, ordure, vomissement* [P, 10-1], *bâillement, crâne* [P, 14], *vice, stérilité* [P, 15], *cervelle* [P, 16], *salive, crève* [P, 24-5], *poux* [P, 52].

7) Borrowings of English terms in *Vers de circonstance*: *Bird'seye* [OC, 156], *Christmas* [OC, 156], *Club* [OC, 93], *cold cream* [OC, 108], *gentleman* [OC, 142], *gentleman speaker* [OC, 142], *old staff* [OC, 157], *select* [OC, 98], *sporting* [OC, 98].

VOCABULARY: 'LES APTES MOTS' 147

8) 'Baby talk' in *Vers de circonstance*: *bibi* {OC, 135], *bobos* [OC, 109], *"paur tit quin"* [OC, 174], *riquiqui* [OC, 95], *Titi* {OC, 169], *Vévette* [OC, 175].

9) Terms or expressions borrowed from slang in *Vers de circonstance*: *cagnard* [OC, 86], *être paf* [OC, 157], *fiche un camp* [OC, 170], *flemmardes et gnolles* [OC, 174], *ma trogne* [OC, 169], *la frousse* [OC, 174], *tu soulages ta tripe* [OC, 163], *salaude* [OC, 153].

10) Use of the adjective *banal*: in 'Les Fenêtres' [P, 10-1], 'Remémoration d'amis belges' [P, 50], 'Plainte d'automne', [OC 270-1], 'L'Ecclésiastique' [OC, 286-8].

110 Use of the adjective *quotidien* in: 'La déclaration foraine' [OC, 280].

II. Prose

1) Neologisms: *contemporainement* [OC, 496], *diamantairement* [OC, 373], *éblouissamment* [OC, 536], *élyséennement* [OC, 535], *irrêvé* [OC, 490], *lyrise* [OC, 252].

2) Vocabulary borrowed from commerce and banking: in 'Or': *banque, numéraire, sommes, cent, procès financier, chiffres, nombres, zéros, milliard, intérêt, coffres en fer, monnaie* [OC, 398-9].

3) Vocabulary borrowed from political and social lexicons: in 'Sauvegarde': *institution, chambre représentative, officiel, décret, société, gouvernement* [OC, 418-9].

4) Use of the adjective *ordinaire*: 'une partie de plaisir *ordinaire*' [OC, 754], 'eau *ordinaire*' [OC, 775], 'courbe *ordinaire*' [OC, 784)] 'un déjeuner *ordinaire*' [OC, 795], 'courier *ordinaire*' [OC, 826], 'Le beau *ordinaire*' [OC, 718)] 'de commodes notions *ordinaires*' [OC, 341], 'Quatre plantes presque *ordinaires* [...] et un aspect bizarre et nouveau dans nos jardins' [OC, 720], 'L'existence *ordinaire* suit déjà son cours' [OC, 734],'Notre journal [...] à sa place *ordinaire* sur les tables de salon' [OC, 755].

5) Use of the adjective *banal*: in 'Symphonie littéraire', 'une âme dédaigneuse du *banal* coup d'aile d'un enthousiasme humain' [OC, 262], 'Crayonné au théâtre', 'le *banal* malentendu' [OC, 294], 'nos impressions issues de *banals* soirs' [OC, 299], 'le

contemporain *banal*' [OC, 305], '*Banal* sacrilège' [OC, 315], 'le *banal* conflit' [OC, 322], in 'Offices', 'la *banale* et vaste place publique' [OC, 391], in 'Médaillons et portraits', 'le site entre tous *banal*' [OC, 484], des milieux, autrement *banals*' [OC, 534], in 'Préface à Vathek', 'un français fautif ou *banal*' [OC, 564], in 'La Musique et les lettres', '[...] un avis à notre usage, éveille au contact étranger; certes *banal*' [OC, 637], in *La Dernière mode,* 'les aventures *banales*' [OC, 717], 'éloge point *banal*' [OC, 735], 'un aspect camelote et *banal*' [OC, 736], 'certains traits un peu *banals*' [OC, 745], 'Londres, clair et *banal*' [OC, 825], 'tapisserie *banale*' [OC, 827].

6) Use of the adjective *quotidien*: 'Le genre ou des modernes', 'choses *quotidiennes*' [OC, 321], in 'Planches et feuillets', 'le pain *quotidien*' [OC, 326], in 'La fausse entrée des sorcières dans Macbeth', 'un jour proche de tous et *quotidien*' [OC, 348], in 'L'action restreinte', une foi en le *quotidien* néant' [OC, 372], in 'Offices', 'la lueur, à portée, *quotidienne* du réverbère' [OC, 391], 'la pratique *quotidienne*' [OC, 392], in 'La cour', 'le spectacle *quotidien*' [OC, 414], in 'Médaillons et portraits', 'une *quotidienne* occupation' [OC, 499], 'des boxeurs *quotidiens*' [OC, 502], 'la *quotidienne* apothéose' [OC, 519], 'la grande presse ou *quotidienne*' [OC, 527], 'enseignement au témoin *quotidien* oublieux' [OC, 532], 'Féerie, oui, *quotidienne*' [OC, 537] in 'Le "Ten o'clock" de Mr. Whistler', 'article d'usage *quotidien*' [OC, 573], in the 'Contes indiens', 'sa visite *quotidienne*' [OC, 603], 'sa résurrection *quotidienne*' [OC, 613], in 'La Musique et les lettres', 'une *quotidienne* vitre' [OC, 636], in 'Autobiographie', 'les ennuis *quotidiens*' [OC, 664], in 'Trois lettres sur l'exposition de Londres', 'contact *quotidien*' [OC, 671], in the third letter, 'décor familier de notre existence *quotidienne*' [OC, 679], 'la forme *quotidienne* de nos lampes' [OC, 685], 'le sentiment *quotidien* de la vie' [OC, 690], in 'Le Jury de peinture pour 1874 et M.Manet', 'un théâtre *quotidien* et national' [OC, 703], in *La Dernière Mode,* 'les us *quotidiens*' [OC, 751]. 'ordonnateur de la fête sublime et *quotidienne*' [OC, 764], 'La presse *quotidienne*' [OC, 786], 'mille affiches *quotidiennes*' [OC, 824], in 'Sur Maupassant', 'l'écrivain, conteur *quotidien*' [OC, 875], in 'Les Mots anglais', 'Termes *quotidiens* et populaires' [OC, 919], 'rapports *quotidiens*' [OC, 978], in 'Les Thèmes anglais', 'la fleur même de l'Anglais, humble et *quotidienne* dans ses phrases de chaque jour' [OC, 1058)] 'l'expérience *quotidienne* du professeur' [OC, 1062], in 'Les Dieux antiques', 'la marche *quotidienne* et annuelle du soleil' [OC, 1213], 'le soleil dans son orbe annuel et *quotidien*'

[OC, 1232], 'une répétition du siège *quotidien* de l'est' [OC, 1265], 'nos impressions *quotidiennes*' [OC, 1277].

7) Use of the adjectives *journalier*: in the second letter from the Exhibition: 'un regard usuel promené sur les objets de nécessité *journalière*' [OC, 670], or in 'Confrontation', des procédés *journaliers*' [OC, 411].

8) Use of the adjectives *commun*: and *vulgaire*: in 'Bucolique', ' un reflet de nuage classique et lieu *commun*' [OC, 404], or as a qualifier: '*commun* alignement' [OC, 371], 'le *commun* fonctionnement' [OC, 391], 'métal *commun*' [OC, 412]. We also find *vulgaire* in 'le piment *vulgaire* de l'actualité' [OC, 254].

9) Use of the adverb *ordinairement*: in 'Offices', 'les messieurs qu'*ordinairement* nous paraissons' [OC, 395], in 'La Cour', 'quelque fidélité suppléant ce qu'on appela, *ordinairement*, le public' [OC, 416], in the preface to *Un Coup de Dés*, 'les "blancs" en effet, assument l'importance, frappent d'abord; la versification en exigea, comme silence alentour, *ordinairement*, au point qu'un morceau, lyrique ou de peu de pieds, occupe, au milieu, le tiers environ du feuillet' [OC, 455], in 'Médaillons et portraits', 'les expositions *ordinairement* de Monet et Renoir' [OC, 533], in 'Contes indiens', 'au ciel *ordinairement* heureux d'une contrée de L'Inde' [OC, 606], in *La Dernière Mode*, 'les grandes amitiés inoubliables de la vie naissent *ordinairement* de ce fait' (OC 717), '*ordinairement*, répertoire: *les Huguenots,* notamment' [OC, 789], 'Rien des Concerts-Populaires, *ordinairement* detaillés ici' [OC, 825], in 'Les Dieux antiques', 'on présente *ordinairement* Hermès un bâton à la main' [OC, 1211], 'La version reçue *ordinairement*' [OC, 1244], in 'L'Etoile de fées', 'on passait *ordinairement* sans prendre garde' [OC, 1304].

10) Use of the adverbial phrase *d'ordinaire*: in 'Un Spectacle interrompu', 'la récompense mystérieuse *d'ordinaire* après ces représentations' [OC, 278], in 'Ballets', 'le librettiste ignore *d'ordinaire* que la danseuse, qui s'exprime par les pas, ne comprend d'éloquence autre, même le geste' [OC, 306], in 'Verlaine', 'La solitude, le froid, l'inélégance et la pénurie [...] *d'ordinaire* composent le sort qu'encourt l'enfant avec son ingénue audace marchant en l'existence selon sa divinité' [OC, 511], in 'Contes indiens', 'on me cède *d'ordinaire*' [OC, 605], in *La Dernière mode*, 'la page accordée *d'ordinaire* à quelques jours' [OC, 721], 'les mères, à qui *d'ordinaire* cette page

importante du journal enseigne les Costumes' [OC, 836], in 'Les Dieux antiques', 'celles que l'on connaît *d'ordinaire*' [OC, 1237], in 'L'Etoile des fées', 'il y a *d'ordinaire* une assez vile engeance là-dedans' [OC, 1305].

11) Use of the adverbs *quotidiennement* and *journellement*: in 'Le Démon de l'analogie: '[...] le reste mal abjuré d'un labeur de linguistique par lequel *quotidiennement* sanglote de s'interrompre ma noble faculté poétique' [OC, 273], in 'Conflit', 'une intelligence robuste de la condition humaine leur courbe l'échine *journellement*' [OC, 359], in 'Médaillons et portraits', 'celui qui *quotidiennement* y tendait l'étoffe de fastueux pensers' [OC, 483], in 'Le "Ten o'clock" de Mr Whistler', 'l'admiration illimitée produite *quotidiennement* par le plus niais coucher de soleil' [OC, 574], in 'La Musique et les lettres', 'La Littérature, d'accord avec la faim, consiste à supprimer le Monsieur qui reste en l'écrivant, celui-ci que vient-il faire au vu des siens, *quotidiennement*?' [OC, 657], in 'Sur l'idéal à vingt ans', 'Le moyen, je le publie, consiste *quotidiennement* à épousseter, de ma native illumination, l'apport hasardeux extérieur, qu'on recueille, plutôt, sous le nom d'expérience' [OC, 883].

CHAPTER IV
Metaphorisation of the ordinary

Writing about vocabulary and syntax inevitably brings us to focusing on the use of metaphor. The study of a process by which Mallarmé characterises the ordinary goes beyond the careful analysis of lexis and syntax, beyond the dissection and study of individual words or grammatical forms to a more synthetic approach. It requires the putting back together of lexis and syntax within the context, on the one hand of poetry and prose, on the other of the ordinary as conceptual tool defined in the introductory chapter by a number of theoreticians and of the 'Mallarmean ordinary' that we have analysed in previous chapters. The metaphoric vocabulary energises and dynamises new frames of reference, just as the ordinary as subject matter, explicit or implied, enriches the Mallarmé world with a powerful emotional charge both positive and negative. The ordinary is characterised in terms of framework, *toile de fond*, and of event or non-event, and to both approaches correspond a number of often ambiguous and fascinating similes and metaphors. In this chapter, I propose, after studying a selection of definitions of metaphor, to isolate the qualities of the Mallarmean metaphor, in particular his metaphors of the everyday, to study his use of ordinary metaphor based on conceptual frameworks used in ordinary French language, and to examine the metaphoric structure of the Mallarmean concept of the ordinary. I shall then analyse a number of examples of metaphors of the ordinary, first in his verse, then in his prose, and concentrate particularly on two richly paradoxical metaphors, often fused together in representing the ordinary world, that of the veil and the rock. I shall conclude by drawing a parallel between Mallarmé's use of lexis, syntax and his paradoxical use of metaphor.

Works devoted to metaphor abound, and there is no lack of theoretical contributions to the study of the figure both in literary and in everyday language. A number of them have appeared to be more helpful and fruitful than others in producing a set of concepts and a method of analysis for the Mallarmean metaphor. Given Mallarmé's predilection for ellipsis, which we have studied extensively in the chapter on syntax,[146] a definition of metaphor, which relies on the idea of absence, loss or lack

---

[146] See above, p.74-8.

would be helpful. Karsten Harries writes in the chapter 'Metaphor and Transcendence' (February 1978): 'Metaphors speak of what remains absent. All metaphor that is more than an abbreviation for more proper speech gestures towards what transcends language. Thus metaphor implies lack.'[147] This understanding of metaphor might seem far removed from the generally accepted definition as expressed by J.J.A.Mooij in *A Study of Metaphor* (1976):[148]

> Metaphors help to cover new situations or to elucidate new aspects of already familiar ones. Metaphors are powerful tools whenever we are exploring, describing, interpreting or elucidating new situations. They enable us to assimilate in the light of the familiar, what was hitherto unknown, undigested or unnamed. They may also contribute to an insight in what is already (all too) well known. (pp.16-7)

The Mallarmé metaphors can be studied both with reference to lack and with reference to added richness and meaning. It is their very ambiguity when either trying to annihilate or to explore the ordinary world, and sometimes balancing between the two in a tension that betrays the poet's difficulty with the concept, which makes a separate study essential in the context of the everyday in the Mallarmé corpus. Whether we understand metaphor as a 'collapsed comparison',[149] a substitution,[150] an emphasis on incompatibility between terms rather then similarity,[151] or whether we place it in the 'category of elliptical utterances'[152] the point of departure is the same: the words on the page, both lexis and syntax, but moulded to the conceptual and imaginary universe of

---

[147] *On Metaphor*, ed.Sheldon Saks (Chicago and London: University of Chicago Press, 1979). This book is based on the papers given at a symposium, 'Metaphor: the Conceptual Leap', February 1978, sponsored by The University of Chicago Extension.

[148] See J.J.A.Mooij, *A Study of Metaphor* (Amsterdam, New York, Oxford: North-Holland Publishing, 1976).

[149] *A Study of Metaphor*, p.24.

[150] For a general review of theories of metaphor, see Andrew Ortony, *Metaphor and Thought*, ed. Andrew Ortony (Cambridge: Cambridge University Press, 1979). The book also reviews Richards tensive view of metaphor (1936), which emphasises the conceptual incompatibility between terms in a metaphor.

[151] See Christine Brooke-Rose, *A Grammar of Metaphor* (London: Secker and Warburg, 1958).

[152] See the chapter by Max Black, 'Metaphor and Meaning' in *Metaphor and Thought* ed. Ortony.

a poet's perception of the ordinary. I shall first study the syntactic characteristics of Mallarmé's metaphors before analysing their conceptual bases and structures.

In *A Grammar of Metaphor*,[153] Christine Brooke-Rose creates a series of syntactic categories within which she divides grammatically different types of metaphors. Deborah A.K.Aish devises a similar study of Mallarmé's metaphors in *La Métaphore dans l'œuvre de Stéphane Mallarmé*.[154] She distinguishes five main types of noun metaphors, from the simple replacement, to the pointing formula where the first noun having been mentioned is replaced but with a demonstrative pointing back to the proper term, the copula in the direct statement, the transformational link where a third noun is involved, and the genitive, in the sense of provenance. The interest of a syntactically based study of metaphors in the context of the ordinary is to isolate a number of grammatical features that are either more frequent, noticeable or even completely absent in the metaphors that relate to everyday life in the Mallarmé corpus. Although the grammatical approach to the study of metaphors of the everyday in the Mallarmé corpus might be seen as having very limited application as far as conceptual structure is concerned,[155] we have already demonstrated in the chapters on syntax and lexis that Mallarmé's predilection for a number of linguistic forms are the tangible evidence of complex mental and emotional attitudes, and are therefore helpful and necessary in determining the areas of philosophical and artistic conflict related to the ordinary world. The consequences and repercussions on the present discussion of grammatical choices in the use of metaphor will have far-reaching effects on the analysis of metaphors of the ordinary on the conceptual, thematic and philosophical levels. Does Mallarmé make greater use of simple replacement metaphors, of copula metaphors, or does he use adjectival and verbal metaphors more frequently in relation to the ordinary? Is it possible to discover a grammatical pattern of preference, as we have in the lexis and

---

[153] Ibid.146.

[154] Deborah A.K.Aish, *La Métaphore dans l'œuvre de Stéphane Mallarmé*, (Paris: Droz, 1938).

[155] See George Lakoff and Mark Turner in *More than Cool Reason* (Chicago and London: University of Chicago Press, 1989), p.133: 'This attempt to define metaphor in terms of syntactic form misses entirely what metaphor is about [...]. On the whole, the syntactic form of an utterance has little, if anything, to do with whether metaphor is involved in comprehending it'.

syntax chapters and to use our observations as the basis for our study?

In the poetic works, the predominance of predicative or verbal metaphors, especially in the juvenilia, is noticeable. We can also isolate a number of clichés, stereotyped metaphors, which are part of 'ordinary' conventional poetic diction:

> La fleur rit aux épis: l'alcyon chante encor,
> Elle seule a passé - Sous un saule elle dort.[156] [P, 117].

Personification and the use of a conventional metaphor of death as sleep are typical examples of metaphors in the early poetic works. If the verbal metaphors are conventional, the noun metaphors are often derivative and a pastiche of Baudelaire or Hugo:

> Chez celles dont l'amour est une orange sèche[157] [P, 150]

or

> Mais la chevelure est une rivière tiède,[158] [P, 19]

The copula lends the metaphor a concreteness, a simple materiality which is directly lifted from Baudelaire's own use of objects and sensory perceptions that belong to the ordinary. In 'Le guignon' [P, 4-6] (1862), the abundance of metaphors transforms a sordid and harsh everyday into a Baudelairian universe of *correspondances*. From genitive metaphors such as 'bétail ahuri des humains' and 'citron d'or de l'idéal amer', to simple replacement metaphors as in '[...] un monarque rageur,/ Le Guignon [...], the poem is replete with images drawn from a number of semantic fields and built on a variety of grammatical structures. Every type of grammatical metaphor used by Mallarmé can already be found in the poem, whether appositional as in

> O Mort le seul baiser aux bouches taciturnes!

or in using a verb which is the pivotal word on which the metaphor hangs:

> Ils tètent la douleur comme ils tétaient le rêve.

---

[156] 'Sa tombe est fermée', 11 July 1859.
[157] 'L'enfant prodigue', Sens, 1861.
[158] 'Tristesse d'été', Tournon, 1864.

METAPHORISATION OF THE ORDINARY 155

The metaphor can also be expressed in an adjective *un noir vent, hasards tortueux, galops cuirassés* or in a genitive:

Mordant au citron d'or de l'idéal amer.

or in the opening line of the poem:

Au-dessus du bétail ahuri des humains.

But the most important term of a metaphor can also be an adverb. We have already studied Mallarmé's extensive use of adverbs in *-ment* in the chapters on syntax and lexis.[159] This predilection can also be traced in his use of metaphor:

Et tu fis la blancheur sanglotante des lys
Qui [...]
Monte rêveusement vers la lune qui pleure![160] [P, 12]

In 'Prose' [P, 44-6],[161] the two adverbs in *-ment* which introduce the second lines of the first and the seventh verse, *triomphalement* and *ordinairement*, take on within the metaphor the transforming, qualifying role that anchors the figure into the recognisable characteristics of the concrete world of the ordinary:

Hyperbole! de ma mémoire
Triomphalement ne sais-tu
Te lever, aujourd'hui grimoire
Dans un livre de fer vêtu:

[...]
Telles, immenses, que chacune
Ordinairement se para
D'un lucide contour, lacune
Qui des jardins la sépara.

In 'Petit air II'[162] [P, 55], the poem opens with an adverb that introduces the metaphor on which the poem rests, and

---

[159] See above, pp.81-3, pp.115-6 and pp.135-7.
[160] 'Les fleurs', Tournon, mars 1864.
[161] Paris, 1884.
[162] Paris, 1894.

immediately establishes both the atmosphere of the text and the quality of the metaphoric world into which we enter:

> Indomptablement a dû
> Comme mon espoir s'y lance
> Eclater là-haut perdu
> Avec furie et silence,
>
> Voix étrangère au bosquet
> Ou par nul écho suivie,
> L'oiseau qu'on n'ouït jamais
> Une autre fois en la vie.
>
> Le hagard musicien,
> Cela dans le doute expire
> Si de mon sein pas du sien
> A jailli le sanglot pire
>
> Déchiré va-t-il entier
> Rester sur quelque sentier!

The metaphoric use of the adverb is then underlined by the use of *comme* at the beginning of the second line of the first quatrain, structuring the following comparison between bird and poet not so much on their common artistic and creative fate as on the quality and intensity of their vocation, and its obsessive, compelling, almost suicidal nature. In this respect, Mallarmé's *oiseau* shares with Keats's nightingale the uniqueness of its song, the agony of its production and the uncertainty of its eventual fate. Nevertheless, the introductory adverb, which opens up the metaphoric framework imprints on to the poem a powerful and positive mark of the energy and vitality of creativity, based on hope despite the strong possibility of ultimate failure.

It must be noted that Mallarmé's use of adverbs in *-ment* seems to become more frequent and more significant in the chronology of his poetic work. So does the use of what appear to be similes, where both terms of the comparison are expressed. Although this figure is sometimes perceived as much more primitive than a metaphor,[163] many of Mallarmé's similes are

---

[163] See Deborah A.K.Aish, *La Métaphore dans l'œuvre de Mallarmé*, p.153: 'Reste un procédé rhétorique des plus ordinaires - la comparaison - beaucoup utilisée par Mallarmé. Un emploi si fréquent d'une forme plutôt primitive détonne un peu dans l'oeuvre de cet auteur. Lui, qui cherche surtout les figures complexes, nuancées, il semble qu'il doive éviter autant que possible cette

complex both from a syntactical and exegetical point of view. Based on a simple construction, the Mallarmean comparison evolves into a precariously balanced *tour de force*, often made up of two metaphors rather than of the usual combination of a non-metaphorical term with a metaphorical one. In 'Autre Eventail',[164] the first comparison is still simple and the two terms clearly distinct, the syntax orthodox, although the exclamatory opening term introduces a possible third term into the simile:

> Vertige! voici que frissonne
> L'espace comme un grand baiser
> Qui, fou de naître pour personne,
> Ne peut jaillir ni s'apaiser [P, 48].

The second comparison is still syntactically simple, but is composed of two metaphors:

> Sens-tu le paradis farouche
> Ainsi qu'un rire enseveli
> Se couler du coin de ta bouche
> Au fond de l'unanime pli!

It seems that the Mallarmean simile becomes more complex when it forms the closing lines of a poem. The final two lines of the poem 'La chevelure vol...' [P, 40],[165] is both semantically and metaphorically ambiguous:

> Une nudité de héros tendre diffame
> Celle qui ne mouvant astre ni feux au doigt
> Rien qu'à simplifier avec gloire la femme
> Accomplit par son chef fulgurante l'exploit
>
> De semer de rubis le doute qu'elle écorche
> Ainsi qu'une joyeuse et tutélaire torche.

The various metaphoric strands of the poem are brought together in a simile shaped by several compressed and condensed metaphors: the fire of her hair, the flamboyance of the woman's display of herself as an incarnation of beauty, the bejewelled

---

tournure directe et simple. Néanmoins, c'est de beaucoup la formule la plus employée de toutes les constructions mallarméennes'.
[164] Paris, 1884.
[165] Published initially in *Le Faune* on 20 March 1889.

crown and gems, a festive and almost timeless atmosphere, the triumph and recognition of a new vibrant dimension of life. Every term employed in the simile is used metaphorically, from the verbs *semer* and *écorche*, bringing together two antithetical metaphoric poles, to the *joyeuse et tutélaire torche*, recalling the *vol d'une flamme* of the opening line and the *doute*, itself a metaphor for the disbelieving, disenchanted crowd.

The simile contained in the closing line of 'Remémoration d'amis belges' [P, 50][166] is complex not because of the metaphoric depth and the abundance of terms as in 'La chevelure vol...' but because of its elliptical and condensed form:

> O très chers rencontrés en le jamais banal
> Bruges multipliant l'aube au défunt canal
> Avec la promenade éparse de maint cygne
>
> Quand solennellement cette cité m'apprit
> Lesquels entre ses fils un autre vol désigne
> A prompte irradier ainsi qu'aile l'esprit.

As in the previous poem, the final simile brings together the metaphoric planes into a particularly tightly woven comparison, in which each term contains a number of references to previous metaphors: *irradier* suggests *l'aube* and the *maint cygne* whose whiteness reflect the light. The *aile* refers back to the swans' wings reflecting the light and thus creating new sunrises on the canal; wings and light are almost synonyms, giving a visual impression in the first tercet, and a spiritual image in the second. Light and wings associated with spirit are not particularly original or innovative metaphors; they can be found in Biblical writings and in Catholic liturgy. It is perhaps more in the absence of the article that would usually precede *aile*, for instance, that the metaphor is 'enacted', dramatised, played out, the wing unencumbered by the ordinary article, free to take off in *un autre vol*.

Not only does Mallarmé use the absence of a term as a metaphor, he also inverts the terms of a comparison. In 'Petit air I',[167] the simile between the white clothes and the bird leaves the reader uncertain as to the term of comparison, and the presence or absence of one or both of the objects described:

[...]

---

[166] Published initially in *L'Art Littéraire* in Brussels in November 1893.
[167] Paris, 1894.

Mais langoureusement longe
Comme de blanc linge ôté
Tel fugace oiseau si plonge
Exultatrice à côté

Dans l'onde toi devenue
Ta jubilation nue. [P, 54].

The absence of swan in the second line of the poem is reflected in the presence of the white clothes, which look like a white bird from a distance. The construction of the simile might lead us to think that the discarded clothes are compared to a bird, but the naked bather of the last two lines would point to the fact that the clothes are part of the description and the *fugace oiseau* is the metaphoric term. The adjective *fugace* might refer to the brief illusion of life in the white clothes, making them fleetingly look like a swan. The term *comme* would be expected to precede the absent object, the bird, but if we remember Mallarmé's habitual recourse to ellipsis and inversion, and the use not of *du blanc linge ôté*, but *de blanc linge ôté*, we can reconstruct the proposition as 'comme un oiseau fait de blanc linge ôté'. The presence of the *linge* is also a guarantee of the presence of the bather. The absence of the clothes, if the comparison were based on the presence of a bird, would then also imply the absence of the bather, and transform the observed scene into a daydream. Both interpretations are of course possible, and it is on this simple and richly ambiguous comparison that the carefully balanced edifice of the poem is constructed.

Having analysed a number of metaphors and similes in Mallarmé's poetry, we are now able to formulate relevant questions about Mallarmé's perception of the ordinary within his poetic works. Can we isolate, behind the carefully balanced, sometimes elliptical metaphors and comparisons, a concept of the ordinary expressed in images? Does the Mallarmean metaphor necessarily refer to a world outside, or does it create a new site able to contain an ideal ordinary environment, entirely self-referential and circular in its trajectory?

The reader's initial reaction when encountering the closing simile in 'La chevelure vol...' or in 'Petit Air I' might well be perplexity rather than immediate recognition of reference to everyday life. One might come to the conclusion that Mallarmé, far from metaphorising the ordinary, is escaping from it into a fantasy world built entirely with complex and unusual imagery. And yet it is not so much what the metaphors are about but how they express a certain perception of the everyday which is the most important focus in our reading. The metaphors and comparisons in the poems form a complex system of echoes and reflections and open up a multitude of possible *rapports* between the images, sounds and meanings of the poems. Metaphors are hidden within metaphors, metaphors within comparisons, words within words, and the specular quality of the Mallarmean metaphor points towards a confined and self-reflective concept of the everyday world, a new and complex reworking of the 'pli selon pli' image. Paradoxically, it also opens up a new perspective, beyond the boundaries of the artistic vision, as in 'Petit Air I', where the inclusion of discarded clothes and bather allow the outside and the 'other' into the world of absence and lack described by the poet. Moving in the opposite direction to the poetic process of pole-vaulting from the ordinary world to a poetic universe beyond, Mallarmé uses metaphor to vault from one mental and aesthetic locality to another, crossing limits and boundaries in the process, eventually to complete his trajectory into a world that is recognisable as the everyday in terms of characteristics, ambiguous quality and its very recalcitrance to definition and stasis. The pole used by the poet is not the ordinary, but his own imaginary world, which provides him with the artistic and creative impetus to cross the bar of his own reluctance, obsessions and fears into a new and limitless world, which he is then able to structure and organise according to a metaphoric system. The inadequacy of language when it comes to giving an account and explaining life and its crises is resolved to a large degree by metaphorising the world and structuring it according to one's own choices. Mallarmé's opting for similes rather than metaphors, for instance, makes clear his need to impose an inner equilibrium on what he often perceives as chaos or emptiness. Rather than Aristotelian substitution, Mallarmé's metaphorising of the world of the everyday in his poems displays Empsonian ambiguities, and a need both to resolve and to re-open his never-ending tussle with the ordinary. Mallarmé's metaphoric system seems to echo another more recalcitrant structure, a microcosm reflecting a macrocosm, and it is in its very extraordinariness and quest for uniqueness that it eventually rejoins the ordinary.

Metaphor is of course a usual part of ordinary language, an integral part of the everyday, belonging to a particular language and tradition. It forms a conceptual framework necessary to language, to an understanding of our experience in the world and to a reflection on that experience.[168] At the level of theory, it is part of the dynamics of thought and existence, part of the schemas that organise our knowledge and our perception of the world. Mallarmé himself is part of a Western tradition that uses a number of conventional metaphors to express various key aspects of life, and we find them throughout the corpus: in his verse, for instance, we find death as sleep [P, 117],[169] youth as the morning of life [P, 91],[170] spring as laughter [P, 14],[171] lies as black [P, 15],[172] the sparkle of gems as fire [P, 48],[173] the lover as a treasure [P, 160],[174] worry as bile [P, 53],[175] to shut an eye for sleeping [P, 158].[176] They appear in the *Vers de circonstance* often in the form of ready-made expressions such as 'broyer du noir' [OC, 88], 'resserrer les doux liens' [OC, 94], 'faire la nique' [OC, 97], 'Aile du Temps' [OC, 109], 'faire la chouette' [OC, 118], 'changer d'an comme de robe' [OC, 136], 'prendre la clé des champs' [OC, 148], 'poivre et sel' [OC, 179], 'pendre la crémaillère' [OC, 180], 'pleurer comme un veau' [OC, 182], 'graisser la patte' [OC, 183], 'le temps des roses' [OC, 186]. We also find a number of traditional or conventional metaphors in the prose works (although significantly fewer than in the poetic works or in the *Vers de circonstance*) of which I shall only list a few examples: in 'Proses de jeunesse' [OC, 251],[177] 'ce plumage d'or, paon fanfaron dont se parent tant de geais', ' tremper curieusement les lèvres dans la coupe de toutes les sensations' [OC, 254],[178] 'entrer de plain-pied dans un chef-d'oeuvre' [OC,

---

[168] See Andrew Ortony's *Metaphor and Thought* (1979), second ed. (Cambridge University Press, 1993) first published in 1979.

[169] In 'Sa tombe est fermée', 11 July 1859: '[...] - sous un saule elle dort'.

[170] In 'La prière d'une mère', Sens, 7 July 1859: 'Au matin de ta vie [...]'.

[171] In 'Renouveau', Sens, May 1862: '[...]-Cependant l'Azur rit sur la haie[...]'.

[172] In 'Angoisse', Tournon, February 1864: 'Et que tu peux goûter après tes noirs mensonges'.

[173] In 'Autre éventail', first published in 1884: 'Contre le feu d'un bracelet'.

[174] In 'Sonnet', first published in 1908: '[...]très grand trésor et tête si petite'.

[175] In 'Billet à Whistler', Paris, November 1890: 'Sans se faire autrement de bile'.

[176] In 'Sonnet', 1877: 'Une veille t'exalte à ne pas fermer l'œil'.

[177] Published in *Le Papillon* on 10 January 1862.

[178] Published in *Le Sénonais*, Sens, 22 March 1862.

257],[179] 'étouffer dans l'oeuf' [OC, 298],[180] 'le coup de pouce' [OC, 412],[181] 'creuser tout cela' [OC, 434],[182] 'le fil rompu d'une existence' [OC, 514],[183] In *La Dernière Mode*, although the articles deal with matters concerned with ordinary life, we find very few metaphors that could be considered ordinary, or part of ordinary language. The following examples might possibly qualify as lacking originality and easily identified as part of a metaphoric framework used by a number of writers: '[...] un prologue en vers, un joyau, de Coppée' [OC, 791], 'Comme deux fils, l'un de soie ou même de laine et l'autre d'or, qui s'interrompent et se rattachent entre eux, mêlés dans leur dessin annuel, alternent ici et l'évolution de la mode durant la Saison, et les fêtes' [OC, 797], 'la flore du songe' [OC, 799], 'les doigts de rose du matin' [OC, 800], 'A quoi songer, quand les chiffons laissent désoeuvrées les femmes?' [OC, 812], 'Les fleurs d'abord; puis, fussent-elles de rhétorique, le bouquet: les mots du language et sa littérature' [OC, 828], 'la face de l'Europe' [OC, 830].

Having listed a number of ordinary metaphors within the various parts of the Mallarmé corpus, it is possible to isolate a few characteristics: they tend to appear in greater numbers in the poetic works, and occur far less in the prose dealing more ostensibly with ordinary matters. It seems that, the more removed from the ordinary the subject matter, the more ordinary the metaphors; the more ordinary the content, the more extraordinary the metaphors. As in the case of lexis and syntax, Mallarmé chooses to create tensions by combining ordinary and extraordinary, by setting the one against the other and by either redeeming or eliminating the one by using the other.

'En dernière analyse, Stéphane Mallarmé ne pense guère que par métaphores' writes Aish.[184] It is therefore within the metaphoric system that I shall look for the conceptual framework, which reveals Mallarmé's perception and response to the ordinary. To what extent are the Mallarmean metaphors and similes concerned with everyday life or about the ordinary world? Do extraordinary metaphors point towards a view of the ordinary that is uniquely Mallarmean, or do they go beyond a narrowly

---

[179] In 'L'Art pour tous', Sens, 1862.
[180] In 'Crayonné au théâtre', Paris 1887.
[181] In 'Confrontation', October 1895.
[182] In 'Igitur', Avignon, 1869.
[183] In 'Arthur Rimbaud', Paris, April 1896.
[184] See *La Métaphore dans l'œuvre de Stéphane Mallarmé*, p.20.

defined personal and imaginary universe into an exploration of the outside world?

It is possibly in the pages of *La Dernière Mode* that the metaphors and similes are most strikingly used either as instruments of original thinking about the ordinary or as the means of creating a new ordinary, more subtle, rich and habitable. In 'Autobiographie', Mallarmé gives the following account of *La Dernière Mode*:

> Si à un moment, pourtant, désespérant du despotique bouquin lâché de moi-même, j'ai après quelques articles colportés d'ici et de là, tenté de rédiger tout seul, toilettes, bijou, mobilier, et jusqu'aux théâtres et aux menus de dîner, un journal *La Dernière Mode*, dont les huit ou dix numéros parus servent encore quand je les dévêts de leur poussière à me faire longtemps rêver [OC, 663-4].

The ideal 'despotique bouquin' has disappeared behind the reality of contemporary living under the guise of a fashion magazine, but a fashion magazine capable of inspiring dreams and worthy of being reread. The characteristic that makes *La Dernière Mode* able 'à me faire longtemps rêver' is its hypermetaphoric quality. Although it is a magazine about the ordinary routine of middle-class French life, it is not an ordinary publication. The difference is in the constant metaphorisation of the ordinary, from the description of clothing to the advice on travel. Mallarmé's poetic imagination was clearly at work on all aspects of life, seeking by the use of metaphors to bring magic to particularly uninspiring aspects of everyday life, or to extract magic from more promising material such as jewellery or evening dresses. Neither approach could be undertaken without metaphors, some of them occuring again and again in the issues, others linked together in a vast interconnected network reminiscent of Mallarmé's spider web.

Mallarmé has an obvious predilection for some materials, such as 'tulle illusion', mentioned a great number of times and combining the advantages of referring to an actual material, but also used as a metaphor and for alliterative purposes. He also mentions *gazes* as a favourite texture, and the most frequent metaphor used in connection with materials is *nuages, nuées, vapeur*, as in the following examples: 'Pas de *nues* dont l'on puisse s'environner, sous la lumière réelle du gaz, autres que la robe de tissus *vaporeux*, froissés dans l'impatience' [OC, 717]. The dress here is set in contrast to the reality of gaslight, with the power of transporting the wearer from the reality of everyday light to an alternate world of cloud. The metaphor is reversed: it is the dress, representing in a sense the ordinary element in the sentence that is the metaphor for the clouds. The trajectory moves yet again from imaginary world to ordinary world, mediated by the reality of gaslight. In the following sentence, Mallarmé attempts to 'define' a ball dress:

> La tradition, à laquelle plus ou moins obéissent toutes les Toilettes de Bal, je la définis: rendre *légère, vaporeuse, aérienne* pour cette façon supérieure de marcher qui s'appelle danser, la divinité apparue en leur *nuage* [OC, 797].

Mallarmé defines what he understands as the expectations that his female readers might have of a ball dress, its effect on the wearer and on her gait transformed into dance. The latter is explained in ordinary terms: 'une façon supérieure de marcher'. The expectation is that the *toilette de bal* will give the wearer an extraordinary lightness, a floating elegance, almost disembodied: 'légère, vaporeuse, aérienne'. The effect of the *toilette* is to transform the wearer into a 'divinité', an apparition within a cloud. Metaphorisation in this instance is working on every aspect of the reality described, including Mallarmé's readers who might well feel that they will find it difficult, if rather flattering, to recognise themselves in his metaphor. Ordinary experience is controlled, re-moulded and recreated by the defining *je*. Weigthlessness and transparency replace body and opacity, as Mallarmé attempts to isolate qualities that are not concerned with the materials or even the colours, but with fleeting perceptions, impressions and responses. It is only after having established the nature of the essential, archetypal *toilette de bal*, that he begins to describe the physical details of individual dresses, in their materiality:

> *Si les tissus classiques de bal se plaisent à nous envelopper comme d'une brume envolée et faite de toutes les blancheurs, la robe elle-même, au contraire, corsage et jupe, moule plus que jamais la personne: opposition délicieuse et savante entre le vague et ce qui doit s'accuser.*[185] [OC, 797]

---

[185] In italics in the text.

Physical presence, weight, definition and shape are recovered; the *brume envolée* does not efface the solidity of the wearer's body, but draws attention to her shape and to her physical attributes. Mallarmé proceeds from dream to reality, from fantasy world to everyday world, having derived from his imaginary universe principles and essences that underlie the ordinary world and lend it roots, but roots that reach upwards towards the poet's own ideal dreams and visions rather than any objective, quantifiable and easily identifiable reality. Mallarmé uses both the same metaphor and the same movement from poetic vision to ordinary description in an article on baby clothes, 'nuage de suaves étoffes, vaste et allongé à l'extrême, pour que la petitesse exquise du doux être y apparaisse mieux' [OC, 813], only to continue immediately with the detailed measurements and materials to produce the garments. His creative intuition is constantly framed and anchored back into the ordinary concerns of his *lectrices*. From the 'nuage de tulle' [OC, 831], or the 'nuage d'un mouchoir orné de dentelles' [OC, 833], he lightly and elegantly steps back into the minute and trivial details that attend daily life, oscillating between the poetic and the prosaic, juggling with the metaphoric and the literal, moving with incongruous speed from the weightless world of clouds and mists to the heavy draperies of interior decoration.

Mallarmé metaphorises not only textures and materials, but also colours and visual effects. Colours are described in metaphoric terms, evocative and referring to a different reality, a reality outside the world of fashion and contemporary modern living. His description of *cachemire* material sounds more like a horticulturist's notebook or a Verlainian *romance* than a practical guide for the busy and elegant housewife:

> Mais la plus exquise des innovations, familière et suave, celle appelée, je le dis! à régner plus qu'une saison, c'est les Cachemires de nuance claire devenus (mieux que les failles et les poults-de-soie) Toilettes du soir; ceux roses et rose thé, bleus et bleu de ciel, les maïs, les réséda, les myosotis, les crème et gris clair de lune [OC, 781].

The subtle rainbow of suggestive nuances is both real and unreal, describing the colour of materials freely available at the recently opened *Bon Marché*, yet providing the poet with rich and seductive matter for dreaming and extracting a kind of magic not from the materials themselves, but from the names of the material and the names of their colours. Mallarmé does not play with the ordinary itself, or with its elements, but with the names that transform ordinary material into the stuff of dreams. He revels in the naming of colours, some easy to imagine, others ambiguous and impossible to define clearly: 'Toutes les teintes, ce sont: mauve tendre, réséda, crépuscule, gris tzarine, bleu scabieuse, émeraude, marron doré...' [OC, 800], or 'robe de taffetas bleu céleste' [OC, 845]. And yet curiously mixed with these descriptions we find a running commentary on consumerism and the effects and spread of the new department stores, for instance. In the fifth issue of 1 November 1874, the 'Gazette de la Fashion' investigates and discusses both these subjects whilst giving a beautifully metaphoric description of 'la robe bleu-rêve':

> Qu'on aille chez M. Worth en équipage à deux chevaux, attiré par les trois nouvelles robes du créateur renommé, ou qu'on aille à la Malle des Indes pour les cachemires, couleur thym, loutre et héron, partout le même ensemble dans un désir immense de dépenser de l'argent.
> Il y a pourtant des gens que cette manière de faire vivre les fabricants fâche beaucoup, et qui disent obstinément que rien ne va plus dans notre capitale. Cela irrite les gazetières, mais il faut savoir écouter les mécontents: tout le monde n'est pas heureux; tout le monde ne peut pas acheter des robes bleu-rêve, chaos et Infante, ni des tuniques loutre en pure laine du Tibet.
> [...]
> Nous avons toutes rêvé cette robe-là sans le savoir. M. Worth, seul, a su créer une toilette aussi fugitive que nos pensées.
> On n'a qu'à le vouloir, pour se figurer une longue jupe à traîne de reps, de soie du bleu le plus idéal, ce bleu si pâle à reflets d'opale, qui enguirlande quelquefois les nuages argentés. [OC, 783].

From considerations of a social nature Mallarmé moves to the description of one dress, prompted by its name to elaborate a system of metaphors and similes. Blue is no longer an ordinary colour found in various shades and nuances, it moves from the *bleu-rêve* to *bleu le plus idéal*, becoming in the process a metaphor for the fleetingness of thought and the unreality of dream. The dress does exist not only as the latest and most successful creation of a famous *couturier*, it also exists at an entirely different level, that of the dreams of the readers, and has therefore all the attributes of perfection with which dream can endow it. However, the reader is still aware of Mallarmé's ironic reminder that 'tout le monde n'est pas heureux; tout le monde ne peut pas acheter des robes bleu-rêve'. The dream has its price, money can buy a dream, but that dream is out of reach for many unhappy people. Reality has broken into the dream, Mallarmé is having a laugh, or at least a smile at the expense of his well-to-do *lectrices*, whose chief happiness resides in the possession of the latest Worth creation. He neatly encapsulates the consumerist aspirations of the modern *Parisienne* in the following sentence: '[...] on peut dire maintenant que quelques établissements universels, à eux seuls, contiennent tout le rêve en pièces et en boîtes et confectionné même, d'une Parisienne' [OC, 816]. Dream comes in boxes for the Parisian woman, and in words that describe that dream for Mallarmé. It is by dreaming into words the ordinary of his *lectrices*, an ordinary that is not his but that he adopts and explores through the use of metaphor, that Mallarmé reinvests the prosaic with a magic that he has himself first extracted from the brute material of his own trade: words.

The metaphors that are dominant in *La Dernière Mode* are part of a system that expresses a uniquely Mallarmean concept of the ordinary. This is not the ordinary of the *vulgaire*, but a subtle, reinvented ordinary, built layer by layer with delicate colours, ethereal materials, dignified by beautiful words. It is essentially feminine, yet contains within the fashion commentary and descriptions a strong philosophical, social and artistic discourse, a discourse concerned with the organisation of everyday life, with its priorities and, maybe more than any other subject, with the passage of time. Many of the metaphors and similes are to do with the changeability of popular taste; the nature of a fashion magazine is to be aware of change, to live in an eternal but unstable present, whilst predicting future changes. The Worth dress is 'fugitive comme nos pensées', elusive both in its colour, material and reality, desired for a few months only. 'avec Paris, tout un mois, n'est-ce pas une période plus vague et moins définie que ne l'est, elle-même, l'éternité?' [OC, 716]. This concern with time is intermingled with a concern for everyday life and its detail. Mallarmé formulates himself the question he imagines his readers asking him in the first issue of the magazine: 'l'Art, toujours, mais la vie, immédiate, chère et multiple, la nôtre avec ses riens sérieux, n'en sera-t-il, dans votre discours, pas question?' [OC, 718]. Mallarmé understands that it will not be possible to write a fashion magazine without dealing with ordinary life, and his response to his readers concern takes this fact into account: 'Rien n'est à négliger de l'existence d'une époque: tout y appartient à tous'. [OC, 719].

The metaphoric system which tries to deal with, and to give an account of *une époque* is not a one way-system, but has often the ambiguous quality of being reversible, and of providing the reader with a choice between literal term and metaphoric term. This is of particular interest when engaging with the ordinary, where the ordinary itself is sometimes the metaphor for a world beyond it, for a specific time dimension or a natural occurrence. Clouds are often the literal term in a metaphor, the material of a dress for instance being the metaphoric term. Mallarmé's preferred *démarche* is to move from dream to ordinary world, rather than to use the ordinary world as a *point d'appui* or a trampoline to move out of its confines and into elevated metaphoric realms. *La Dernière Mode* is ultimately, a metaphor of time and its effects and constraints on life, an exploration of ways to make both time and everyday life more habitable, to infuse it with a timeless sense of beauty in its very fleetingness, instability and changeability. It grapples with the difficulty inherent in any project that proposes to give an account of contemporary society at a given moment in time. The shortsightedness that results from a close and detailed study of one aspect of modern life, also has the benefit of envelopping harsh contours in a pleasant haze, blending distant lines into gentle harmonies, and absolving the writer from the need to be overly precise. Long-term vision does not matter, it is the micro-changes of present and immediate future that are all important: 'Aussi bien, maintenant, les yeux éblouis par des irisations, des opalisations ou des scintillements, ne pourrions-nous regarder, sans peine, quelque chose d'aussi vague surtout que l'Avenir' [OC, 715].

After a detailed study of the way in which Mallarmé metaphorises the ordinary in *La Dernière Mode*, the analysis of a number of metaphors of the ordinary elsewhere in his prose writings will underline several interesting points. In the prose poems, the reader will immediately note some derivative Baudelairian metaphors, which are clearly part of a Baudelairian concept of the ordinary. In 'Le Phénomène futur',[186] the crowd is characterised in terms of an alienated, diseased people, unable to appreciate beauty, totally estranged from any form of art, or creativity other than procreation: 'maint réverbère attend le crépuscule et ravive les visages d'une malheureuse foule, vaincue par la maladie immortelle et le péché des siècles, d'hommes près de leurs chétives complices enceintes des fruits misérables avec lesquels périra la terre' [OC, 269]. Ordinary life is seen entirely as negative, destructive, and irredeemable. Its temporal dimension is

---

[186] Written in December 1864, published eleven years later in *La République des Lettres*.

an eternal form of hell, the symptom of which is 'la maladie immortelle et le péché des siècles'.

The contrast with the ordinary described and metaphorised in 'Plainte d'Automne'[187] [OC, 270-1] is striking. From a harsh, sinful and diseased picture, we move on to a bittersweet domestic familiarity, an everyday that contains within loss and loneliness the consolation of memory. The mood of the everyday is melancholy, its melody 'un air joyeusement vulgaire et qui mit la gaîté au cœur des faubourgs, un air suranné, banal: d'où vient que sa ritournelle m'allait à l'âme et me faisait pleurer comme une ballade romantique?' The writer's own everyday is interrupted by another everyday, that of time past, made more poignant by the disembodied sound of the barrel organ. The metaphor stands both for past and present, an ideal ordinary and a real ordinary, an everyday where the 'crépuscule du souvenir' is as real as the almost mystical presence of the cat and the books. It becomes multilayered, with the quality of a palimpsest, or of a gallery of mirrors, one metaphor calling forth another, as one melody brings back another, as present and past merge, autumn and spring have the same atmosphere, and as 'un air joyeusement vulgaire' and 'une ballade romantique' have the same effect on the poet.

'Frisson d'hiver' [OC, 271] isolates within the everyday world of the poet, metaphorised by the *pendule*, the *bahut* and the *glace*, the unfamiliar, the *unheimlich* in a Heideggerian experience of the ordinary. Again it is the time dimension that brings into the poem both the familiar and the unfamiliar: the characters are far more at ease in the past, yet the past itself contains unknown elements. The present, which should be perfectly known and familiar, also contains an unsettling, almost threatening potential and it is the combination of past and present, familiar and unfamiliar expressed in a complex metaphoric web, which lends the poem its haunting and nostalgic quality. Newness, 'les objets neufs', is perceived as vulgar and unappealing. Yet age also has its negative, defamiliarising side. The everyday environment of the poet and his companion is one that has lost a clear temporal locus, settling in a shadowy in-between, a 'circle of being' which is also a circle of non-being.

The Proustian quality of 'La Pipe' [OC, 275] is evident in the description both of temporal and geographical displacement. The ordinary of 'l'hiver dernier' becomes the extraordinary of today, the picture of settled domesticity changes into that of travel

---

[187] Written in May 1864.

and uncertainty. The pipe is not only a part of the writer's winter routine, it is both its symbol and its recreator. One ordinary action summons up an ordinary that is no longer; by its location in time it loses its ordinariness, and yet its resurrection also brings back the flavour, emotions and sensations of last winter's everyday life.

'Un Spectacle interrompu' [OC, 276] deals with ordinary and extraordinary perception of an event, and explores the philosophical implications and consequences of an ordinary view of the extraordinary, and an extraordinary understanding of the world of the ordinary: 'Je veux, en vue de moi seul, écrire comme elle frappa mon regard de poëte, telle Anecdote, avant que la divulguent des *reporters* par la foule dressés à assigner à chaque chose son caractère commun'. Although the writer clearly distances himself and his perception both from *la foule* and *les reporters*, paradoxically, he intends to 'jouir comme la foule du mythe inclus dans toute banalité, quel repos et, sans voisins où verser des réflexions, voir l'ordinaire et splendide veille trouvée à la rampe par ma recherche assoupie d'imaginations ou de symboles'. His perception of the extraordinary depends first on a perception of the ordinary, and an ability to enjoy the show in the same unambiguous manner as the crowd. And yet the crowd is often used as a metaphor for the most negative form of the ordinary, *le commun, le vulgaire*. The image of the crowd as a negative, vacant and destructive force occurs throughout the critical prose works. However, as the poet recounts the *Anecdote*, the crowd is metamorphosed into an emblematic absence, becoming the necessary condition for the incident to take place, and acquiring therefore a spiritual dimension not generally attributed to *la foule*:

> La foule s'effaçait, toute, en l'emblème de sa situation spirituelle magnifiant la scène: dispensateur moderne de l'extase, seul, avec l'impartialité d'une chose élémentaire, le gaz, dans les hauteurs de la salle, continuait un bruit lumineux d'attente. [OC, 277-8].

Le gaz provides the continuity of ordinary time and circumstance, a metaphor of the modern age, both ordinary but also provider of the extraordinary, 'dispensateur moderne de l'extase'. The writer's perception of the event described in the prose poem is never divorced from his perception of the crowd and of the ordinary circumstances that surround the incident. The fatal outcome is interpreted by the writer as being caused by the environment unfamiliar to the bear, rather than by any instinct in the animal. He deliberately enters the inner processes of the bear's responses, almost bypassing the emotions and reactions of the mime artist, and linking together the crowd's perception and that of the bear. The two provide a strangely self-reflexive metaphor of each other in terms of brute force and reaction to stimuli.

The crowd also has a major role in 'La déclaration foraine' [OC, 279-83], introduced initially by its noise, 'rire strident ordinaire des choses et de leur cuivrerie triomphale: au fait, la cacophonie à l'ouïe de quiconque, un instant écarté, plutôt qu'il ne s'y fond, auprès de son idée, reste à vif devant la hantise de l'existence'. It is characterised by 'ce déchaînement exprès et haïssable de tout ce que j'avais naguères fui dans une gracieuse compagnie', and concerned mainly with the task of getting value for money, 'la certitude pour chacun de n'être pas refait'. The effect of the crowd on the writer is to force him into producing the sonnet, 'mais ceci jaillit, forcé, sous le coup de poing brutal à l'estomac, que cause une impatience de gens auxquels coûte que coûte et soudain il faut proclamer quelque chose fût-ce la rêverie...'. The metaphor of physical assault tellingly underlines the poet's perception and reaction to the crowd, a crowd which seems generally favourably disposed but implacably present and demanding.

'Réminiscence' [OC, 278-9] explores the theme of loss and displacement together with that of childhood, placing side by side different perceptions of the ordinary, that of the orphan and that of the circus children. They find a common ground of recognition and understanding first in the 'tartine de fromage mou', then in a short conversation about family life. In the prose poem, it is the ordinary 'sous l'aspect d'une tartine de fromage mou' which is a metaphor for whiteness, and its absorption by the child, echoed later in the text by the 'chaste régal'. The ordinary food has less reality than the 'neige des cimes, le lys ou autre blancheur constitutive d'ailes au-dedans'. These form the first term of a kind of comparison, finding in the simple food the metaphoric term that brings the imaginary universe right into the heart of the ordinary.

'L'Ecclésiastique' [OC, 286-8] gives an amusing example of extraordinary behaviour by an ordinary minister, rather unflatteringly described as 'plus heureux qu'un âne' [...] 'dans la béatitude de sa simplicité native'. Yet by his unorthodox behaviour, he becomes 'le héros de ma vision' only to disappear almost immediately into the crowd, 'pour rentrer, inaperçu, dans la foule, et les habitudes de son ministère [...]'. Ordinary life reaffirms its claim on him, and having become for a few moments a metaphor for the unconventional, he is translated back into just one of the anonymous members of *la foule*.

'La Gloire' [OC, 288-9] describes an ordinary journey on the train, and is replete with metaphors of modern life and its encroachment into the inner world of the poet, perceived as a violation. The outside world is characterised in terms of noise: *discord, cri, aboi, vociférateur*. It evokes within the poet an equally violent response:

> Si discord parmi l'exaltation de l'heure, un cri faussa ce nom connu pour déployer la continuité de cimes tard évanouies, Fontainebleau, que je pensai, la glace du compartiment violentée, du poing aussi étreindre à la gorge l'interrupteur: Tais-toi! Ne divulgue pas du fait d'un aboi indifférent l'ombre ici insinuée dans mon esprit, aux portières de wagons battant sous un vent inspiré et égalitaire, les touristes omniprésents vomis [OC, 288].

And yet the train is itself a dream, the poet needing to negate its reality in order to bring to life his own dream and substitute it to what seemed initially an overwhelming and undeniable manifestation of modern life. Ordinary life slowly recedes as:

> [...] lent et repris du mouvement ordinaire, se réduisît à ses proportions d'une chimère puérile emportant du monde quelque part, le train qui m'avait là déposé seul [OC, 289].

It is ordinary life which becomes 'une chimère puérile', dismissed and reduced to a non-threatening childish fantasy, lacking in substance, disconnected from the poet's own ordinary world.

To conclude this study of metaphors in the prose poems, it is necessary to distinguish between the type and quality of metaphors used. At the simplest and most immediately noticeable level, a number of metaphors substitute ordinary familiar objects for the ordinary world, effectively bringing in metonymy: *le bahut, la glace,* etc... But this is a very specific, contained ordinary, that of the poet and his companion, an ordinary that is perceived as positive, both familiar and unfamiliar, but accepted and loved. Parallel to it, and often in tension with it, we can isolate another ordinary, metaphorised by the *objets neufs*, or the *foule*, an ordinary that is alien, often seen as entirely negative, and sometimes repulsive as in the Baudelairian 'Le Phénomène futur'. It is possible to isolate yet another level and quality of metaphor of ordinary modern life, which has neutral, sometimes rather positive attributes, *le gaz* and *le train*. Within the concrete metaphoric representation of the ordinary, we move from one level to another, from one quality to another, the whole process of metaphorisation of the ordinary acquiring a complex layered system of relationships, tensions and paradoxes between the various strata of metaphors. But we also find instances where the metaphoric term is an abstract term, a concept or a quality that stands as metaphor of the ordinary, often a quality of sound (*discordant, criard*) or a level or form of violence (*coup de poing à l'estomac, violentée, étreindre du poing*). Mallarmé confides in 'Conflit'[188] that he is particularly sensitive to noise, and loud noise is *par excellence* the metaphor of the crowd, itself a metaphor of the ordinary as a negative and threatening force. Together with sound, we find a number of metaphors referring to forms of violence, and they seem particularly significant in terms of Mallarmé's own perception and response to the ordinary world. The violence is not always part of the ordinary, occasionally, as in 'La Gloire', it is part of the poet's response to the ordinary, a form of rebellion and defence against its encroachment on his own imaginary universe, often re-enacted as we have seen in previous chapters at the level of syntax.

It is in Mallarmé's critical writings, and in particular in 'Variations sur un sujet', that we find a strongly structured and consistent metaphorisation of the world of the ordinary. A large number of the articles are concerned with one or other aspect of modern life, and the style in all the texts is highly metaphorical, possibly more complex and demanding in its many ramifications than in the prose poems. The process of metaphorisation in the articles goes through several stages, in a parallel development to the layers in the poetic works. Not only can we identify several stages in one process, we can also isolate different processes of metaphorisation. In the next few pages, I shall analyse a number of different processes and stages based on examples taken mainly from 'Variations sur un sujet', before studying in detail a particularly significant metaphor in the Mallarmé corpus, that of the veil.

The processes of metaphorisation are often structured around the crowd and the daily newspaper as physical manifestation and representations of *le commun* in 'Variations sur un sujet'. It is therefore particularly interesting to study the way in which metaphors of the ordinary work in relation to those themes, how these themes become metaphors of the ordinary, and to analyse the aspect of the everyday that Mallarmé associates them

---

[188] 'Je suis le malade des bruits et m'étonne que presque tout le monde répugne aux odeurs mauvaises, moins au cri' [OC, 356].

with. In 'Plaisir sacré'[189] [OC, 388-90], he brings the two together: 'Cette multitude satisfaite par le menu jeu de l'existence, agrandi jusqu'à la politique, tel que journellement le désigne la presse;'[OC, 389]. In the first stage of the process of metaphorisation, Mallarmé perceives the crowd's satisfaction with the trivialities of life, *le menu jeu de l'existence*, as all pervasive, reflected and magnified in the press under the name of politics, a metaphor of physical and literary commonness. But his own observation of the crowd and his need to find an answer to the following question lead him to look beyond its obvious superficiality and its inevitable vulgarity: 'comment se fait-il - est-ce vrai - cela repose-t-il sur un instinct que, franchissant les intervalles littéraires, elle ait besoin tout à coup de se trouver face à face avec l'Indicible ou le Pur, la poésie sans les mots!' Far from dismissing the crowd as an embodiment of the ordinary, he is drawn into a further stage of metaphorisation:

> La foule qui commence à tant nous surprendre comme élément vierge, ou nous-mêmes, remplit envers les sons, sa fonction par excellence de gardienne du mystère! Le sien! elle confronte son riche mutisme à l'orchestre, où gît la collective grandeur. Prix, à notre insu, ici de quelque extérieur médiocre subi présentement et accepté par l'individu [OC, 390].

In a positive and almost sympathetic second stage, Mallarmé hangs a new metaphor on the image of the crowd and its representation of triviality, and from the rather threatening and uninteresting *multitude*, we move to the more complex and ambivalent *foule* to end with an awareness of *l'individu* which forms the crowd. The crowd is both *élément vierge* and *gardienne du mystère*, the crowd as metaphor being itself perceived in metaphoric terms both in relation to its nature, and in relation to its function. Mallarmé usually associates uncomfortable discordant noises with the crowd, but its physical manifestation here is 'son riche mutisme'. The positive function of the crowd resides in its protecting its own mystery, the mystery of the *élément vierge*, and this protection manifests itself in a silence which is not a sign of vacancy but of positive enrichment. Yet Mallarmé takes the metaphorisation one stage further, picking out of the crowd and the individuals forming the crowd, the detail that reflects the mysterious *accord* between the crowd and the music,

---

[189] Published in *Journal*, 5 December 1893.

the intricacies of lace on shoulders becoming a metaphor for the complexities of melody:

> Parure - si la foule est femme, tenez, les mille têtes. Une conscience partielle de l'éblouissement se propage, au hasard de la tenue de ville usitée dans les auditions d'après-midi: pose, comme le bruit déjà de cymbales tombé, au filigrane d'or de minuscules capotes, miroite en le jais; mainte aigrette luit divinatoire. L'impérieux velours d'une attitude coupera l'ombre avec un pli s'attribuant la coloration fournie par tel instrument. Aux épaules, la guipure, entrelacs de la mélodie [OC, 390].

From the macrocosm of a general ordinary without nuance or detail, Mallarmé moves to an ordinary characterised in terms of ornamentation. The crowd becomes one, not the anonymous and ungendered *individu* but *femme*, a metaphor for beauty, ornament and fashion. The passage is reminiscent of *La Dernière Mode* in its attentive description of adornment, but with the added richness of patterns and light synaesthetically reflecting the qualities of the music. It is this interaction that lifts the whole process of metaphorisation onto yet another plane, that of the *rapports multiples* that Mallarmé is forever trying to express in all their complexity.

It is in the press that Mallarmé sees the most negative effects of banality, stripping all events of their potential poetic interest. In 'Un Spectacle interrompu', he writes: 'on doit par exemple s'étonner qu'une association entre les rêveurs, y séjournant, n'existe pas, dans toute grande ville, pour subvenir à un journal qui remarque les événements sous le jour propre au rêve' [OC, 276]. Several of the articles in 'Variations sur un sujet' deal with the subject of the press, often comparing unfavourably newspapers to books. The newspaper is seen as the voice of *le commun*, a metaphor of the ordinary in its most negative manifestation, the literary pendant to the crowd: '[...] les déversoirs à portée maintenant dans une prévoyance, journaux et leur tourbillon, y déterminer une force en un sens, quelconque de divers contrariée, avec l'immunité du résultat nul' [OC, 369].[190] In 'Le Livre, instrument spirituel'[191] [OC, 379] the newspaper is also described as a 'déversoir, indifférent'. The metaphor conjures up images of refuse, reinforcing the negative

---

[190] In 'L'Action restreinte', published in *La Revue Blanche*, 1 February 1895.
[191] Published in *La Revue Blanche*, 1 July 1895.

characteristics of daily papers. They are also characterised in terms of noise, 'cri de journaux',[192] 'une incohérence de cris inarticulés'[193] [OC, 379]. Their lack of mystery is yet another negative quality; 'Journal, la feuille étalée, pleine, emprunte à l'impression un résultat indu, de simple maculature: nul doute que l'éclatant et vulgaire avantage soit, au vu de tous, la multiplication de l'exemplaire et, gise dans le tirage' [OC, 380]. This multiplication renders them hopelessly banal, in the same way as *la foule* in its number and generality is irredeemably ordinary. It is also the newspaper's failure to engage with time that gives it a flat one dimensional banality: 'Hors des premier-Paris chargés de divulguer une foi en le quotidien néant et inexperts si le fléau mesure sa période à un fragment, important ou pas, de siècle' [OC, 372]. It is reduced for Mallarmé to 'Un commerce, résumé d'intérêts énormes et élémentaires, ceux du nombre, emploie l'imprimerie, pour la propagande d'opinions, le narré du fait divers et cela devient plausible, dans la Presse, limitée à la publicité, il semble omettant un art' [OC, 375-6]. And yet, as in the image of the crowd, Mallarmé is able to discern a positive and enriching aspect:

> Ainsi, strictement, un "quotidien" avant qu'à la vision, peu à peu, mais de qui? paraisse un sens, dans l'ordonnance, voire un charme, je dirai de féerie populaire. Suivez - le faîte ou premier-Paris, dégagement supérieur, à travers mille obstacles, atteint au désintéressement et, de la situation, précipite et refoule, comme par un feu électrique, loin, après les articles émergés à sa suite, la servitude originelle, l'annonce, en quatrième page, entre une incohérence de cris inarticulés [OC, 379].

The metaphoric universe initially structured around one or two negative images, splits into two conflicting perceptions of manifestations of the ordinary. As for the image of the crowd, the process of metaphorisation moves from a general monolithic and negative system of images to a far more detailed and consequently positive system of metaphors. Although the negative images coexist with the more positive ones, the new strand stands out almost incongruously within a system that seemed initially

---

[192] In 'Etalages', [OC, 377], published in *The National Observer*, 11 June 1892.

[193] In 'Le Livre, instrument spirituel'.

strongly structured and closed against any form of change or new vision. In the verse, we tend to find a *galerie de glaces* or 'Russian dolls' process of metaphorisation, whereby one metaphor contains within itself a number of related metaphors; the process in the articles seems to be one of moving from the general to the detail, as a photographic zoom lens would pick out the interesting detail, and of creating within the metaphoric system a tension between the general negative characterisation, and the one positive redeeming detail.

If the images of the crowd and the newspaper are representations of the ordinary for Mallarmé, the image of the veil is often associated in his writings with the banal. The implication is that behind or beyond the banal resides either reality or art as divorced from a threatening quotidian world. He writes in 'Crayonné au théâtre':[194]

> [...] il a fallu formidablement, pour l'infatuation contemporaine, ériger, entre le gouffre de vaine faim et les générations, un simulacre approprié au besoin immédiat, ou l'art officiel qu'on peut aussi appeler vulgaire; indiscutable, prêt à contenir par le voile basaltique du banal la poussée de cohue jubilant si peu qu'elle aperçoive une imagerie brute de sa divinité [OC, 298].

The striking image of the banal as a dark opaque veil goes counter to the far more usual image of the mysterious as a veil. Mallarmé's reversal might well indicate that he finds the banal mysterious also, with a dark threatening quality emphasised by the alliteration. The paradoxical association of *voile* (usually light and diaphanous) with *basaltique* (black, referring to volcanic stone) might be a further indication of Mallarmé's awareness of the ambiguous quality of the banal, both transparent and opaque, light and yet rock-like and ever-present, with a Heideggerian quality of dark and alien materiality. In his article on 'L'Œuvre poétique de Léon Dierx',[195] Mallarmé uses a similar image: '[...] c'est en tant qu'un séculaire et granitique orgueil, inaccessible à la ruine, que se condense, au contraire, le sentiment quotidien de la vie' [OC, 690]. In his poem 'Les fenêtres' [P, 10-1], 'la blancheur banale des rideaux' provides a different image of the veil, hiding behind its ordinariness a metaphoric and promising window of art and *mysticité*. The image of the banal as veil is

---

[194] Published in *La Revue Indépendante* in July 1887.
[195] Published in *La Renaissance artistique et littéraire* on 16 November 1872.

implied in this passage on ballet: 'Toujours une banalité flotte entre le spectacle dansé et vous' [OC, 308], and this metaphoric expression of the ordinary as veil is further developed in 'Le genre ou des Modernes' [OC, 321], as Mallarmé reflects on the modern novel:

> Ce voile conventionnel qui, ton, concept, etc., erre dans toute salle, accrochant aux cristaux, perspicaces eux-mêmes son tissu de fausseté et ne découvre que banale la scène, il a comme flambé au gaz! et ingénus, morbides, sournois, brutaux, avec une nudité d'allure bien dans la franchise classique, se montrent des caractères.

The veil of banality is also one of inauthenticity, rendering ordinary a set of characters whose unpleasant traits are disclosed only when the veil disappears, and it can also blur and banalise more promising material as in 'le voile de généralité' [OC, 311], or in 'des détails très-neufs enveloppés de généralité comme par le voile' [OC, 763]. The veil has a standardising effect, the cover of uniformity masking the interesting and original detail. And yet this veil is also seen as the indispensable protection of the sacred element that should not be exposed to the *vulgaire*. In 'Crise de vers', Mallarmé writes:

> on assiste, comme finale d'un siècle, pas ainsi que ce fut dans le dernier, à des bouleversements; mais, hors de la place publique, à une inquiétude du voile dans le temple avec des plis significatifs et un peu sa déchirure [OC, 360].

The quality and function of the veil is a positive, protective one, rather than a negative, threatening one. It becomes itself the object of focus and importance, hiding not the spectacular and artistic, but providing a defence against vacancy and hiding in its folds the sacred meaning that oozes out of a near-Biblical rent. Events of cosmic importance find symbolic expression in the metaphoric veil, whilst ordinary time at the close of the century brings with it an end time anxiety which underlines the uniqueness of the moment.

But anxiety also inhabits the poet's thought processes, which need the mist of a veil-like cloud to blur and cover the potential vacancy of the workings of his inner conscience. In 'Le

Mystère dans les lettres' [OC, 382-7][196] the poet writes of 'tendre le nuage, précieux, flottant sur l'intime gouffre de chaque pensée'. Vacancy is no longer an outside, cosmic event, but an inner reality. He further explores the metaphor in his conclusion to 'Les Mots anglais'[197] when he brings together the image of the veil in the context of language: 'ici comme transparente [la langue] et recherchant les tons neutres, voile presque pareil à la pensée elle-même; là plus riche d'un éclat familier, émaillé, bariolé, multiple comme la vie' [OC, 1047]. The veil has become the thought, not hiding or protecting anything, but with intrinsic value.

It is possible to draw a parallel between Mallarmé's use of syntax and lexis, and his use of metaphor. The fundamental paradox studied in the chapters on syntax and vocabulary re-emerges at the level of metaphor: extraordinary metaphors tend to describe the most ordinary events, whereas ordinary metaphors are applied to the extraordinary. The prose language in particular is hypermetaphorical, offering a number of processes and stages of metaphorisation within a text, moving from patterns of internal comparisons to interactions of completely separate metaphoric systems. Inevitably, as with syntax and lexis, a number of tensions arise within the texts, as the interactions not only between systems but also between concepts of the ordinary clash and jostle with each other, occasionally finding a rather harmonious equilibrium as in some of the prose poems. Mallarmé as a compulsive metaphorist seems driven by his own difficulty in coping with everyday life. His obsessive metaphorisation enables him to face and occasionally confront the ordinary by affording him a sense of choice and control. If he is not able to gain full and ultimate mastery over the ordinary world itself, he is able to control the words that describe and express his perception and experience of it. Most important to the present discussion is the discovery, on close study, of the trajectory from imaginary universe to ordinary world through the medium of metaphor. Mallarmé's point of departure is generally his own ideal vision, ending with an ordinary that is subtly reinvented and shaped by the poet's initial dream. Metaphor is not simply a story of flight from the ordinary, or even a story of flight back to the ordinary, but a complex process in which the poet alternates between his own personal vision of the ordinary which at times coincides with the Heideggerian concept, an ideal ordinary that is occasionally

---

[196] Written in Valvins, 1896.

[197] Written in Paris, 1877.

acknowledged as such a carefully constructed and a Cavellian outside ordinary used as reference, bridge, 'subject of a quest' or 'object of an inquest'.[198]

What is the purpose of this insistent metaphorisation of the ordinary? Firstly, Mallarmé imposes on recalcitrant, sometimes unpromising material, his own personal aesthetic and artistic vision, making habitable, and enlarging, a world that he often finds confining and stifling. Where the reader would be tempted to see an eclipse of the ordinary, Mallarmé has infiltrated it with a system of images that both displaces and replaces the ordinary, giving it breadth and depth, subtly redefining the one according to the other. Behind the metaphoric system designed to make poetic sense of reality lies a thought system that undergirds all of Mallarmé's *œuvre*, creating alongside the process of metaphorisation of the ordinary world an ideological discourse, which will be the subject of the last chapter of this study.

---

[198] Stanley Cavell, *The Quest of the Ordinary: Lines on Skepticism and Romanticism* (Chicago and London: University of Chicago Press, 1988), p.149, quoted above, p.18.

CHAPTER V
An Ideology of Ordinary Life

A close study of Mallarmé's lexis and syntax as they relate to ordinary life, and an analysis of some of the significant metaphors that are a Mallarmean figuration of the ordinary lead us from an understanding of it as necessary element within language and as referent within which language performs its more extraordinary syntactic and lexical evolutions, to an analysis of the rhetoric that attends the subject. I shall use the word rhetoric in its sense of doctrinal discourse, Mallarmé's attempt to wrestle intellectually with the concept of the ordinary, and the philosophical framework within which he deals on the one hand with his observation of contemporary society, on the other with his own response to the ordinary world of his day. I am therefore moving from a study of the ordinary defined by textual linguistic and internal parameters to the ordinary of contemporary public life that the poet necessarily inhabited. In the process of ambiguous response to modern society, the ordinary becomes caught up in an ideology, a worldview that informs all of the poet's writings, in particular the journalistic writings. The reader is aware of the manipulative effects of rhetoric in action, a metaphysical position in constant shift, and a dynamic convergence towards a creative point within an argumentative composition. It goes beyond the presentation of a point of view, the stating of a philosophical or metaphysical stance. It points towards a process of controlling and manipulating, of seducing, embellishing but also of distancing and ironising. This textual, intellectual and philosophical discourse does not belong singly to one type of text. We are aware, even as we read the *Vers de circonstance*, that there is a larger project at work, a project that has to do with the poet's self-conscious engagement with the everyday life of his time. We recognise a typically Mallarmean response to the ordinary in its public expression, that of excitement and recoil.

In his book *La Religion de Mallarmé*,[199] Bertrand Marchal refers to 'tout un système de pensée'[200] and states that

---

[199] Bertrand Marchal, *La Religion de Mallarmé* (Paris: Corti, 1988). My research has been greatly stimulated by the author's insights into Mallarmé's relationship with modern society.

his aim is to 'exhumer le substrat idéologique'.[201] Marchal's argument is that behind and beyond Mallarmé's aesthetic and poetic project lies the undergirding of a religious (in the broadest of senses) perception of history, art and modern society. Marchal powerfully presents Mallarmé's political and social views as finding coherence and unity in the poet's religious apprehension of reality. But Mallarmé's preoccupation with ritual, be it mass, concerts, or political gatherings, his need to 'rendre à l'homme moderne, sous la forme d'une célébration poétique, la double dimension cosmique et sociale, qui le constitue, et la conscience de sa divinité fictive',[202] has an obsessive and paradoxical side which points to yet another fundamental grappling, a deep-seated anxiety which promotes in the poet a discourse that can sound reactionary and violent at times. Religion is both a symptom of Mallarmé's need to re-create poetically the ordinary world, to endow it with divine attributes in order to make it habitable, and proof of the possibility of redemption of even the most ordinary of circumstances or events.

In this chapter, I shall use a number of Mallarmé's texts and draw a sequence of examples from the journalistic writings, *La Dernière Mode* and *Vers de circonstance*. I shall attempt to identify within the texts the worldview from which Mallarmé's expressive, creative and poetic characteristics spring, an ideology which informs all his writings and which has at its centre the poet's intellectual, emotional and ultimately textual response to the world of the ordinary. I shall focus within the texts on the process of ideological recuperation of the ordinary: in the public sphere as embellishment and as metaphysical search, and also as manipulation and as quest towards a reconciliation between what Mallarmé perceives as a flawed and at times uninhabitable society, and a seductive and invigorating modernity. I shall argue that it is at the point of tension and cleavage between a recoil from the banalisation offered by the new industries, and the excitement that the possibilities of a wide distribution and democratisation of goods with artistic value stimulates, that the poet's own recuperative and fertile creative powers are thriving. Although he is placed in a painful double postulate, his imagination readily investing modernity with dynamic potential, but also pointing out the possibility of the loss of the rare and the unique, the inner and outer rifts perceived within the contemporary world and his own

---

[200] *La Religion de Mallarmé*, p.9.
[201] *Ibid.*
[202] *Ibid*, p.551.

response has the useful consequence of providing the necessary intellectual and emotional sting to drive the writer on towards a sustained and often divided evaluation of the cultural, social and ordinary life of his time.

I shall first of all study Mallarmé's discourse on the quotidian as ingredient of a domestic everyday life, drawing examples from the 'Trois lettres sur l'Exposition Internationale de Londres',[203] the *Vers de circonstance* (1881-1898) and *La Dernière Mode* (September to December 1874). Can we isolate within texts ostensibly devoted to the domestic the expression of a negative attitude towards everyday living, or a discourse aimed at emptying the quotidian of quality and undermining any creative potential? One is entitled to claim with some confidence that the ordinary events of daily life provided the writer with a wealth of material for the wordplay, amusement and ingenuity of the *Vers de circonstance* right up to the month preceding his death.[204] We can recognise, recycled or embryonic, a number of images and metaphors which appear in his verse, trimmed, subverted or disguised to fit the circumstances of ordinary life, and to extract from them their pun-and-fun potential:

Rue, ouïs! 22 Lavoisier
Madame Degrandi qui lance
La richesse de son gosier
Aussi haut que notre silence. [OC, 91]

---

[203] The three letters appeared in the newspaper *Le National*, in the 29 October, 14 and 29 November 1871 editions. Mallarmé used the pseudonym of L.S.Price to sign the letters. Mallarmé wrote a further article on the 'Expositions Internationales de Londres', which appeared in *L'Illusion* on 20 July, and was signed by the poet. The letters and the article, although representative of the style of writing popular with contemporary reviews, nevertheless display typically Mallarméan stylistic features and are of interest because of the way they exemplify Mallarmé's ability to adapt to the current trends in journalistic writings. They also give interesting indications as to Mallarmé's tastes by the very choices he makes for the focus of his descriptions.

[204] The 'Notes et Variantes' of the Pléiade edition states that 'en 1920 parut, sous ce titre, aux éditions de la *Nouvelle Revue Française*, un volume dans lequel le gendre et la fille du poëte, le Dr et Mme Edmond Bonniot, avaient réuni les "vers familiers" composés par Stéphane Mallarmé à des époques diverses de sa vie, en des occasions amicales, entre 1881 et le mois qui précéda sa mort'. [OC, 1502] The Pléiade edition also quotes Jean Royère: 'Dans les *Vers de Circonstance*, [...] je vois comme le pouls de sa vie quotidienne...' [OC, 1503] from *Mallarmé*, vol. I, Messein éd., Paris, 1931, p.114.

The rhyme and last words of lines 2 and 4 are identical to the lines 2 and 4 of 'Petit Air II' [P, 55], pointing to the fact that the type of work involved in writing the pieces was not vastly different, and that the exploitation of ordinary situations, and the stimulation they provided were a rewarding source of material for the poet. The investment is one not only of pleasure in words and the amusement provided for friends, but one of implicit recognition of the potential of everyday life for creativity and exploration of sounds, words and the process of shaping the grey quotidian from 'monotone littérature'[205] [OC, 119] to 'azur barbaresque' [OC, 127]. Mallarmé's response to the ordinary events that stimulate his linguistic *pirouettes* is one of warm-hearted enjoyment of communication within the safe circle of friends and family. They form the secure terrain of his own social exchanges, largely untouched by the problematic encroachments of industrial change. It is when the poet is confronted not so much with the comfortable fabric of the ordinary routine of a life of urbanity but with the insistant and shrill demands made by a particularly dynamic modern society that his response of fascination and fear stimulates a creative if painful reflection.

In his letters and article on the 'Expositions Internationales de Londres' Mallarmé includes a number of revealing sentences on his attitude towards the domestic objects that are part of the 'décor familier de notre existence quotidienne' [OC, 679]:

> Nos exposants ne s'étonneront pas de notre sollicitude pour leur tentative - vraiment celle de l'âge moderne tout entier - d'une fusion de l'art et de l'industrie. N'est-ce pas un réciproque devoir, que l'art décore les produits requis par nos besoins immédiats, en même temps que l'industrie multiplie par ses procédés hâtifs et économiques ces objets embellis autrefois par leur seule rareté? Je me propose de rechercher, sous l'heureuse inspiration de votre programme, qui est celui que je viens d'abréger, toutes choses participant de ce double aspect. [OC, 666-7]

---

[205] 'Dons de fruits glacés au Nouvel An'. For a stimulating introduction on the *Vers de circonstance*, see Yves Bonnefoy's preface of *Vers de circonstance* (Gallimard, 1996), pp.7-51.

The acknowledgement that art and industry do, indeed have to, complement each other, and that their complementarity is both pleasing and a trait of the modern age has a ring of pragmatism and acceptance of the changes inherent in industrialisation that might surprise coming from the writer reputed to be the poet of the rarefied and the refined. He is acutely aware of the modern environment, willing to see in its manifestation the positive qualities that enhance everyday life. He is of course part of a vastly optimistic mood, which ascribed industrialisation in the last decade of the nineteenth century the power to transform everyday living and to usher in an age of unending and blissful comfort. Theodore Zeldin describes in the second volume of *France 1848 - 1945*,[206] the birth of the consumer society and the hopes and ambitions of the newly born modern consumer. It is particularly with the phenomenon of the international exhibitions, and the importance they assumed as diffusers and promoters of new industries and techniques applied to the quotidian that contemporary society became acquainted with the advances of science and technology. The public was also able to enjoy displays of articles of daily use, often manufactured with the use of new tools, which reduced their cost. Mallarmé chooses to write particularly on the ornamental and aesthetic qualities of the objects exhibited in the French pavilion. He finds the quality of newness as attractive as the reproduction of older styles. He describes 'le charme inhérent aux choses neuves' as well as the 'réminiscences surannées' [OC, 667], he admires 'deux pièces véritablement modernes' [OC, 667] and eventually recognises his

---

[206] Zeldin devotes several pages to a description of the international exhibitions, and their effects on the public (pp.612-8):

> The masses could get a sight of the latest advances in technology and the practical results of science in the international exhibitions, which were events of great importance in several different ways. The exhibitions were voluntarily attended by more people than went to any other attraction or entertainment that was organised in this period. [...] The exhibitions brought the industrial portion of the nation out of its traditional secretiveness and enabled it both to boast of its achievements and to receive public acknowledgement of the value placed on them, despite all the attacks on profiteering and chimney smoke. They drowned, even if only while they lasted, the pessimistic complaints of the poets and moralists in exclamations of awe and self-congratulation; and the delight in technical progress that they stimulated should not be overlooked simply because there were few great writers who echoed it.'.

inability to define clearly the imprint of modernity, 'un cachet indéfinissable auquel convient seul le nom de: moderne qui exprime quelque chose, également, d'occidental.' [OC, 685]. He analyses the inevitable implications of mass production, the question of authenticity, and seems to be able to accept happily the resulting reduction in rarity as well as cost: 'J'avoue que, devant ces reproductions admirables, le mot d'*authentique*,[207] fréquemment prononcé par le collectionneur exigeant, perd singulièrement de sa valeur à nos yeux.' [OC, 674]. The hallmark of contemporary genius is not so much the creation of new forms but the ability to reproduce, the '[...]vulgarisation des modèles plus anciens, dont le prix de fabrication seul baissera [...]' [OC, 676], the process of recapturing a past that is made modern by the ability of contemporary techniques of recreating beautiful 'objets de nécessité journalière' [OC, 670] cheaply, quickly and *ad infinitum*. Zeldin's commentary echoes Mallarmé's own very modern evaluation: 'The immediate result of technical improvements [...] was greater productivity, more goods on the market and eventually more money to buy them with.' (p.613) Mallarmé is curiously without regret when he states: 'Je le prédis: le mot d'*authentique*, qui fut, pendant maintes années, le terme sacramentel de l'antiquaire, avant peu n'aura plus de sens.' [OC, 684] Exclusiveness and rarity are not qualities that he recognises as essential anymore, the possession of beautiful objects that were not available to the majority is now the mark of the past. Modern society and the progress of industry bring the benefit of the availability of beauty in its everyday forms of furniture and familiar objects to the masses.[208] The writer's imagination is attracted to the potential for a kind of universal, perpetual and huge fête, a new form of collective *réjouissances* in a kinder and more aesthetically pleasing environment. Mallarmé applauds the aim of enhancing the quotidian environment, making it quite literally more habitable for a greater number of people: 'Quant à l'Industrie, qui est la préoccupation visible de ce temps, son but, actif et généreux, sera la multiplication populaire de ces merveilles, célèbres ou uniques, enfouies longtemps dans quelques résidences héréditaires.' [OC, 683-4] The egalitarian aims of industry, qualified as active and generous, are unhesitatingly

---

[207] In italics in the text.

[208] Zeldin writes in *La France 1848 - 1945*, p.615: 'Above all, it was the enormous reduction in prices of articles of daily use, which were once luxuries, and which now came within the reach of the masses, that seemed important. Industrialisation meant, more than anything else, cheaper goods.'

sanctioned as a worthy endeavour, the benefits of 'la multiplication populaire de ces merveilles' opening up the possibility of a more attractive vision of the everyday world.[209] *La Dernière Mode* is dominated by one expression, 'le monde contemporain'. Mallarmé's preoccupation with the manifestations of modernity in their more domestic expressions and interests is apparent throughout the issues, understandably enough for a magazine claiming to bring the latest in fashion and entertainment to the discerning female reader. Yet this concentration on *la nouveauté, la modernité* on the part of a poet reputed to be aloof and isolated from the concerns of ordinary life deserves a careful study, a re-reading of the magazine that looks at the underlying rhetoric purpose and at the dynamic process of recreating a totalising experience in an ever-changing quotidian, offered as the ultimate way of life to the unsuspecting French *femme d'intérieur*. In the first issue (6 September 1874), Mallarmé, signing as Ix, sets out the aims of the magazine: to bring to his *lectrices* 'les produits de la dernière heure' in every possible domain, addressing himself to 'la personne moderne', and 'attentif à la somme de plaisir que peut, de ces usages nouveaux, tirer une personne contemporaine' [OC 718]. He imagines a possible argument between his readers and himself on the contents of the magazine, keen to underline his own interest in the latest and most modern expressions of art and everyday life:

> "Intéresser aux habitudes du beau ordinaire, c'est un peu notre objet; mais encore plus l'utilisation directe à de délicates jouissances de toute visée manifestée par un artiste."
> "Livres, théâtre et simulacres obtenus avec la couleur ou les marbres: l'Art, toujours, mais la vie, immédiate, chère et multiple, la nôtre avec ses riens sérieux, n'en sera-t-il, dans votre discours, pas question?"[OC, 718]

The writer, attempting to imagine his readers' response, sets up an opposition between Art and life, between *simulacres* and *vie immédiate*, between *livres* and the *littérature particulière* that he condescendingly imagines is his female readers' foremost interest: [...]listes de danseurs perdues avec les fleurs effeuillées, programme du concert ou carte des dîneurs, composent, certes, une littérature particulière, ayant en soi l'immortalité d'une

---

[209] See also Walter Benjamin, *Charles Baudelaire: A Lyric Poet in the Era of High Capitalism* trans.Harry Zohn (London: NLB, 1973) pp.163-6.

semaine ou de deux. Rien n'est à négliger de l'existence d'une époque: tout y appartient à tous' [OC, 718-9]. Mallarmé professes an interest in the detail of everyday life, and in its value as an expression of a historical period of time. Its very fleetingness, 'l'immortalité d'une semaine ou de deux', confers on it the aura and the seduction of constant change, and brings with it an anxiety of loss which drives the writer to try and capture it in his magazine. Each detail of life, from the menus to the fashion in hats, to the latest book of poems, contributes to 'l'existence d'une époque'. To dismiss any aspect of it as négligeable or unrepresentative, or simply too trivial to be mentioned would be to rob an unspecified all (*tous*, Mallarmé's contemporaries) of a part of everything (*tout*, every detail that constructs the ordinary life of an epoch), thereby making the picture incomplete. The reader is aware of a globalising intention on the part of Mallarmé, of the constructing of a discourse aimed at explaining and justifying the whole enterprise of *La Dernière Mode*. Whilst the whole project has a totalising ambition in the diversity of the aspects of modern life that it deals with, it is also fragmented and dispersed as it jumps from dresses to gardens to menus, cold remedies and the poetry of François Coppée. Behind the competent voice that seems able to deal with every possible educational or decoration problem, we guess at the metaphysical anxiety that throws the writer into a whirlpool of words in an attempt to circumscribe the dimension and variety of everyday life within time:

> Un Mois et plus encore était derrière nous, avec son vaste rien qu'il fallait raconter: car comment, sans faire cela d'abord et sans remettre enfin à la quinzaine future le tableau de ce qui poind aujourd'hui et brillera alors d'un éclat très vif, rattacher nos paroles de maintenant à l'écho d'une causerie lointaine, en même temps qu'à celles de bientôt; et pour la première fois, prendre date? Tout le passé, cette fois; pour l'autre, le présent, mêlé à l'avenir. [OC, 734]

The difficulty and the charm of writing about the new, the contemporary, the modern world, has to do with its uncertain, unstable place in time, a locus where the quotidian routine is endlessly renewed and renewable, where change is the only certainty, and where past and future have little meaning. Yet even as fashion writer Marguerite de Ponty, he aspires to be 'historiographe des Toilettes' [OC, 780], claiming the distance and prestige of placing his writing in a respectable temporal perspective, the details of colours, textures, cuts and designs dignified by their belonging to a present already perceived as part of history. The panic and disorientation caused by the fleeting and the unstable is exorcised by the claiming of a temporal perspective which, by its very magnitude is not subject to the same changeability. The dimension of the everyday becomes eternal, 'l'immortalité d'une semaine ou de deux' stretching backwards and forwards, made up of a multitude of aspects of life into an endless kaleidoscopic vision. The domestic everyday world described in *La Dernière Mode* is redeemable because of its diversity, of its many enjoyable facets, and of its constant changes. But its creative potential, the worth that is conferred on it by investing the everyday with the qualities of a social discourse and a rhetoric that claims that modern life must be recorded, examined and recreated with the testimony of words - 'Rien n'est à négliger de l'existence d'une époque' - is based on Mallarmé's awareness of a different dimension, that of 'Le Tombeau d'Edgar Poe' [OC, 70], that of the poet 'Tel qu'en Lui-même enfin l'éternité le change.'

The clearest and most positive attitude towards industry is found in the 'Trois Lettres sur l'Exposition Internationale de Londres'. As we have seen in the preceding paragraph, industry is characterised in terms of progress and modernity, and brings the advantages of mass production, reproduction and low cost. This leads to a more even distribution of useful and beautiful everyday objects, and enables a greater number of people to enjoy the benefits of a pleasanter domestic environment. 'L'âge moderne tout entier' is characterised by an attempt to fuse art and industry, and there is no doubt that within the context of the exhibition at least, Mallarmé approved and encouraged such a project. Progress is equated with a higher standard of living for a majority through the spread of Industry, 'qui est la préoccupation visible de notre temps'. Multiplication, reproduction and mass production in the context of everyday objects are seen as 'le but actif et généreux' of industry. Mallarmé concentrates on these objects, only mentioning *en passant* the exhibition of industrial machinery: 'Quant aux Galeries artistiques et industrielles, elles contiennent [...]des machines ordinaires: sauf un canon qui intéresse les princes et les souverains et une charmante et exacte machine à composer, à l'usage d'une imprimerie. Cela sous la rubrique: Beaux-Arts et Inventions Scientifiques, qui forment le fond permanent des dix *seasons*' [OC, 682]. His obvious lack of interest in 'machines ordinaires' is counter-balanced by the two objects he chooses to mention specifically: a war machine which he seems to think is only of interest to rulers (possibly a reference to the Emperor's disastrous war against Prussia), and a printing machine which is, perhaps not so suprisingly for a lover and writer of books, qualified as *charmante*. There is a further and negative reference to machines in the third letter, hinting at Mallarmé's disenchantement with Napoléon III's military ambitions:

> Les inventions nouvelles de la Science viennent compléter cette section permanente du musée contemporain que ramènera chaque été.
> Hélas! on sait à la découverte de quels engins spéciaux la science s'est adonnée chez nous depuis une année: notre participation au concours des machines est restreinte, pour ne pas dire nulle. [OC, 674]

Industry, apart from military industry, is seen entirely as a positive contribution to society. It is a sign of modernity that opens up the age of access to the beautiful for all.

In his essay 'Sur le Beau et l'Utile',[210] Mallarmé introduces a number of new ideas on the subject of modern inventions. If he reiterates his understanding of modernity as a fusion of the beautiful and the useful, '[...]comme l'objet se présente, pour plaire et servir, causant une impression, toute moderne, de vérité' [OC, 880], he also introduces a new criterion, '[...]ce terme moyen le Vrai'. Both the beautiful and the useful possess only limited qualities without this extra dimension: 'Le Beau, gratuit tourne à l'ornement, répudié: l'Utile, seul ou qui l'est, alors, à des besoins médiocres, exprime une inélégance' [OC, 880]. Only the combination of the two tempered by the addition of *le vrai* can truly claim to be modern. What does Mallarmé understand by *le vrai* in the context of industry and manufacture? First of all, it seems that the combination of the beautiful and the useful is likely to produce *le vrai*, a new conception of creativity that is applied to ordinary objects:

> Cette transformation du sens créateur ne s'accomplit pas, actuellement, sans inconscience et bavures; mais, telle merveille, dans la réussite, qu'un parapluie, un habit noir, un coupé. Une bicyclette n'est pas vulgaire menée à la main hors du garage, étincelante bientôt de sa rapidité.' [OC, 880]

---

[210] This essay does not seem to have been published. The Pléiade editors give the following explanation: 'C'est un manuscrit de la Collection H.M. Vraisemblablement, une réponse à un enquêteur. Nous n'avons pas encore découvert le texte imprimé. Peut-être cette page a-t-elle été confiée à Ch. Morice pour une de ses conférences' [OC, 1641].

If Mallarmé acknowledges the successes of modern invention, he also points out the failures due not to the inventive spirit, but to the lack of inventive ability. Invention is perceived as always positive, it is the second rate effort to adapt old procedures to new techniques that creates what the writer calls a 'erreur momentanée'. 'Il s'agit non de dénaturer, mais d'inventer', he reminds the *ingénieur* who invented the first motor car. Mallarmé also claims the right for the non-specialist to take part in the inventive process. His own view on the motor car, if we might now find it amusing and hardly practical, is qualified as 'Vision de passant homme de goût, laquelle remet à point les choses' [OC, 880-1]. He imagines that the verdict passed on the latest inventions could be entrusted not to the specialists but to '[...] un jury d'artistes, et de quelques littérateurs, fonctionnerait précieusement, à des concours: outre que son intervention ne détruirait jamais le laid tout à fait (car il importe de le conserver, à titre d'exception, pour un décor, à des âmes qui sont, elles-mêmes, camelote) [OC, 881].

In his lecture 'Le "Ten O'clock de Whistler"'[211] Mallarmé gives an altogether different view of art and industry applied to everyday life. He retraces the origins of art, using for the epic description of the first attempts of artists and artisans a pastiche of Biblical diction. This ironic display of a weighty and occasionally archaic use of language leaves the reader with the sense that the writer is more concerned to entertain, with a wealth of rhetorical effect, his fashionable audience than to conduct a serious discussion on the question of the artistic and the functional. The premise of his argument is that art was present as part of everyday life because no objects that were not beautiful existed at the time. If the majority of people were not able to appreciate the beauty of useful objects, this made no difference to ordinary life:

> Et les siècles se passèrent en ces coutumes, et le monde fut inondé de tout ce qui était beau, jusqu'à ce que se leva une classe nouvelle qui découvrit le bon marché et prévit la fortune dans la fabrication du faux.
> Alors jaillirent à l'existence le clinquant, le commun, la camelote.
> Le goût du commerçant supplanta la science et l'artiste, et ce qui était né de mille et mille leur retourna, et les

---

[211] Written in Paris, March to April 1888, and published in *La Revue Indépendante* in May 1888.

charma, car c'était d'après leur propre coeur; et les grands et les petits, l'homme d'état et l'esclave, prirent pour eux l'abomination offerte et la préférèrent - et ont vécu avec, toujours, depuis lors! [OC, 573]

The humour that is obviously present in the adoption of a pseudo-Biblical register undermines the seriousness of the argument. Yet the rest of the discussion cannot be dismissed on the grounds of a humorous introduction. Mallarmé does not claim any scientific or anthropological truth, he simply exploits an imaginative and playful description of the origins of art, beauty, and ugliness in our everyday environment. He discusses the relationship of the people to art and industry, and the dominance of the latter over the former: 'Et le peuple - maintenant - eut beaucoup à dire en cette affaire et chacun fut satisfait. Et Birmingham et Manchester se levèrent en leur puissance - et l'Art fut relégué dans la boutique de bric-à-brac' [OC, 573]. This plainly contradicts the statements on the exhibition, where Mallarmé sees art and industry not in competition, but as complementary. The differences in the aims and style of the pieces, the ones serious reports on a particularly brilliant event, designed to display the very best achievements and most modern developments in art and industry, and the other a speech conceived for the amusement of an audience, make a comparison difficult. The contradictions could be explained not as a complete change in Mallarmé's opinion, but as different response and form of expression to a different situation, and to a typically ambiguous stance. The one has more to do with *reportage*, with the added bonus of Mallarmé's occasional commentary stimulated by the very real achievement of the combined efforts of art and industry. The other is an imaginative and rhetorical discussion which finds its basis in hypotheses and its conclusion in Mallarmé's tongue-in-cheek sense of occasion and desire to excite a response in his audience. He nevertheless expresses in humorous form the deep anxiety he feels when confronted with the huge changes that technical progress heralds, changes that are reflected at the level of everyday life.[212]

---

[212] See Rachel Killick's 'Mallarmé's Rooms: 'The Poet's Place in "La Musique et les Lettres"' in *French Studies*, vol.51:'The significance of the experience overall lay not so much, however, in its revelation of difference *per se* as in its confirming and crystallising effect on Mallarmé's own sense of ongoing cultural upheaval brought about by scientific and industrial development and the consequential changes in the economic, social and political climate and the intellectual and aesthetic spheres.'

It is really in the area of literary production, of the modern press and of the mass printing of books[213] that Mallarmé departs from a positive view of industry and commercial enterprise, and points out in the articles gathered under the title 'Quant au Livre' [OC, 369-87][214] the perversions and negative effects of consumerism and the pursuit of profit. In 'L'Action restreinte',[215] we find a definition of the book as object and as archetype, totally independent once written both from author and reader, existing without having to be read and understood:

> Le Livre, où vit l'esprit satisfait, en cas de malentendu, un obligé par quelque pureté d'ébat à secouer le gros du moment. Impersonnifié, le volume, autant qu'on s'en sépare comme auteur, ne réclame approche de lecteur. Tel, sache, entre les accessoires humains, il a lieu tout seul: fait, étant. Le sens enseveli se meut et dispose, en choeur, des feuillets. [OC, 372]

It is against this vision of the book as having an independent and eternal life, detached from the vagaries both of readers' demands and of marketing pressures, that Mallarmé constructs a negative discourse on the commerce of books and newspapers. In 'Etalages'[216] [OC, 373-8] Mallarmé introduces the subject by drawing a parallel between a *krach* of the book industry and autumn, a symbolic wind having both bared the trees of leaves and littered the floor with books: 'Les volumes jonchaient le sol, que ne disait-on, invendus; à cause du public se déshabituant de lire probablement pour contempler à même, sans intermédiaire, les couchers de soleil familiers à la saison et beaux' [OC, 373]. However, this is pure supposition, and the writer turns to the realities of the commerce of books to demonstrate that written matter, and particularly poetry, should not be subjected to the indignities of the market place:

---

intellectual and aesthetic spheres.'

[213] For a discussion of the circumstances of the newspaper industry in the second half of the nineteenth century, and of the role of the *feuilleton* and the *réclame*, see Benjamin's *Charles Baudelaire: A Lyric Poet in the Era of High Capitalism*, pp.27-33.

[214] In 'Variations sur un sujet', Paris-Valvins, January to October 1895. The articles appeared on a monthly basis in *La Revue Blanche*.

[215] The article appeared under the title 'L'Action' in *La Revue Blanche* on 1 February 1895.

[216] First published in *The National Observer*, on 11 June 1892.

> La mentale denrée, comme une autre, indispensable, garde son cours et je rentre [...]; n'ayant, en le trajet, éprouvé, que devant les modernes épiceries ou les cordonneries du livre, un souci mais aigu et que proclame l'architecture demandée, par ces bazars, à la construction de piles ou de colonnades avec leur marchandise. [OC, 374]

The reader has become a consumer, eager to feed his need for reading matter, and the bookstores are transformed into shops that sell a cheap and abundant fare of cheaply and badly written and produced material. The main concern of the shopkeepers is to display their wares, stacked into piles resembling the pillars of a glitzy palace. The crude advertising of 'la mentale denrée' offends the writer; books are sold *en plein air* like vulgar vegetables on a market stall, with the implication that they have descended to the same status. Mallarmé attempts to understand the intricacies of supply and demand, and the peculiar case of the book of poetry. He acknowledges the enormous commercial superiority both of the novel and of the newspaper, but infers that their real value is in inverse proportion. Mass production here has none of the qualities of mass production of everyday objects. Although books are part of the everyday, they also belong to a different category: they have the potential to encompass the whole world in their pages: 'tout, au monde, existe pour aboutir à un livre' [OC, 378].[217] The mass production of books denies its spiritual and unique quality:

> Un commerce, résumé d'intérêts énormes et élémentaires, ceux du nombre, emploie l'imprimerie, pour la propagande d'opinions, le narré du fait divers et cela devient plausible, dans la Presse, limitée à la publicité, il semble, omettant un art. [OC, 375-6]

The book industry is concerned mainly with producing as much written material as possible, in every possible form. It has lost the ability to use discernment in the literary sphere, 'le discrédit, où se place la librairie, a trait, moins à un arrêt de ses opérations, je ne le découvre; qu'à sa notoire impuissance envers l'œuvre exceptionnelle' [OC, 377]. Mallarmé claims that the writer will

---

[217] From 'Le Livre, instrument spirituel', published in *La Revue Blanche* on 1 July 1895.

never be able to make a fortune from his trade, and might as well give up the attempt to sell what the poet calls the unsaleable:

> L'auteur, la chance au mieux ou un médiocre éblouissement monétaire, ce serait, pour lui, de même; en effet: parce que n'existe devant les écrits achalandés, de gain littéraire colossal. La métallurgie l'emporte à cet égard. Mis sur le pied de l'ingénieur, je deviens, aussitôt, secondaire: si préférable était une situation à part. A quoi bon trafiquer de ce qui, peut-être, ne se doit vendre, surtout quand cela ne se vend pas.' [OC, 377-8]

If the book market displays the power of greed and responds to the worst pressures of consumerism, it can also benefit from the advances of modern industrialisation. Mallarmé is able to isolate, within a rather negative analysis, the dynamic, positive and redeeming features of an otherwise money-oriented enterprise: 'A jauger l'extraordinaire surproduction actuelle, où la Presse cède son moyen intelligemment, la notion prévaut, cependant, de quelque chose de très décisif qui s'élabore: comme avant une ère, un concours pour la fondation du Poëme populaire moderne, tout au moins de *Mille et Une Nuits* innombrables: dont une majorité lisante soudain inventée s'émerveillera' [OC, 376]. Mass production can also herald a new reading and writing era, as it has done for quotidian objects, giving access to expression to a greater number of people. The future prospects of the book market are bright, even the lesser form of literature found in newspapers has a dynamic and unstoppable quality: 'Tout ce que trouva l'imprimerie se résume, sous le nom de Presse, jusqu'ici, élémentairement dans le journal: [...]Ainsi, strictement, un "quotidien" avant qu'à la vision, peu à peu, mais de qui? paraisse un sens, dans l'ordonnance, voire un charme, je dirai de féerie populaire' [OC, 379]. The spring of its dynamism is both its constant change and its mass production. Although these attributes are the exact opposite to the qualities of the *Livre*, Mallarmé has enough awareness of the structures, demands and pressures of the society in which he lives to recognise the potential within modern technology. Printing and typography possess attractions simply because they transform one object into a number of identical objects without affecting the uniqueness of their content: 'Rien de fortuit, là, où semble un hasard capter l'idée, l'appareil est l'égal: ne juger, en conséquence, ces propos - industriels ou ayant trait à une matérialité: la fabrication du livre, en l'ensemble qui s'épanouira, commence, dès une phrase' [OC, 380]. The writer is part of a creative process that finds its completion in the printing process. The beauty and uniqueness of the work resides first in the carefully crafted 'labeur linguistique' of the author, whereas in the case of the newspaper, it is in fact the process of mass production and the typography elevated to *un rite* which dignify an otherwise undistinguished enterprise:

> [...]nul doute que l'éclatant et vulgaire avantage soit, au vu de tous, la multiplication de l'exemplaire et, gise dans le tirage. Un miracle prime ce bienfait, au sens haut ou les mots, originellement se réduisent à l'emploi, doué d'infinité jusqu'à sacrer une langue, des quelque vingt lettres - leur devenir, tout y rentre pour tantôt sourdre, principe - approchant d'un rite la composition typographique. [OC, 380]

Mallarmé is caught once again in a painfully and characteristically divided response: the excitement of mass distribution of printed matter cannot fail to stimulate his modern imagination, whilst the vulgarisation of precious and invaluable literary contributions induces in the writer a self-protective and almost uncontrollable horror. But the rift that causes intellectual and emotional turmoil also liberates new and powerful energies, a dynamic charge that enables Mallarmé to express with vigour and originality the anxious shifts in his evaluation of contemporary society.

The newspaper has becomes *un déversoir* [OC, 369; OC, 379] eager to reproduce 'une incohérence de cris inarticulés' [OC, 379], attempting to take commercial and intellectual precedence over the book, the very principle of its existence lying in mass production and the relation of *faits divers*. Yet it is redeemed to a degree not only by the techniques of its production, but also by its use of a more imaginative type of writing, the serial. The potential for creativity involved in the writing of fiction, and the predilection that the public shows towards this type of writing covers a multitude of sins in Mallarmé's eyes:

> Mieux, la fiction proprement dite ou le récit, imaginatif, s'ébat au travers de "quotidiens" achalandés, triomphant à des lieux principaux, jusqu'au sommet; en déloge l'article de fond, ou d'actualité, apparu secondaire. Suggestion et même leçon de quelque beauté: qu'aujourd'hui n'est seulement le remplaçant d'hier, présageant demain, mais sort du temps, comme général, avec une intégrité lavée ou neuve. [OC, 376]

As in the case of *La Dernière Mode*, the production of a 'daily' inevitably raises the question of its use of time and its long-term value. The life span of its immediate interest is too restricted and its implied comment on the value of yesterday or tomorrow too superficial to acquire the dignity of a book. But the serial, with its continuous flow over a number of weeks, which in terms of a "quotidien", has a flavour of eternity, lifts the time bound publication out of the slavery of an elusive present.

Far worse in Mallarmé's opinion is the fate of the book, the reduction of the volume to a consumer goods, in particular the novel, written to please the modern reader: 'Voilà ce que, précisément, exige un moderne: se mirer, quelconque [...] [OC, 375]. To pander to the pressure exercised by the consumers is a debasing of the book, substituting a potential 'instrument spirituel' to the already vulgar newspaper.

> Leur malaise, c'est beaucoup! de la gêne - les ferait, ces lettrés, plus qu'au cri de journaux, hâter le pas ou détourner la vue devant un encanaillement du format sacré, le volume, à notre gaz; qui en paraît la langue à nu, vulgaire, dardée sur le carrefour. [OC, 376-7]

L'encanaillement is not so much due to the contents of the volumes as to the sales methods, closer to that of newspapers than to the book as expression of creativity, repository of a unique use of language and as object which contains in its very materiality, in the folding and unfolding of its pages, in the ordinary details of its manufacture, a mystery.

Mallarmé's attitude towards labour, both as physical work and intellectual work, shows him to be particularly aware of the social implications first of the necessity of work, and of its effects on the worker. In the essay 'Conflit',[218] Mallarmé carefully analyses the relationship of the labourer to his work, his own relationship to the workers and to his own work. He places his reflexion within the social context of the *fin-de-siècle*, demonstrating his sharp understanding of social issues and his broad interest in questions of work ethics and class divisions. The sensitivity of his response to the issues raised by the presence of the labourers near his *villégiature* proves that he has thought long and hard on a topic that one might not immediately connect with the poet of 'Hérodiade'. His initial reaction to the invasion of 'une bande de travailleurs' [OC, 355] is one of fear and

---

[218] Published on 1 August 1895 in *La Revue Blanche*.

hesitation, his first encounter a reinforcing of stereotypes he has owned for some time: 'ce les sont, mes co-locataires jadis ceux, en esprit, quand je les rencontrai sur les routes, choyés comme les ouvriers quelconques par excellence' [OC, 355-6]. His knowledge of manual workers was restricted to an image, carefully cultivated as the archetypal image of the labourer.

His experience in 'Conflit' forces him to re-evaluate his knowledge of and response to the world of work, embodied in a group of *ouvriers* displaying the characteristics of their work and leisure. He is forced into the realities of their lives: 'Cette cohue entre, part, avec le manche, à l'épaule, de la pioche et de la pelle: or, elle invite, en sa faveur, les émotions de derrière la tête et force à procéder, directement, d'idées dont on se dit *c'est de la littérature!*[219,] He cannot avoid studying his own responses, and the discoveries he makes are as much about himself as about his momentary neighbours. He realises that his own reaction to the noise they bring might be interpreted as 'inanité', and that he does display a measure of 'dédain'. Yet he is able to appreciate the whole experience as positive. Although he has no choice, he only rents the place, and is not able to order the diggers off the land, he does not regret the fact: 'il faut que je l'aie manquée, [la Propriété] avec obstination, durant mes jours - omettant le moyen d'acquisition - pour satisfaire quelque singulier instinct de ne rien posséder et de seulement passer, au risque d'une résidence comme maintenant ouverte à l'aventure qui n'est pas, tout à fait, le hasard, puisqu'il me rapproche, selon que je me fis, de prolétaires' [OC, 357]. His violent confrontation with one member of the proletariat gives him an insight into the underlying problems of social exchange: resentment, hatred, aggression, provocation, Mallarmé acknowledges the difficulties and unpleasantness of the encounter. He does not attribute the difficulties to what he calls 'la lutte des classes' [OC, 357] but simply to the state of inebriation of the worker: 'Très raide, il me scrute avec animosité. Impossible de l'annuler, mentalement: de parfaire l'œuvre de la boisson, le coucher, d'avance, en la poussière et qu'il ne soit pas ce colosse tout à coup grossier et méchant' [OC, 357-8]. He is keen despite this unpleasant incident to establish a contact with the men: 'Pour faire au groupe des avances, sans effet. Toujours le cas: pas lieu de se trouver ensemble; un contact peut, je le crains, n'intervenir entre des hommes'. He imagines possible answers to the workers complaints that they are working for the benefit of others, for the middle classes that demand a railway. He feels that his own work is

---

[219] In italics in the text.

also worthwhile, although he anticipates a lack of understanding on the part of the labourers: 'Tristesse que ma production reste, à ceux-ci, par essence, comme les nuages au crépuscule ou des étoiles, vaine'. Not only does Mallarmé understand possible objections to his kind of production, he finds the thought saddening, and feels deeply the isolation in which it places him. He does not at any point hint at any superiority of his poetic work over manual labour, but he recognises the width of the gap between the perceptions and ambitions of the labourers on the one hand, and of the poet on the other.

It is this lack of explicit or implicit hierarchy that confers on the essay a quality of openness and willingness on the part of the writer to measure his own production by standards other than literary ones, which might not always show his own achievements as crucially important. His willingness to draw a comparison between his own work and the most basic, heavy and unskilled labour gives an indication of his own need to evaluate what he calls in unromantic terms his production. The social value of work - for the labourers it is a double necessity ('vous le faites, afin qu'on vous paie et d'être légalement, quant à vous seuls') to be payed and to exist legally - is not a simple matter of pride in one's effort and just reward for hard labour. Mallarmé is aware of the complexities the subject holds, and he is also aware of the alienation hard physical and repetitive work can inflict. He mentions 'l'hébétement de tâches' [OC, 359], 'une rude corvée' [OC, 356], and the need to forget in drink and sleep. He re-interprets the need to drink as a form of acknowledging 'la part du sacré dans l'existence' [OC, 359], a search for a more satisfying and wonderful dimension, 'avec le sens, pochards, du merveilleux [...]' [OC, 356]. Far from a condescending and paternalistic attitude, he attempts to see in the sleeping group the qualities that have enabled them to survive the demands of their lives:

> Ces artisans de tâches élémentaires, il m'est loisible, les veillant, à côté d'un fleuve limpide continu, d'y regarder le peuple - une intelligence robuste de la condition humaine leur courbe l'échine journellement pour tirer, sans l'intermédiaire du blé, le miracle de vie qui assure la présence: d'autres ont fait les défrichements passés et des aqueducs ou livreront un terre-plein à telle machine, les mêmes, Louis-Pierre, Martin, Poitou et le Normand, quand ils ne dorment pas, ainsi s'invoquent-ils selon les mères ou la province; [OC, 359-60]

The 'travailleur' has been dignified by the title 'artisan', a word beginning with 'art', a recognition that the physical labour of digging holes in 'la réalité des terrains' [OC, 359] can confer on the worker the same sense of achievement, the same awareness of working towards an important goal ('fondation, certes, de temple' and 'aqueducs') that drives the poet and the artist. This is a far cry from the elitist view of the poet unconcerned and undisturbed by the realities of hard physical labour as they affect a majority of his contemporaries. Mallarmé acknowledges, with a degree of humility, the intrinsic value of work and its dignity.

In 'Confrontation',[220] Mallarmé once again measures his own production against that of a worker digging the earth. Against the visible effort and result of the worker - 'Il extrait une brouettée de terrain, pour la vider peu loin, il a produit et refaire l'inverse implique besogne nouvelle, payée' [OC, 409] - he sets his own production, less easily defined as worthy of effort and reward:

> Un autre, que je veux incarner, serait, dont le labeur ne vaut pas au détail parce que, peut-être, acceptant l'hésitation. La page, écrite tantôt, va s'évanouir, selon - n'envie pas, camarade - qu'en moi un patron refuse l'ouvrage, quand la clientèle n'y voit de tare.' [OC, 409]

The poet himself is a harsh judge of his own work, ready to destroy it without any form of reward, indeed with the sense of a death, or the loss of a day. 'Anéantir un jour de la vie ou mourir un peu, le sachant, quels cris jetterais-tu: quoique une divination pareille, au nom de quelque supériorité, t'interrompe, souvent, de la tâche, ivre mort' [OC, 410]. If the sense of working in vain is acute for the poet, he is willing to concede that the labourer too has a similar sense of the vanity of effort, and seeks to blot it out in drink. The conditions of production are not so different that poet and manual worker cannot sympathise and understand each other - Mallarmé addresses the workers both in 'Conflit' and in 'Confrontation' as *camarade* - both seeking dignity, value and reward in the task, both experiencing discouragement and fatigue. But more than in 'Conflit', Mallarmé explores the social and economic repercussions of payment, which he sees alternately as a substitute for the sun, golden, life giving and implacable, and as

---

[220] The title 'Confrontation' replaces in *Divagations* the earlier title of 'Cas de conscience' published in *La Revue Blanche* in October 1895.

the piece of gold, a smaller reflection of solar power. It exercises the same fascination and the same adoration:

> L'or frappe, maintenant, d'aplomb la race; ou, comme si son lever ancien avait refoulé le doute, chez les hommes, d'un pouvoir impersonnel suprême, plutôt leur aveugle moyenne, il décrit sa trajectoire vers l'omnipotence - éclat, l'unique, attardé pour un midi imperturbable.' [OC, 410]

Both the sun and money are necessary to sustain life, and the link between the one and the other provides an explanation and a justification of man's fascination with gold as a reward for work and as a sanction of his effort and production: 'que faire, en l'occasion ou supprimant une foule intermédiaire directement de soi au dieu, que le forcer de reconnaître la pensée, essence, par le résidu, monnaie - tous, ensuite, agiront, sans honte, sous la loi visée d'un paraphe privé' [OC, 410]. The necessity of payment is almost sanctified by the symbolic value of gold, its ordinariness transformed by its sun like qualities: 'La poignée indispensable du métal commun lui sert, professionnellement, avant qu'il ne pense d'en vivre, à accomplir son tour, jongleur sacré, ou éprouver l'intelligence de l'or' [OC, 412]. Thus gold takes on a mythic dimension not just as social reward but as the god Mammon on the one hand, and as meaningful and meaning-giving social element on the other. One might even see a glimmer of embryonic Marxist theory in Mallarmé's awareness of the social impact of production and of its exchange value as opposed to the 'bourgeois' concept of work as purely personal. He recognises the socio-economic system that exchanges money for labour, that measures production in the form of labour, and that integrates within society the mythical bond between labour and money.

Work is part of everyday life, the work of the labourer and the work of the poet. Mallarmé's discourse is one that seeks to redignify and transcend the alienation of routine, the discouragement of failure and fatigue by the awareness of the essential contribution work brings to human experience and to the wider construction of social exchange. Its intrinsic value is completely divorced from any form of hierarchy, neither the method of production nor the product justify a view of work as more or less worthy of effort. The *camaraderie* between the poet and the workers of 'Conflit' or the labourer of 'Confrontation', although unacknowledged by the manual workers, is still real in terms of effort and ultimate appreciation of the intrinsic value of labour. Even the awareness of routine, alienation and lack of productivity are part of the dignifying process. Work is necessarily hard and demanding for the poet and the manual worker. The process of digging the earth, or digging in one's brain, as the poet writes in 'Las de l'amer repos'[221] brings one to the limits of one's resources, mental or physical, and demonstrates both the limits and the extent of man's capacity for endurance.

As a social critic, Mallarmé has engaged with a number of contemporary issues, centred initially on the question of the role of the poet within society, but extending to a commentary on a variety of subjects related to political, economic and social aspects of everyday life: the value and necessity of work, the role of government, the power of money, the problems of life in cities, the effects of industrialisation. 'Grands faits divers'[222] in particular focuses on a number of important social and economic issues. In 'Magie'[223] the poet examines the strange mixture of history that goes to make the modern age and attributes a common origin to the modern financial world and to poetry. He acknowledges the difficulty in defining 'modernity', paradoxically and intimately linked in with the most obscure of historical periods, the Middle Ages: 'Le moyen-âge, incubatoire: tout depuis, alliage, avec l'antique, pour composer cette vaine, perplexe, nous échappant, modernité - outre la législation pétrifiée romaine stagne une religion, celle des cathédrales, parallèlement' [OC, 399]. The main domains of inquiry are seen as initially linked, both originating with a form of alchemy: 'Comme il n'existe d'ouvert à la recherche mentale que deux voies, en tout, où bifurque notre besoin, à savoir l'esthétique d'une part et aussi l'économie politique: c'est, de cette visée dernière, principalement, que l'alchimie fut le glorieux, hâtif et trouble précurseur' [OC, 399-400]. The beginnings of world finance are as mysterious as the beginnings of poetry, and the influence of the one as far reaching as that of the other. The transfer of capital was first transfer of dreams, and the lack of understanding of the origins of financial trade brings with it a useless frenzy: 'La pierre nulle, qui rêve l'or, dite philosophale: mais elle annonce, dans la finance, le futur crédit, précédant le capital ou le réduisant à l'humilité de monnaie! Avec quel désordre se cherche cela, autour de nous et

---

[221] [...]et plus las sept fois du pacte dur
De creuser par veillée une fosse nouvelle
Dans le terrain avare et froid de ma cervelle [P, 16].
[222] 9 essays belonging to *Divagations* published between January 1893 and November 1895.
[223] First published in *The National Observer* on 28 January 1893.

que peu compris!' [OC, 400] Mallarmé measures the value of the aims of society by comparing them to the aims of art. In 'La Cour'[224] he exposes the totalitarian aims of a press that operates a kind of cultural dictatorship:

> On a dit, par vociferation et le silence, à des masses "Tout appartient - en le domaine - se doit à votre admiration" et, faute de quelque chose à désigner, on les lâcha sur l'art. Non, qui trafique, non, qui pioche, combien cette journée fut lourde à la gent, elle dormira ouïe au sac où le métal, intérieurement, sert de rêve; sans, au reste, s'inscrire à l'immortalité de chaque jour qu'éclaire la soirée... Ou, du moins, repose, toi, dans ta simplicité bénie de tâche assurant ce qui est aussi, le pain, dont toute trompette de clartés répercute, avec magnificence, la gerbe juste initiale. [OC, 413-4]

The harsh realities of life, the necessity of work, of earning money, are the first concerns of *la gent*. To promise them more in the form of art, and to order them to admire it, is practising a form of deceit: 'Oh, qui leurra vers ici une émeute affamée' [OC, 414]? To give the impression that art and the artist can be dealt with in terms of laws, votes and popular choices is yet another form of deceit, and the expression of the need to exclude mystery from an area that is essentially mysterious: 'L'élection, vous la prônez, le vote aux doigts, assimilée au travail de l'usine; attendu que vous craignez particulièrement, je le sais, une ingérence de mystère, ou le ciel, dans tel choix' [OC, 415]. Both the 'aristocratie' of art and the 'démocratie' of popular choice are necessary to feed the dynamic processes of the life of a nation. The one is dependent on the other, they are both necessary in order to avoid a collapse of state and social order. Mallarmé indicates that it is the clash of those two aspects of society that keeps the wheels of the social state going:

> Aristocratie, pourquoi n'énoncer le terme - en face du tant vagi de démocratie: réciprocité d'états indispensable au conflit, national, par quoi quelque chose tient debout, ils se heurtent, se pénètrent, sans vertu si l'un fait défaut.

---

[224] Published in March 1895 in *La Revue Blanche*.

> La pièce de monnaie, exhumée aux arènes, présente, face, une figure sereine et, pile, le chiffre brutal universel. [OC, 415]

In 'Le Jury de peinture pour 1874 et M. Manet'[225] Mallarmé pleads for the freedom of the public to decide for itself the value of a work of art, in a curiously anti-paternalistic article. He exclaims ironically: '[..] il faut, certes, avoir le courage d'abuser pleinement et absolument, d'un pouvoir conféré dans un autre but. Ces habitudes anciennes et quelque temps oubliées, de régenter le goût de la foule, pourquoi ne les évoquer qu'à demi, et soit même aux deux tiers' [OC, 695]? The decision of the jury to refuse to accept two of Manet's paintings is interpreted by the poet as an abuse of power. He gives the public the right to decide on the value of a work of art, without interference from experts:

> L'esprit dans lequel a été conçu un morceau d'art, rétrospectif ou moderne, et sa nature, succulente ou raréfiée, en un mot, tout ce qui touche aux instincts de la foule ou de la personne: c'est au public, qui paye en gloire et en billets, à décider si cela vaut son papier et ses paroles. Il est le maître à ce point, et peut exiger de voir *tout ce qu'il y a*[226]. [OC, 699]

Mallarmé is of course indignant on behalf of his friend. Yet his argument complements his views on the dishonesty of the press, eager to deceive the public on matters of art, and to exercise a monopoly of taste. Mallarmé is clearly disturbed by any kind of dictatorship, particularly in the artistic domain, even if it masquerades as benevolent paternalism: 'Le jury a préféré se donner ce ridicule de faire croire, pendant quelques jours encore, qu'il avait charge d'âmes' [OC, 700]. Mallarmé recognises and approves the need for experiment and new forms of art, and applauds the public's taste for the new and the artist's aim of 'contenter le juste goût du neuf. La foule, à qui l'on ne cèle rien, vu que tout émane d'elle, se reconnaîtra, une autre fois, dans l'œuvre accumulée et survivante: et son détachement des choses passées n'en sera cette fois, que plus absolu [OC, 700].

If Mallarmé recognises the rights of *la foule*, both to exist and to make decisions, he does not associate the same advantages with the term *société*:

---

[225] Published on 12 April 1874 in *La Renaissance Artistique et Littéraire*.
[226] In italics in the text.

> La Société, terme le plus creux, héritage des philosophes, a ceci, du moins, de propice et d'aisé que rien n'existant, à peu près, dans les faits, pareil à l'injonction qu'éveille son concept auguste, en discourir égale ne traiter aucun sujet ou se taire par délassement. [OC, 419]

Mallarmé denies the existence of society as an entity, cut off from the human dimension in all its familiar detail and rejects a concept that has the empty ring of theoretical peroration rather than the resonance of real social concern. *La foule* has a life and a vitality, which are both attractive and repulsive, mysterious and vulgar. But *la Société*, elaborated in the minds of philosophers, does not even possess, as Bertrand Marchal suggests, 'une existence négative',[227] but has no autonomous existence at all. Mallarmé is fascinated by any gathering of people, in any form, whether in theatres and concert halls, in art exhibitions, in cities or in institutions such as l'Académie or l'Institut. His response is by no means one of rejection, but a finely differentiated one, which ranges from suspicion to enthusiastic acceptance. In 'Bucolique,'[228] Mallarmé meditates on the disadvantages of cities, built on a scale that lacks beauty, quietness and the accommodation of the needs of the human spirit:

> Longs faubourgs prolongés par la monotonie de voies jusqu'au central rien qui soit extraordinaire, divin ou totalement jailli du sol factice en échange des lieues d'asphalte, de nouveau, à piétiner, pour fuir. [OC, 402]

The city lacks any redeeming features that might help the inhabitant to forget the 'sol factice', it is characterised by an inherent '[...] défaut de sociales bases et d'un couronnement par l'art' [OC, 402]. Mallarmé intriguingly associates the social foundations of the city and art, the one as a solid base, and the other as a visible crowning. The lack of both these aspects leads to the poet's criticism of a fundamental lack and emptiness at the very heart of the city. The alienating aspects of life in cities are a modern reality that the poet has grasped and experienced, offering *la Nature* and *la Musique* as antidotes to the annihilating effects of city dwelling.[229]

---

[227] In *La Religion de Mallarmé*, p.554.
[228] Published in *La Revue Blanche* in June 1895.
[229] For an exploration of life in nineteenth-century Paris, see Christopher

Mallarmé builds around the manifestations of modern life a typically ambiguous discourse, and demonstrates by the diversity of his subjects and interests that 'Rien n'est à négliger de l'existence d'une époque: tout y appartient à tous' [OC, 719]. The process by which Mallarmé accounts for 'l'existence d'une époque' is not so much a rhetoric of everyday life, a coherent ideology or worldview, as a dynamic principle which, applied to a variety of aspects of contemporary life, invests it with the powerful energy and creativity that we perceive in the *Vers de circonstance* as well as in the *Poésies*. The ambiguous discourse about the ordinary that is particularly at work in the journalistic writings is not an applied social theory, but rather a re-energising by the use of a complex syntactic, lexical and metaphorical language, of one man's experience of contemporary life.

The study of Mallarmé's discourse on ordinary life, evolving from a close textual analysis of syntax and lexis, has led us to identify a number of processes, mechanisms and systems at work within the corpus and forming the background but also the springboard to the poet's expressed observation and response to the everyday world of his time. The process of constructing a discourse around the world of domesticity and routine involves a twofold process: a distancing through an often complex and ornate use of language, as in the examples from *La Dernière Mode*, or through the use of wordplay, puns and rhyme in *Vers de circonstance*, and also an appropriation and recreation of the world of the familiar and the ordinary by investing that world with positive qualities of linguistic elegance and choice of detail in subject matter (as in the texts on the Great Exhibition in London in 1874). These eventually mirror the poet's own ideal view of an ordinary made habitable by his own creative powers. Thus the mechanism by which the poet effects both distancing and appropriation are one and the same, expressed in a number of choices both at the linguistic and content levels. Transformation rather than transcendence, trampolining rather than flying, the constant return to make contact with the ordinary in order to leap higher into transforming creative linguistic activity seem to me to be the mechanics which operate the poet's process of exploiting ordinary experience.

The underlying discourse about ordinary life which is a constant in the texts rests on a systematised attitude of mind characterised by Lefèbvrian ambiguity, both in use of language as seen previously, and in ideology, a systematised hesitation that is

---

Prendergast's *Writing the City: Paris and the Nineteenth Century* (Oxford and Cambridge, Massachusets: Blackwell, 1992), pp.74-101.

itself a worldview without dogmatic certainty. It has at times the painful force of a deep rift, a fertile cleavage, which is a source of essential strength. Self-division and anxiety about the poet's own response to the cultural, social and industrial changes in the Parisian *fin-de-siècle* become the very condition of creative production. This oscillatory movement within the discourse expresses on the one hand a belief in the possibility of redemption of the ordinary, on the other a belief in its hopelessness. This hesitation is magnified into a conflicting, paradoxical movement, fascination and repulsion, which translated into ideological terms, are expressed both in engagement with modern society and search for features that are potentially redeemable, in an almost Taylorian recognition of 'the good life', and withdrawal, reaction, sometimes even abhorrence and condemnation.

However, the process by which the poet wrestles with the difficulty of a double postulate vis-à-vis the ordinary never entails denial or ignorance of the realities of modern life and contemporary society, but rather the elaboration of a flexible system of intellectual reflection and emotional response, grown from the strengthening creative tension of self-division.

CONCLUSION

The end of the twentieth century has been a particularly propitious time to revisit the works of a poet that has been internationally fêted on the anniversary of his death by an impressive set of celebrations led not only by specialists, conference after conference, in Europe, the States and the Antipodes, but also with events meant to attract the *Tout-Paris* at the Musée du Quai d'Orsay. More than ever, the name of Mallarmé works as a trigger, a talisman, a magic word not only in the realms of literature but also in art and music. A number of recent critical studies draw stimulating parallels and comparisons between these areas.[230] This underlines the fact that Mallarmé has acquired and accumulated over the years immense artistic and scholarly currency. As a name and an emblem of high culture, of literary achievement and as the father of modernity, not just in French but also in continental poetry, he is a familiar figure. For his perceived lack of engagement with the ordinary world, and for his textual difficulty often interpreted as extraordinary, he is revered or reviled, but always named with that same assumption of familiarity. Dozens of movements, literary or other throughout Europe claim acquaintance with, or indebtedness to, the poet's innovative genius. This might well be the most puzzling paradox yet: Mallarmé, apostle and exorcist of the ordinary, is himself becoming so well-known at one level and part of the cultural baggage of so many that the risk is not, and never has been, of ultimate obscurity, but of disappearance into the characteristics of his own fame and of his own thematic and linguistic concerns. His name has become 'la chose du monde la mieux partagée', whilst retaining the sense of mystery and enigma that attracted and infuriated the very first Mallarmé critics, and still has the same effect on the more recent generation of Mallarmists. This is a strange and in some ways an appropriate destiny for the 'prince des poètes' who is also the author and editor of a fashion magazine, a journalist and a competent and passionately interested witness of his time in its ordinary as well as extraordinary aspects.

A study of Mallarmé's verse and prose works using the ordinary as a necessary referent and sometimes as a significantly absent or disguised ingredient, has shown that the concept is never ignored or bypassed. Against a certain strain in traditional Mallarmé criticism, which has examined the poet's works in their

---

[230] See Jean-Michel Nectoux, *Mallarmé. "Un clair regard dans les ténèbres". Poésie, peinture, musique,* éd. Adam Biro, 1998.

relation to the obscure, the hermetic or the irrelevant and removed from the quotidian, I have established the strong links, whether positive or negative, that the poet entertains with the ordinary in the textual detail of his œuvre. Particularly useful to the initial task of defining the ordinary as a philosophical concept and as a helpful critical tool have been the models offered by Charles Taylor in a historical perspective of a valorisation of the everyday, by Heidegger and his dialectic of concealment and refusal, by Stanley Cavell in his view of the ordinary as object of a quest and subject of an inquest, and by Henri Lefèbvre and ambiguity as a category of the everyday. In order to study the ordinary within the Mallarmé corpus, it was crucial to define what has traditionally been called his difficulty. The taxonomy of difficulty established by Steiner has been a useful tool in the determination not only of the type, but also of the nature of difficulty encountered in the poet's work and of its impact on the relationship between the ordinary as concept and as critical category within the texts and the syntactic, lexical and thematic choices made by the poet.

I have chosen particular aspects of Mallarmé's writing which showed a number of ways in which the poet deals with the ordinary both within the scriptural fabric of the verse and prose, and within the metaphorical and rhetorical world he builds in order to control it. The concept of the everyday in Mallarmé's texts is destabilised by several converging linguistic and philosophical patterns: the complex syntax, the occasional use of unusual lexis, the elaboration of an intricate web of metaphors and the constructing of a paradoxical ideological system. Mallarmé's use of language offered a particularly fascinating challenge, starting from his indebtedness to his predecessors, Hugo and more particularly, Baudelaire. This places him firmly within a literary genealogy, and a tradition, which made use of the quotidian world both at the level of subject matter, and at the level of response. But his appropriation of a number of themes, stereotypes and characteristics of Hugolian and Baudelairian diction in the early verse in particular develops into a profoundly individual way of responding to the ordinary within the textual or social framework. With a Baudelairian love of risk-taking, and a Hugolian sense of the moral dimension of the quotidian, Mallarmé describes a typically oscillatory and ambiguous trajectory. On the one hand, his whole writing project is one of exorcism of the ordinary, a powerful and occasionally obsessive rejection and carefully elaborated word charm, with the evil-deflecting quality of a talisman, 'une sorcellerie évocatoire' that also works as protection against the potentially empty and mind-numbing triviality of the quotidian. The magic lies not so much in the complexity or obscurity of the writing, as in the power to make the ordinary disappear, leaving in its place an absence that still bears its imprint. On the other hand, his work can also be interpreted as a supremely artful and artificial way of reintegrating the ordinary world, but an ordinary that has been explored and re-invented by the author and that has been made habitable by a number of textual and intellectual devices.

It is within the rich complexities and taunting contradictions of the verse and prose that I have isolated moments of particular interest in the study of Mallarmé's relation to the world of the ordinary: in his complex syntax, marked by hesitation between a subversion of the Kristevian symbolic and an embracing of the anarchic powers of the semiotic; in his usually straightforward lexis, in which more than at any other level he expresses his delight in the creative potential of words and terminologies; in his metaphorical world governed by a constellation of paradoxical images and comparisons, and in a rhetorical system flexible enough to allow for a wide range of intellectual positions. All of these facets of Mallarmé's work have been shown to reveal his own response both to everyday life and to the concept of the ordinary, and I shall examine each of these in turn, reminding my reader of the conclusions I have reached in each area of my study.

Within the syntax, as we have seen, Mallarmé favours interpolation and disjunction. These have both a simplifying and a complexifying role, effecting both a distancing from ordinary language and an encompassing of it in the folds of the long, sinuous sentence which often displays free associative qualities and betrays in the hesitancy of its many incidental clauses the anxiety of an author oscillating between fascination and revulsion. Yet the poet still claims an intellectual attachment to syntactic order, and to the unifying dominance of the symbolic. However, in his obsessive use of ellipsis, which leads to condensation and ambiguity at the level of syntactic function, he transgresses a number of grammatical laws. In his widespread use of ellipsis, he tends to eliminate some of the basic elements of syntax: the pronoun *je*, the verb *être*, possessive adjectives. These are the visibly invisible signs of Mallarmé's fear of engagement with the ordinary, translated at the syntactic level by the systematic disappearance of the banal word needed to make sense of a sentence. But its very absence draws attention to it, its significance multiplied by the demand on the reader to replace it within the Mallarmean phrase in order to complete it. The prominence it attains by the need for the reader's contribution in the deliberate process of re-introduction after deliberate authorial suppression produces a meaningful presence in its very absence. If obliquity and complexity are augmented by the use of ellipses, the underlying structures of the textual construction of a syntactical ordinary are made visible, like the mark left on a wall after the removal of a picture. Several processes unfold simultaneously within the syntactic ballet: on the one hand, Mallarmé attempts to remove syntax from the ordinary by using a number of complexifying devices. On the other, he also removes the ordinary from syntax, often by the use of ellipsis. The two processes are separate, although they can be found in the same sentence. The one affirms the functional importance of absence, and endows it with a kind of meaningful hovering presence *dans les coulisses*, whilst the process of removing the syntax from the ordinary involves a different device, that of embeddedness.

With the use of apposition and adjacency, Mallarmé isolates words and syntactic structures whilst also bringing words closer together than they would normally be. We are left with conflicting effects, enriched possibilities of connections and meanings on the one hand, and potential for threatening and possibly irretrievable vacancy on the other. The deliberate cultivation of, and search for, meaningful links promotes both a sense of simplification through loss of textual matter, and a greater complexity through unexpressed connections. The structures and processes involved in writing become apparent, in a skeletal schema devoid of the connective tissue of banal syntactic elements. The Cavellian task of retrieval, restoration and reconstruction falls to the patient reader who faces the challenge of, quite literally, recovering the sinews and 'délicate ossature' of the Mallarméan sentence.

Mallarmé's predilection for the use of adverbs in *-ment* is a particularly fascinating feature, from the syntactic point of view and from the lexical point of view, and I have discussed their impact on a number of occasions in my book. Their sheer length and syntactic isolation makes them quite extraordinary, and particularly the adverbs connected semantically with the ordinary: *ordinairement, quotidiennement, journellement.* This strong adverbialisation of the quotidian introduces the dimension of the ordinary as an inescapable referent within which less ordinary syntactic events take place, as a kind of backdrop, a Heiddegerian continuum. The ordinary is named not as a substantive but as a quality, a less tangible but unavoidable all-pervading presence.

The isolative and dislocatory syntax that the poet uses point to the possibility of conflicts and disharmony within the sentence. A persistent determination on the part of the poet to foster new and unusual connections is often translated at the level of pragmatics in a complete removal of links, forcing a violent proximity of inimical terms which jostle and overlap, bringing together different qualities and orders of experience. The tension that this engenders is often the point of creative innovation, and also at times the place of collapse and vacancy. But the effect is equally one of self-generated energy, a re-endowing the ordinary with a sense of contained power, even violence which teeters precariously on the edge of collapse, in a carefully arbitrated equilibrium. The tearing apart of groups of nouns that belong together speaks of a syntax of violence, where, from the point of forceful separation, the dynamic *épanchement* of meaning originates.

The constant truncations, interpolations, deferrals and embeddednesses create grammatical ambiguities, which can at times discourage even the most sympathetic reader. They require on the part of the reader an exercise in re-uniting the dislocated elements, a rebuilding of the carefully dismembered sentences, in an Isis-like search for the dispersed parts of the body of the text. This exercise in retrieval once again points to a Cavellian sense of quest and inquest. As for the dimension of the ordinary, nothing is given; active and intense participation and engagement with the textual matter is demanded. This will therefore lead to a number of constraints on the reading of the texts: in terms of time, and in terms of method, demanding a reading that takes a diagonal, lateral as well as forwards and backwards course, a reading alert to alternation, oscillation, intermittence, pulsation and gradation. The spatial disordering of the words on the page reproduces the processes of dream and memory, a non-linear, often searching process, with a significant proportion of *oubli* as well as remembrance, clearly encouraging a semiotic interpretation.

The punctuation is the visible sign of the texts' organic breathing life, and also the visible sign of silence and truncation. The scarcity of punctuation in the poetry points to an unwillingness on the part of Mallarmé to resolve syntactic ambiguities. In the prose, on the contrary, it is its superabundance that leads to ambiguity. Thus, in both cases, Mallarmé subverts the elucidating role of punctuation, lending instead a curiously porous texture to his prose works, cutting the text into a jigsaw puzzle, tantalisingly set out to be re-invented and re-interpreted. The infiltration of silence into the text brings in the dimension of the inexpressible, and the pulsation of arduous labour.

In its highly performative task, syntax in Mallarmé crucially underlines his relationship with a textual and social ordinary. He is caught in a double imperative: the need to explore the ordinary through textual means, and the need to escape it also by textual means. It is within syntax that he enacts the paradox of his perception and response to the ordinary: a Heideggerian awareness of the potential of concealment and refusal mixed with a Cavellian sense of quest. Syntax provides Mallarmé with a way of reworking time and his relation to the quotidian, and of creating ways of going towards it as well as running away from it. In its more unfamiliar and disorientating effects, Mallarmean syntax skirts the abyss of vacancy as he moves away from syntactic guarantee and grammatical order, taking the textual risk of a violence and a subversion too great to stem the haemorrhage of meaning.

It is within syntax that the temporal and the quotidian meet in an oscillatory movement between the quasi-immobility of Hérodiade's world, the micro-movements of 'Sainte' and the erratic yet inevitable pendulum swing of time in 'Le vierge, le vivace et le bel aujourd'hui'. Mallarmé's representation of the temporal is expressed not so much as a succession of moments, but rather as a past, present and future experienced conjointly, or as an eternal present of varying value. The verb as the word in the sentence that bears the dynamic mark of time is often in the present tense, or in the infinitive, or avoided altogether, presenting a weakened form of time indication. Although there is a sense in which the poems seek to describe the forward flight of time, it is possible to conclude, after a close study of a number of prose and poetry texts, that Mallarmé systematically avoids making a strong temporal choice, leaving all the temporal possibilities as past and future potentially present in his favoured verbal forms. Instead of attempting to circumscribe and define time by syntactic means, the poet is concerned with keeping the whole gamut of temporal possibilities uncurtailed, so that past, present and future, within the tantalising indeterminacy of an infinitive or a lyric present, often displayed in unspecific verbs, possess a simultaneous and merged life. The effect is one of a shimmering backdrop, the oscillations between the different aspects of time evoked too fleetingly to enable the reader to discard any of them. But it is also possible to conclude that with these choices, Mallarmé is keeping open a way of escaping the contingencies of time, the constraints of a dimension that is not just the locus of dynamic events, but also that of destruction, decay, death and vacancy. By a systematic choice of infinitives, the poet also avoids naming a specific subject, preferring the dispersal and infiltrating diffuse presence of an unidentified subject to the unifying dominance of a clear syntactic agent.

Far from being represented as a linear, stream-like, gentle and uniform flux, time is perceived as restless, moving from present to past to future, textually marked by an abundant use of indexicals. Its quality is that of a type of performance as opposed to a sequential stream of time, in which temporal layer after temporal layer is shed. The often contradictory responses on the poet's part are again characterised by fear and fascination, by a dynamic and driving need to explore it, but also by the desire to exorcise it, and to annihilate its power by literarily and literally squeezing it out of his work. By the use of innovative and diverse syntax, Mallarmé attempts, sometimes simultaneously, to escape and to reconcile himself to the inevitable contingencies, the creative potential and the destructive power both of ordinary time and of the time of the ordinary.

Mallarmé's vocabulary has often been seen as too ordinary, except for a relatively small category of spectacularly extraordinary terms, to deserve sustained attention. The poet himself claims a surprisingly democratic use of vocabulary, which he considers to be a national heritage. The most interesting factor in the poet's use of rare or archaic lexical material lies in the way in which he interweaves rare terms and ordinary words, highlighting the one by the use of the other. As with syntax, where the intriguing mix of complex and simple clauses produces a rich pattern of interfused ordinary and extraordinary formulation, leading the reader to re-appraise the one against the other, Mallarmé's use of vocabulary sets up a series of nodal points of creative tension within the corpus: everyday versus unfamiliar, presence versus absence, reality versus dream. The use of a startlingly alien or rare word jolts the reader out of his complacent reading and forces him to redefine the limits of the textual ordinary exposed to the pressure of the unusual. Within the fabric of the ordinary lexical material, we discover epiphanic moments that highlight dramatic lexical events.

Although his generally ordinary use of vocabulary has largely been ignored by critics understandingly focusing on his hugely innovative syntax, the variety of non-literary terminologies from which it originates gives Mallarmé's writing a sense of rootedness in the life and issues of his time. Many aspects of contemporary life are represented at the level of lexis, from the world of banking, commerce, politics, and anatomy to the world of mathematics and botany. It is the juxtaposition, overlap and alternation between literary and non-literary vocabulary that enriches and re-energises the textual matter, infusing it with a sense of lively and modern inquiry and response. It also enables the poet to imaginatively explore the comic potential of the mixing of registers, and to uncover in the process new and delightful aspects of the ordinary

As a lexical feature adverbs in *-ment* are given a role that can be defined as one of anchoring the original substantives into the sentence by the length and substance of their very notable presence. This anchoring down, giving weight and body to often abstract concepts underlines the inescapable infiltration of the extraordinary dimension of life by that of the ordinary, of the encroachment and incrustation into the literary of everyday experience. But we also find that, as the adverbs are used with increasing frequency in the chronology of the poet's writings, prosaic terms are rendered extraordinary by this adverbialising, and that a sense of the alien rather than the familiar surreptitiously invades the well-known lexical matter.

The vocabulary of *La Dernière Mode* displays an extraordinary abundance of terms drawn from a very wide range of terminologies, and although ostensibly dedicated to the description of the minutiae of contemporary everyday life, it encompasses a wide range of terms drawn from the poetic, effectively turning the short-lived and rather extravagant fashion magazine into a poetics of the prosaic. The literary and non-literary lexicons are constantly jostling for supremacy, infiltrated by a significant number of terms from ethical, liturgical and anthropological domains. The poeticising of the trivial and the banal by using a complexly intertwined network of terminologies, as well as a variety of registers, invests the day to day *reportage* of the Parisian fashion scene and the up-to-the-minute review of novelties in the field of home-making and entertaining with a wealth of lavishly recreated textual intricacies, both lexical and metaphorical; the everyday of *La Dernière Mode* is both undermined and rehabilitated by the use of such diverse terminologies. Its dynamic principle, as with fashion as described by Mallarmé, is extravagance and sheer enjoyment of the infinite potential of word combination.

Mallarmé also uses a number of terms belonging to the casual, the colloquial, the vulgar and to slang. *Vers de circonstance* displays a fascinating mixture of registers, as do a number of poems. Mallarmé's sense of humour, his penchant for wordplay and puns, for paraphonic games, add yet another dimension to the exploration of his relationship with the ordinary. He is also able to exploit the comic potential it offers, to uncover a playful and amusing quality within the everyday which is then translated at the textual level into the *jeux de mots* of the *Vers de circonstance* or 'Petit Air (Guerrier)'.

The proliferation of terms taken from a huge variety of terminologies is affected by the ordinariness of the subject matter. The more ordinary the subject, the more extraordinary the language; the more extraordinary the themes, the simpler and more ordinary the lexis. Mallarmé favours a mixture of either ordinary theme and extraordinary diction, or of ordinary use of language and unusual subject. The tensions that are created by this inverse pattern inevitably leave the reader torn between recognition of the rootedness of language in the everyday, and alienation from the ordinary world. The betrayal of Mallarmé's own ambivalent attitude towards the ordinary, following the Lefèbvrian pattern of ambiguity, is clearly revealed within the text in the conflicting levels of complexity and banality of his lexis. Recognition of his need of ordinary words, used at the level at which they are employed to negotiate the vicissitudes of everyday living, but also acknowledgement of his attraction towards a distanced and unthreateningly removed ordinary, viewed from the safety of poetic diction, build into the texts a systematised ambivalence. Mallarmé's art lies in the masterful and at times risky exploitation of this ambivalence.

As he himself has noted, it is not possible to eliminate the ordinary from one's use of language, even for a writer as well versed in the intricacies of scriptural acrobatics as Mallarmé. When the linguistic pirouetting stops, the ordinary realities of the poet's routine of authorial tasks are not only recognised by Mallarmé, they form a central metaphor in his *œuvre*. The image of the poet as a labourer working with the material and tools of his trade, words, is a familiar Mallarmean comparison, and it is within language and through the use of words that poet and labourer meet. The need to anchor the language within the ordinary experience of life, in order to be safely able to experiment with the extraordinary, and to measure its validity and its risks against a known background are part of the writer's 'labeur de linguistique'. The extraordinary comprehensiveness of his lexis demonstrates his willingness to explore a number of aspects of contemporary life, and to build a textual and multi-faceted ordinary by mixing ordinary and extraordinary linguistic means.

By his use of a variety of terms explicitly naming the ordinary, Mallarmé expresses a compulsive need to designate a level of existence and a way of being in time and space that reaches far beyond an incidental recognition of a lower mode of life. The abundant use of a metalanguage that reinforces and multiplies the heavy encrustation of lexical and syntactical concern with the ordinary reveals sensitive areas of Mallarmé's poetic world particularly invested with emotional and conceptual tensions and paradoxes, an anxiety of life created by the ambiguities of different and often intermingling levels of experience. The most obvious effect of naming the ordinary is its abstracting of its reality in the very naming, the transforming of tangible and specific life situations and circumstances into concept or models, moving from the level of pragmatics to that of theory. This is often a level that Mallarmé perceives as being more habitable, and more controllable. By abstracting and theorising in the naming of the dimension of the ordinary, Mallarmé is able to manipulate it, to apply censoring criteria, to ensure that its explicit appearances within the corpus exorcise a more implicit and infiltrating presence. The more insidious and all-pervasive qualities of the everyday are therefore denied by an explicit naming that categorises without characterising and that labels without specifying. The widespread use of words such as *ordinaire*, *banal* and *quotidien* has the comforting quality of a safety mechanism, a way of acknowledging while at the same time ordering and subduing powerful affective energies, and rewriting frightening circumstances into a recognisable pattern. It acts like a safety net, enabling the acrobat to perform his highly skilled and dangerous stunts with the confidence afforded by the knowledge of its reassuring presence, and freeing him therefore to attempt ever more ambitious displays.

On the other hand, the naming of the ordinary is also a way of making contact with the world of ordinary human engagements by moving from the concept of the everyday towards an acknowledged reality. Within the framework of the concept, the process of recognition can take place, a guarded acquaintance or re-acquaintance with the positive and negative aspects of the quotidian, a building of bridges between the observation of empirical raw material and philosophical explanation. With great flexibility and versatility, Mallarmé moves between the concept of the ordinary as a critical category against which to measure interesting departures, and the listing of ordinary components of life: objects, feelings, relationships characterised as ordinary or banal. He does not, however, offer a clear definition of his understanding of *le quotidien*, *le banal*, *l'ordinaire*, and never consciously and deliberately queries his own perception or problematises the use of these terms. The reader is left with a range of ambiguous responses on the part of the poet, which have to be deciphered and interpreted almost between the lines. Concept and observation interact uneasily as the poet switches from the specific to the vague, from category to quality, and from referend to detail of everyday life.

The reader, faced with the insistent and explicit naming of the ordinary, eventually has to ask the questions: what ordinary is Mallarmé writing about? Whose ordinary is it? Is it uninhabited, or uninhabitable? The boundaries of what Mallarmé designates as ordinary are impossible to define within the texts. The instability of the concept does not allow for the existence of an absolute form of the ordinary, leaving the responsability to deal with and to define the dimension to individual perception. This relativism in Mallarmé's interpretation of the concept accounts for the variations in levels of meaning and in connotations. Mallarmé names not *the* ordinary, but *an* ordinary, and in the process of naming it, he distances himself from it and turns what is perceived as the ordinary into an 'ideal ordinary', a reworking of the Platonic world of the cave, where perception is not of direct reality but of a re-invented and idealised view of the world.

The process of naming the ordinary is paralleled by a process of metaphorisation of the everyday. The instability of the concept within the texts forces the writer to find new means of manipulating, circumscribing and characterising the word, means that will take into account the complexities of dealing with a dimension that is both familiar and unfamiliar, fascinating and repulsive, inescapable and yet open to potential transformations and re-creations. The metaphoric structures and vocabulary dynamise new frames of reference, either as backdrop or framework, *toile de fond*, or as event and non-event, and to both approaches correspond a number of powerful similes and metaphors. I have isolated within the corpus a number of stereotyped metaphors, which are part of conventional poetic diction, and a number of derivative metaphors, taken either from Baudelaire or Hugo. These form a kind of *degré zéro* of poetic writing, from which Mallarmé's own metaphoric constructs originate; they do not necessarily refer to a world outside the frame of the text, but can also create a new locus able to contain an ideal ordinary. The poet uses metaphor to vault from one mental and aesthetic locality to another, crossing limits and boundaries in the process, eventually to complete his trajectory into a world that is recognisable as the everyday in terms of its ambiguous Lefèbvrian qualities and its very recalcitrance to definition and stasis. The pole used by the poet is not the ordinary, but his own imaginary world, which provides him with the artistic, dynamic and creative impetus to cross the bar of his own reluctance, obsession and fear into a new, threatening and seemingly empty world, which he is then empowered to structure and organise according to his own metaphoric system. As in the lexis, the pattern of metaphoric usage shows that the more removed from the ordinary the subject matter, the more ordinary the metaphors; the more ordinary the theme, the more extraordinary the metaphors. Mallarmé chooses to create tensions by perversely combining ordinary and extraordinary at two different levels, by setting the one against the other, and by either redeeming or eliminating the one with the other. The two terms of the equation, however, because of essential differences in levels and nature, do not always add up to a perfectly balanced absence or presence. The reader often feels as if the elevator he has just taken has stopped between two levels, and although the doors are open, there is no possibility of stepping out.

It is in the pages of *La Dernière Mode* that the process of metaphorisation, or even hyper-metaphorisation is most clearly at work. Mallarmé's poetic imagination engaged with all aspects of everyday life, seeking by an abundant use of metaphor to bring magic to particularly uninspiring facets of the quotidian, or, in an inverse process, to extract magic from such promising, shimmering and glittering material as jewellery or evening gowns. Neither approach could possibly be envisaged without the extensive use of metaphors, forming in their often inter-related imagery a Mallarmean spider's web. The poet frequently proceeds from dream to reality, from fantasy world to everyday world, having derived from his imaginary universe principles and essences that undergird the ordinary world and lend it roots, but roots that reach upwards towards the poet's own ideal dream and visions, rather than towards a simple quantifiable reality.

Mallarmé as a compulsive metaphorist is often driven to a hyper-metaphorisation of the ordinary by his own difficulty in coping with the everyday, and by an obsessive use of the trope he is given the means to choose and control, not the ordinary himself, but the words that describe and express his own perception and experience of it. Mallarmean metaphor is not simply a sometimes hysterical expression of flight from the ordinary, or even an expression of a reintegration of the ordinary by the re-inventing of a habitable locus, but a complex process in which the poet alternates between his own personal vision of the ordinary, an ideal ordinary that is occasionally acknowledged as such and an outside ordinary used as reference, a bridge, in Cavell's words, 'subject of a quest or object of an inquest'. Mallarmé has infiltrated it with a system of images that both displaces and replaces the ordinary, not in the sense of eclipsing it, but in the sense of giving it breadth and depth, subtly redefining the one according to the other, and vice-versa.

Mallarmé also deals with the ordinary of his day, in its social, political and economic manifestations. He elaborates, from his observation of the contemporary *fin-de-siècle* society, a personal ideology, a worldview which, if it is not a systematically coherent philosophical and theoretical framework, attempts nevertheless to account and interpret the main features of nineteenth-century modern life. This goes beyond the presentation of a point of view, it is the stating of a metaphysical stance vis-à-vis the quotidian of his day, and of a self-conscious intellectual and emotional engagement with the public face of the ordinary. It possesses a wide enough intellectual base to allow for a number of divergent, sometimes paradoxical views, whilst at the same time affording the poet the locus of philosophical and sociological reflection and engagement with decidedly modern issues.

In his letters and article on the 'Expositions Internationales de Londres', Mallarmé's intellectual and emotional responses to the display of industrial and consumer goods reveals yet again his own ambivalence. He is acutely aware of the excitement and advantages that the new techniques are able to bring to the comfort of everyday life, in particular the production of cheap goods that are now available to the masses. Beautiful objects for everyday use are now accessible to many, and Mallarmé unhesitatingly sanctions this egalitarian endeavour as a generous and worthwhile enterprise, bringing into the everyday lives of a greater number of people the potential to own beautiful objects, and to transform their own quotidian environment, making it literally more habitable.

Mallarmé's preoccupation with *modernité* is particularly evident in the pages of *La Dernière Mode*. In a totalising view of the ordinary, he claims that no detail is unimportant that gives an account of contemporary life. The domestic everyday described in the fashion magazine is redeemable precisely because of its many facets, its constant change, and yet the short term vision under the magnifying glass of the ubiquitous editor of the publication can only survive because it is re-placed into a long term historical perspective. The minutiae of everyday living cease to have an ordinary quality, they become removed and extraordinary to the reader of the twentieth century *fin-de-siècle*. The everyday of *La Dernière Mode* can therefore only survive at the cost of its own ordinariness, gaining with the distance of time a new and alien quality.

Mallarmé builds around the manifestations of modern life a typically ambiguous discourse: he is caught in a painful ambivalence, aware on the one hand of the potential and excitement of contemporary advances in industry, but horrified on the other at the implications of mass production and at the inevitable loss of the rare, the precious and the unique. The difficult rift within his own response accounts for his problematic approach to the socio-economic dimension of the ordinary. The rhetoric, which Mallarmé develops concerning the ordinary within the public sphere, does not claim in any way to possess the coherence of a complete theoretical system. Rather, it has the qualities of a dynamic principle, which informs all the journalistic writings of the poet. Applied to a variety of aspects of contemporary life, it invests it with the powerful creative energies that we perceive in *Vers de circonstances*, *Divagations* as well as *Poésies*. The underlying discourse about the ordinary which is a constant in the texts both finds its origins and rests on a systematised attitude of mind characterised by Lefèbvrian ambiguity, by the awareness in Mallarmé of a deeply antithetic response, releasing from the very point of painful self-division the tension and energy necessary to generate creative production.

This antithetic response is in itself a manifestation of modernity, and consecrates Mallarmé as the high priest and the *figure de proue* of most self-respecting modernist artists of the following century. Modernity, as characterised by a 'volatile relationship between high art and mass culture',[231] by its insistence on the autonomy of the work of art and by its fear of engulfment by mass culture, has recognisable forunning signs in Mallarmean discourse. But it is also possible to argue that the Avant-garde's challenge to those beliefs in the form of exploration of potential integration of life and art, of a breaking down of walls between art and the everyday, also finds precursory notes in the later prose texts. Mallarmé was, as were many of his contemporary artists and writers, swept up in the contentious relationship between modernity as a sociological phenomenon and modernism[232] as an aesthetic concept, but attempts to bridge the divide by the fascinated attention he brings to contemporary life as described in *la Dernière Mode*, *Divagations* or his study of the world expositions as symbol of mass culture and large-scale commodity production. He can be seen therefore as father of modernism and avantgardism, but also in tandem with Nietzsche's concept of modernity, and already modelling the experimentalism of Apollinaire and Cendrars. Indeed, as Christopher Butler points

---

[231] Andreas Huyssen, *After the Great Divide: Modernism, mass Culture and Postmodernism* (London, Basingstoke: Macmillan, 1986), p.vii.

[232] For a discussion of the meaning of the term I shall refer my reader to the seminal work by Astradur Eysteinsson, *The Concept of Modernism* (Ithaca, London: Cornell University Press, 1990) and the series of papers on Modernism published in *The Turn of the Century: Modernism and Modernity in Literature and the Arts*, ed. Christian Berg, Frank Durieux, Geert Lernout (Berlin, New York: De Gruyter, 1995).

out in his study of early modernism in Europe,[233] 'twentieth century verse makes very few technical changes which go far beyond those to be found in the French Symbolist poetry of the nineteenth century, which had already experimented with free verse, typographical rearrangement, and an irrationalist association of ideas' (p.4). This takes place well before Marinetti's typographical revolution and his futurist manifesto. Common objects and everyday experiences continue to feed the creative imagination, as in Gertrud Stein's *Tender Buttons* (1914) or in Robert Delaunay's painting 'Fenêtres' (1912) where the study of simultaneity and the theme are directly borrowed from Mallarmé's poem.

Mallarmé has not only been called 'modernist', but also 'cubist' and even 'post-modern'. These readings might well be closer to 'misreadings', but fruitful nonetheless in their establishing a form of genealogy and positive affirmation of the new generation of poets and artists. Even if 'the impression of Mallarmé as a cubist author – as creating a new disjointed reality by juxtaposed elements – results from incomplete comprehension', as Roger Shattuck underlines,[234] the fact of his relevance as reference for such a large and diverse community of writers and artists confirms his status as 'modern', in the sense of eternal and undeniable presence and influence on the following generations. More specifically, in his tussle with the ordinary of his day, in a response that is both innovation, exploration and rejection, he can indeed be seen as the prophetic voice with which all the great European literary movements recognise a form of kinship. 'Two things seem modern to us today: the analysis of life and the retreat from life'. According to Hofmannsthal's oft quoted phrase, Mallarmé was supremely modern, not only in the Baudelairian sense 'qui exige seulement que l'artiste soit de son temps, qu'il ne méprise pas les sujets contemporains, qu'il s'applique au contraire à tenir compte de la mode, de l'actualité fugitive, de ce qu'on a vu une fois et qu'on ne reverra plus' (*Œuvres complètes* vol. 2, p.695)[235] but also in his very modern,

---

[233] For a comprehensive study of early European modernist art, music and literature, see Christopher Butler, *Early Modernism: Literature, Music and Painting in Europe 1900-1916* (Oxford: Clarendon Press, 1994).

[234] See Roger Shattuck, *The Banquet Years: the Origins of the Avant-Garde in France, 1885 to World War I* (New York: Vintage Books, 1968) p.335.

[235] Quoted in Yves Vadé's excellent article, 'Modernisme ou Modernité', p.54, in *The Turn of the Century: Modernism and Modernity in Literature and the Arts*.

some would say post-modern sense of the deep and unresolvable difficulty arising from the relationship between art and everyday life. 'Cette vaine, perplexe, nous échappant toujours, modernité' [OC, 399] echoes the constant questioning of the everyday which underlies the poet's work.

The ordinary relocated within the works of Mallarmé has an essential role, then, first as backdrop to more extraordinary textual events, as ingredient within the use of syntax and lexis, as a necessary controversial generator of metaphoric constructs and as the subject of a reflection on its place within contemporary society. The possibly dangerous versatility and the instability of the concept are in themselves positive assets. They enable Mallarmé to explore the negative and positive potential of the ordinary at a number of different levels and to discover its palimpsestic as well as chameleon like qualities. This forces the poet into ever more extraordinary linguistic feats in order to define the limits both of his art and of the quotidian. Mallarmé constantly seeks to enlarge his perception and his powers of expression in an attempt at exploring and exploding the inescapable. In his *Tractatus*, Wittgenstein links apprehension of the limits of one's language and of one's world: 'Die Grenzen meiner Sprache bedeuten die Grenzen meiner Welt'.[236] Mallarmé's subversion of syntactic rule, his experimenting with lexis and his dramatic *mise en scène* of textual events all gesture towards a basic quest for knowledge and engagement with both his material and his environment. Paradoxically, the measure of his awareness of the negative qualities of potential vacancy of the ordinary also promotes a powerful reactionary creative dynamism. It is at the point of tension, at the point of fear and repulsion, at the point of refusal and rejection, that the poet discovers his own power to manipulate, control, structure and re-invent a more habitable ordinary. To pastiche Mallarmé, one could say that 'il n'y a pas d'ordinaire, un ordinaire n'existe pas', an absolute ordinary other than complete vacancy is not part of the Mallarmean conception of the ordinary. However, an individually tailored ordinary, accepted not only as critical tool with an essential performative and ambivalence-creating role, but also as the necessary inimical environment within which Mallarmé has to resolve a number of painful and risk-laden conflicts, spurs the poet on to innovative ways of interpreting the ordinary and transforming it into an ideal ordinary, the locus of fascinating and

---

[236] L.Wittgenstein, *Tractatus Logico-Philosophicus,* German text with trans. By D.F.Pears and B.F.McGuiness (London, 1961).

extraordinary linguistic events, made habitable by a huge creative investment. It is at the very point of rift and tension, fascination and exorcism, that the centrally fruitful and productive role of the ordinary at the syntactical, lexical, metaphorical and ideological levels is clearly and crucially active.

LIST OF WORKS CONSULTED

Editions of Mallarmé:

Poésies, ed. Bertrand Marchal (Paris: Gallimard, 1992)

Poésies, ed. Lloyd James Austin (Paris: Flammarion, 1989)

Œuvres complètes, ed. Henri Mondor and G.Jean-Aubry (Paris: Bibliothèque de la Pléiade, Gallimard, 1945)

Œuvres complètes, ed. Bertrand Marchal, vol.1 (Paris: Bibliothèque de la Pléiade, Gallimard, 1998)

Igitur, Divagations, Un coup de dés (Paris: Gallimard, 1976)

Vers de circonstance, ed. Bertrand Marchal (Paris: Gallimard, 1996)

Documents Stéphane Mallarmé, ed. Gordon Millan (Saint-Genouph: Nizet, 1998)

Propos de Mallarmé sur la poésie (Monaco: Editions du Rocher, 1946)

Correspondance, ed. Henri Mondor and L.J. Austin, 11 vols (Paris: Gallimard, 1959-85)

Pour un 'Tombeau d'Anatole', ed. Jean-Pierre Richard (Paris: Seuil, 1961)

Les Gossips de Mallarmé, ed. Henri Mondor and L.J. Austin (Paris: Gallimard, 1962)

Books and Articles on Mallarmé:

Aish, Deborah A.K., *La Métaphore dans l'œuvre de Stéphane Mallarmé* (Genève: Slatkine reprints, 1981)

Audi, Paul, *La Tentative de Mallarmé* (Paris: Presses Universitaires de France, 1997)

Austin, Lloyd James, '"Le principal pilier", Mallarmé, Victor Hugo et Richard Wagner', *Revue d'Histoire Littéraire de la France*, avril-juin 1951, pp.154-180

Austin, Lloyd James, 'Mallarmé et le Rêve du Livre', *Mercure de France*, January-April 1953, pp. 81-108

Austin, Lloyd James, 'Mallarmé disciple de Baudelaire', *Revue d'Histoire Littéraire de la France*, vol. 67, 1967, pp. 65-74

Beausire, Pierre, *Mallarmé, Poésie et poétique* (Lausanne: Mermod, 1949)

Bellet, Roger, *Stéphane Mallarmé: l'encre et le ciel* (Seyssel: Champ Vallon, 1987)

Bénichou, Paul, *Selon Mallarmé* (Paris: Gallimard, 1995)

Bernard, Suzanne, *Mallarmé et la musique* (Paris: Nizet, 1959)

Bersani, Leo, *The Death of Stéphane Mallarmé* (Cambridge: Cambridge University Press, 1982)

Bowie, Malcolm, *Mallarmé and the Art of Being Difficult* (Cambridge: Cambridge University Press, 1978)

Cellier, Léon, *Mallarmé et la Morte qui parle* (Paris: Presses Universitaires de France, 1959)

Chadwick, Charles, *Mallarmé, sa pensée dans sa poésie* (Paris: Corti, 1962)

Chassé, Charles, *Les Clefs de Mallarmé* (Paris: Aubier, 1954)

Chisholm, A.R., *Mallarmé's Grand Œuvre* (Manchester: Manchester University Press, 1962)

Cohn, Robert Greer, *Mallarmé's Prose Poems: a Critical Study* (Cambridge: Cambridge University Press, 1987)

Cohn, Robert Greer, *Toward the Poems of Mallarmé* (Berkeley and Los Angeles: University of California Press, 1965)

Davies, Gardner, 'Stéphane Mallarmé: Fifty Years of Research', *French Studies*, vol. I, 1947, pp. 1-26

Davies, Gardner, *Les 'Tombeaux' de Mallarmé* (Paris: Corti, 1950)

Davies, Gardner, *Mallarmé et le drame solaire* (Paris: Corti, 1959)

Davies, Gardner, *Mallarmé et le rêve d'Hérodiade* (Paris: Corti, 1978)

Dayan, Peter, *Mallarmé's Divine Transposition* (Oxford: Clarendon Press, 1986)

Delfel, Guy, *L'Esthétique de Stéphane Mallarmé* (Paris: Flammarion, 1951)

Dragonetti, Roger, *Un fantôme dans le kiosque: Mallarmé et l'esthétique du quotidien* (Paris: Seuil, 1992)

Durand, Pascal, *Poésies de Stéphane Mallarmé* (Paris: Gallimard, 1998)

Florence, Penny, *Mallarmé, Manet and Redon* (Cambridge: Cambridge University Press, 1986)

Fontainas, André, 'Mallarmé et Victor Hugo', *Mercure de France*, 15 août 1932, pp.63-78

Fowlie, Wallace, *Mallarmé* (Chicago: University of Chicago Press, 1953)

Gengoux, Jacques, *Le Symbolisme de Mallarmé* (Paris: Nizet, 1950)

Gill, Austin, 'Les deux pauvres de Mallarmé', *Revue d'Histoire Littéraire de la France*, vol. 73, 1973, pp. 1045-1048

Gill, Austin, *The Early Mallarmé* vol.I (Oxford: Clarendon Press, 1979)

Gill, Austin, *The Early Mallarmé* vol.2 (Oxford: Clarendon Press, 1986)

Giroux, Robert, *Désir de synthèse chez Mallarmé* (Sherbrooke: Naaman, 1978)

Hambly, Peter, 'An approach to the Language of Mallarmé', *Parnasse*, vol. 3, published by Parnassian Study Circle, Oxford, October 1987, pp. 1-39

Huot, Sylviane, *Le 'mythe d'Hérodiade' chez Mallarmé* (Paris: Nizet, 1977)

Kaufmann, Vincent, *Le Livre et ses adresses* (Paris: Méridiens-Klincksieck, 1986)

Kaufmann, Vincent, *L'Equivoque épistolaire* (Paris: Minuit, 1990)

Kravis, Judy, *The Prose of Mallarmé: the Evolution of a Literary Language* (Cambridge: Cambridge University Press, 1976)

LaCharité, Virginia A., *Un Coup de dés: the Dynamics of Space* (Lexington, Kentucky: French Forum, 1987)

Lawler, James R., 'Mallarmé et le "poison tutélaire"', *Australian Journal of French Studies*, 1979, pp. 226-232

Lawler, James R., 'On "L'Assaut"', *French Forum*, supplement 1, 1989, pp. 55-63

Lestringant, Frank, 'Rémanence du Blanc: à propos d'une réminiscence hugolienne dans l'œuvre de Mallarmé', *Revue d'Histoire Littéraire de la France*, vol. 81, 1981, pp. 65-74

Lloyd, Rosemary, *Mallarmé: Poésies* (London: Grant & Cutler, 1984)

Lund, Hans Peter, 'L'Itinéraire de Mallarmé', *Revue Romane*, numéro spécial, 1969

Marchal, Bertrand, *Lecture de Mallarmé* (Paris: Corti, 1985)

Marchal, Bertrand, *La Religion de Mallarmé* (Paris: Corti, 1988)

Marvick, Louis Wirth, *Mallarmé and the Sublime* (Albany: State University of New York Press, 1986)

Mauron, Charles, *Mallarmé l'obscur* (Paris: Corti, 1968)

Mauron, Charles, *Introduction à la psychanalyse de Mallarmé* (Neuchâtel: La Baconnière, 1968)

Michaud, Guy, *Mallarmé: l'homme et l'œuvre* (Paris: Hatier-Boivin, 1953)

Millan, Gordon, *Mallarmé: A Throw of the Dice* (London: Secker & Warburg, 1994)

Mondor, Henri, *Vie de Mallarmé* (Paris: Gallimard, 1941)

Mondor, Henri, *Mallarmé plus intime* (Paris: Gallimard, 1944)

Mondor, Henri, *Mallarmé lycéen* (Paris: Gallimard, 1954)

Noulet, Emilie, *L'Œuvre poétique de Stéphane Mallarmé* (Paris: Droz, 1940)

Olds, Marshall C., *Desire Seeking Expression* (Lexington, Kentucky: French Forum, 1983)

Patri, A., 'Mallarmé et la musique du silence', *La Revue Musicale*, janvier 1952, pp. 101-111

Paxton, Norman, *The Development of Mallarmé's Prose Style* (Geneva: Droz, 1968)

Pearson, Roger, *Unfolding Mallarmé: the Development of a Poetic Art* (Oxford: Clarendon Press, 1996)

Rancière, Jacques, *Mallarmé: la Politique de la sirène* (Paris: Hachette, 1996)

Richard, Jean-Pierre, *L'Univers imaginaire de Mallarmé* (Paris: Seuil, 1961)

Robb, Graham, *Unlocking Mallarmé* (New Haven and London: Yale University Press, 1996)

Sartre, Jean-Paul, *Mallarmé or the poet of Nothingness*, trans. Ernest Sturm (London: Pennsylvania State University Press, 1986)

Scherer, Jacques, *L'Expression littéraire dans l'œuvre de Mallarmé* (Paris: Droz, 1947)

Scherer, Jacques, *Grammaire de Mallarmé* (Paris: Nizet, 1977)

Shaw, Mary Lewis, *Performance in the Texts of Mallarmé: the Passage from Art to Ritual* (Pennsylvania: Pennsylvania State University Press, 1993)

Soula, Camille, *Gloses sur Mallarmé* (Paris: Diderot, 1947)

Sugano, Marian Zwerling, *The Poetics of the Occasion: Mallarmé and the Poetry of Circumstance* (Stanford: Stanford University Press, 1992)

Temple, Michael, *The Name of the Poet* (Exeter: University of Exeter Press, 1995)

Temple, Michael, ed. *Meetings with Mallarmé in Contemporary French Culture* (Exeter: University of Exeter Press, 1998)

Thibaudet, Albert, *La Poésie de Stéphane Mallarmé* (Paris: Gallimard, 1926)

Thibaudet, Albert, 'A l'ombre des *Contemplations*: Baudelaire et Mallarmé', *Nouvelle Revue Française*, 1er juin 1933, pp. 865-872

Valéry, Paul, *Ecrits divers sur Mallarmé* (Paris: Gallimard, 1950)

Verdin, Simone, *Stéphane Mallarmé le presque contradictoire* (Paris: Nizet, 1975)

Walzer, Pierre-Olivier, *Mallarmé*, Nouvelle édition (Paris: Seghers, 1973)

Watson, Lawrence J., *Mallarmé's Mythic Language* (Oxford: Tallents Press, 1990)

Zayed, G., 'Réflexions sur les variantes "d'Aumône" et l'hermétisme mallarméen', *Revue d'Histoire Littéraire de la France*, vol. 72, 1972, pp. 85-100

Other Books and Articles consulted

Austin, Lloyd James, *L'Univers poétique de Baudelaire* (Paris: Mercure de France, 1956)

LIST OF WORKS CONSULTED 233

Austin, Lloyd James, *Poetic Principles and Practice: Occasional papers on Baudelaire, Mallarmé and Valéry* (Cambridge: Cambridge University Press, 1987)

Alquié, Ferdinand, *Philosophie du surréalisme* (Paris: Flammarion, 1977)

Arbid, Michael A., and Mary B. Hesse, *The Construction of Reality* (Cambridge: Cambridge University Press, 1986)

Barlow, Norman H., *Sainte-Beuve to Baudelaire: a Poetic Legacy* (Duke University Press, 1964)

Barrère, Jean-Bertrand, *La Fantaisie de Victor Hugo* , vol.2 (Paris: Klinksieck, 1972)

Barrère, Jean-Bertrand, *La Fantaisie de Victor Hugo*, vol. 3 (Paris: Klinksieck, 1973)

Baudelaire, Charles, *Les Fleurs du mal* ed. Henri Lemaître (Paris: Garnier-Flammarion, 1964)

Benjamin, Walter, *Charles Baudelaire: a Lyric Poet in the Era of High Capitalism*, trans. Harry Zohn (London: New Left Books, 1973)

Bersani, Leo, *Baudelaire and Freud* (Berkeley and Los Angeles: University of California Press, 1977)

Blanchot, Maurice, *L'espace littéraire* (Paris: Gallimard, 1955)

Bonnefoy, Yves, *Entretiens sur la poésie* and *La Présence et l'image* (Paris: Mercure de France, 1983)

Breton, André, *Les Manifestes du surréalisme* (Paris: Editions du Sagittaire, 1946)

Brombert, Victor, *The Hidden Reader* (Cambridge, Ma. and London: Harvard University Press, 1988)

Brooke-Rose, Christine, *A Grammar of Metaphor* (London: Secker and Warburg, 1958)

Butler, Christopher, *Early Modernism: Literature, Music and Painting in Europe 1900-1916* (Oxford: Clarendon Press, 1994)

Cavell, Stanley, *The Quest of the Ordinary: Lines on Skepticism and Romanticism* (Chicago and London: University of Chicago Press, 1988)

Caws, Mary Ann, *The Art of Interference: Stressed Readings in Verbal and Visual Texts* (Princeton: Princeton University Press, 1989)

Cellier, Léon, *Baudelaire et Hugo* (Paris: Corti, 1970)

Chaillet, Jean, *Etudes de grammaire et de style* (Paris: Bordas, 1969)

Chatman, Seymour, *The Later Style of Henry James* (Oxford: Basil Blackwell, 1972)

Chiari, Joseph, *Symbolism from Poe to Mallarmé: the Growth of a Myth* (London and Colchester: Spottiswood, Ballantyne, 1956)

Coburn, Robert C., *The Strangeness of the Ordinary: Issues and Problems in Contemporary Metaphysics* (Maryland and London: Rowman & Littlefield, 1990)

Cogman, Peter, *Hugo: Les Contemplations*, (London: Grant & Cutler, 1984)

Compagnon, Antoine, *Les Cinq paradoxes de la modernité* (Paris: Seuil, 1990)

Cook, E., *The Ordinary and the Fabulous* (Cambridge: Cambridge University Press, 1969)

Coppée, François, *Œuvres complètes*, vol.I (Paris: Hébert, 1885)

Davie, Donald, *Articulate Energy: an Inquiry into the Syntax of English Poetry* (London: Routledge & Kegan Paul, 1955, reprinted 1965, added postscript 1976)

Eysteinsson, Astradur, *The Concept of Modernism* (London, Ithaca: Cornell University Press, 1990)

Freud, Sigmund, *The Psychopathology of Everyday Life* (London: The Hogarth Press, 1960)

Freud, Sigmund, *Art and Literature* (London: Penguin, 1988)

Frey, John A., *Les Contemplations de Victor Hugo: The Ash Wednesday Liturgy* (Charlottesville: University Press of Virginia, 1988)

Froidevaux, Gérald, *Baudelaire, représentation et modernité* (Paris: Corti, 1989)

Gaudon, Jean, *Le Temps de la contemplation* (Paris: Flammarion, 1969)

Gibson, Robert, *Modern French Poets on Poetry* (Cambridge: Cambridge University Press, 1961)

Glauser, Alfred, *La Poétique de Victor Hugo* (Paris: Nizet, 1978)

Gordon, Rae Beth, *Ornament, Fantasy and Desire in Nineteenth-Century French Literature* (Princeton: Princeton University Press, 1992)

Guiraud, P., *Index du vocabulaire du symbolisme* (Paris: Klincksieck, 1953)

Guiraud, Pierre, *Langage et versification d'après l'œuvre de Paul Valéry* (Paris: Klincksieck, 1953)

Guiraud, Pierre, *Essais de stylistique* (Paris: Klincksieck, 1969)

Hawkes, Terence, *Metaphor* (London: Methuen, 1972)

Heidegger, Martin, *The Origin of the Work of Art*, trans. Albert Hofstadter (London: Harper and Row, 1975)

Henry, Albert, *Langage et poésie chez Paul Valéry* (Paris: Mercure de France, 1952)

Herrnstein Smith, Barbara, *Poetic Closure: a Study of how Poems End* (Chicago and London: University of Chicago Press, 1968)

Holdheim, W.Wolfgang, *The Hermeneutic Mode* (Ithaca and London: Cornell University Press, 1984)

Houston, John Porter, *French Symbolism and the Modernist Movement: a Study of Poetic Structures* (Baton Rouge: Louisiana State University Press, 1981)

Houston, John Porter, *Patterns of Thought in Rimbaud and Mallarmé* (Lexington, Kentucky: French Forum, 1986)

Hugo, Victor, *Châtiments* (Paris: Garnier-Flammarion, 1979)

Hugo, Victor, *Les Contemplations* (Paris: Gallimard-Poésie, 1973)
Huyssen, Andreas, *After the Great Divide: Modernism, Mass Culture and Postmodernism* (London, Basingstoke: Macmillan, 1986)

Johansen, Svend, *Etude sur le style des symbolistes français* (Copenhague: Einar Munksgaard, 1945)

Johnson, Barbara, *Défigurations du langage poétique* (Paris: Flammarion, 1979)

Kristeva, Julia, *La Révolution du langage poétique: L'Avant-garde à la fin du XIXe siècle: Lautréamont et Mallarmé* (Paris: Seuil, 1974)

Kuhn, Thomas S., *The Structure of Scientific Revolutions,* second edition (Chicago and London: University of Chicago Press, 1970)

Laforgue, Jules, *Poésies complètes,* (Paris: Gallimard, 1970)

Lamartine, Alphonse de, *Œuvres complètes* (Paris: Bibliothèque de la Pléiade, Gallimard, 1963)

Langer, Susanne K., *Problems of Art: Ten Philosophical Lectures* (London: Routledge & Kegan Paul, 1957)

Lakoff, George and Mark Turner, *More than Cool Reason* (Chicago and London: University of Chicago Press, 1989)

Lawler, James, *The Language of French Symbolism* (Princeton: Princeton University Press, 1969)

Lefèbvre, Henri, *Critique of Everyday Life,* trans. John Moore (London and New York: Verso, 1947)

Lehmann, A.G., *The Symbolist Aesthetic in France 1885-1895* (Oxford: Blackwell, 1968)

Lemaire, Michel, *Le Dandysme de Baudelaire à Mallarmé* (Montréal: Presses de l'Université de Montréal, 1978)

Lesage, Laurent, *The Rhumb Line of Symbolism* (Philadelphia: Pennsylvania State University Press, 1978)

Levin, Harry, *The Gates of Horn* (New York: Oxford University Press, 1963)

Lloyd, Geneviève, *Being in Time: Selves and Narrators in Philosophy and Literature* (London and New York: Routledge, 1993)

Lucas, J.R., *An Essay on God, Temporality and Truth* (Oxford: Blackwell, 1989)

Michaud, Guy, *Le Message poétique du symbolisme,* ed. in one vol., (Paris: Nizet, 1978)

Mooij, J.J.A., *A Study of Metaphor* (Amsterdam, New York, Oxford: North-Holland Publishing Company, 1976)

Mossop, Deryk J., *Pure Poetry, Studies in French Theory and Practice* (Oxford: Oxford University Press, 1971)

Nash, Suzanne, *Les Contemplations de Victor Hugo* (Princeton: Princeton University Press, 1976)

Ortony, Andrew, ed. *Metaphor and Thought* (Cambridge: Cambridge University Press, 1979)

Parkes, Malcolm B., *Pause and Effect: an Introduction to the History of Punctuation in the West* (Cambridge: Scolar Press, 1992)

Poulet, Georges, *La Distance intérieure* (Paris: Plon, 1952)

Pourbaix, Joël, *Le Simple Geste d'exister* (Québec: Noroît, 1989)

Prendergast, Christopher, *Writing the City: Paris and the Nineteenth Century* (Oxford and Cambridge, Massachusetts: Blackwell, 1992)

Raymond, Marcel, *From Baudelaire to Surrealism* (London: Peter Owen, 1957)

Ricœur, Paul, *La Métaphore vive* (Paris: Seuil, 1975)

Rifelj, Carol de Dobay, *Word and Figure: the Language of Nineteenth-Century French Poetry* (Columbus: Ohio State University Press, 1987)

Sainte-Beuve, Charles-Augustin de, *Poésies complètes*, vol.I (Paris: Lemerre, 1929)

Segal, Naomi, *The Banal Object: Themes and Thematics in Proust, Rilke, Hofmansthal and Sartre* (London: Institute of Germanic Studies, Bithell Series of Dissertations, 1981)

Smith, Quentin, *Language and Time* (Oxford, New York: Oxford University Press, 1993)

Jacobs, Steffen, 'Er lebe den Alltag', *Neue Rundschau* 107, 1996, pp.22-34

Steiner, George, *On Difficulty and Other Essays* (Oxford: Oxford University Press, 1978)

Taylor, Charles, *Sources of the Self: the Making of the Modern Identity* (Cambridge: Cambridge University Press, 1989)

Thomä, Dieter, 'Die Pharmakologie des Banalen', *Neue Rundschau* 107, 1996, pp.15-21

Turquet-Milnes, G., *The Influence of Baudelaire in France and England* (London: Constable, 1930

Veyne, Paul, 'Das Alltägliche und das Interessante', *Neue Rundschau* 107, 1996, pp.9-14

Vigny, Alfred de, *Œuvres complètes* (Paris: Bibliothèque de la Pléiade, Gallimard, 1986)

Williams, Roger L., *The Horror of Life* (Chicago and London: University of Chicago Press, 1980)

Zeldin, Theodore, *France 1848-1945*, vol.I (Oxford: Clarendon Press, 1973)

Zeldin, Theodore, *France 1848-1945*, vol.II (Oxford: Clarendon Press, 1977)

INDEX

'L'Action restreinte': 80, 101, 133, 148, 175, 193
'A la nue accablante tu': 84
Aish, Deborah A.K.: 153, 156, 162
'L'Albatros' (Baudelaire): 51
'Angoisse', 47, 50, 161
Apollinaire, Guillaume: 103, 222
'L'Après-midi d'un faune': 61, 69, 80, 138
Aristotle: 160
'Au lecteur' (Baudelaire): 56
'Aumône': 47, 53, 58
'Autobiographie': 47, 127, 139, 148, 163
Austin, L.J.: 47, 50
'Autre éventail': 157
Avant-Garde: 222
'L'Azur': 46, 59, 115

Baudelaire, Charles: 17, 25, 36, 41, 44-61, 107, 109, 120-2, 154, 187, 193, 210, 219
Beckett, Samuel: 92
Bellet, Roger: 15
Bergson, Henri: 101
Bersani, Leo: 40, 83, 90
'Berthe Morisot': 32, 73, 83, 112, 116
Bettelheim, Bruno: 40
'Billet': 120
Bon Marché: 134, 165, 191
Bonnard, Pierre: 44
Bonnefoy, Yves: 24, 27, 36-9, 41, 43, 184
Bowie, Malcolm: 14, 41
Breton, André: 35, 40
'Brise marine': 43, 46, 49, 54-6, 66
Brooke-Rose, Christine: 152-3
'Bucolique': 149, 205
Butler, Christopher, 222-3

Catholic: 158

Cavell, Stanley: 20, 25, 36, 42-3, 75, 180, 210, 212-4, 220
Cendrars, Blaise: 222
'La chevelure vol...': 74, 80, 115, 154, 157-9
Chisholm, A.R.: 13, 20, 36
Coburn, Robert C.: 27
'Conflit': 116, 126, 142, 150, 173, 197-8, 200-1
'Confrontation': 149, 162, 200-1
'Conseils sur l'éducation': 119
Constant, Benjamin: 103
'Contes indiens': 137, 148-9
contingent difficulty: 12, 20, 28-30, 32, 34, 111
Coppée, François: 48, 107, 109, 114, 162, 188
Coronation Street: 45
Un Coup de dés: 11, 33-4, 38-9, 66-7, 85, 95, 113, 121, 136, 139, 146, 149
'La Cour': 135-6, 148-9, 203
'Crayonné au théâtre': 66, 133, 147, 162, 177
'Le crépuscule du matin' (Baudelaire): 56
'Crise de vers': 30, 80, 114, 126, 141, 178

Dante, Alighieri: 18
'La déclaration foraine': 134, 140, 147, 171
Delaunay, Robert: 223
'Le démon de l'analogie': 82-3, 136
La Dernière Mode: 48, 77, 82, 116-21, 125, 129, 132, 135, 137, 141, 145, 148-9, 162-3, 167-8, 175, 182-3, 187-8, 197, 216, 220-2
Desbordes-Valmore, Marceline: 109
'Diptyque': 127, 133

Divagations: 23, 43, 200, 202, 222
'Don du poème': 50, 56-7
Dragonetti, Roger, 16

Eastenders: 45
'L'ecclésiastique': 140, 147, 171
'Edouard Manet': 84
Entre Quatre Murs: 47
'Etalages': 131, 134, 176, 193
'Eventail': 97
'Exposition internationale de Londres', 128, 148, 183-4, 189, 221
Expositions universelles: 15, 83

'Les fenêtres': 46, 48-9, 53, 58, 72, 112, 138, 147, 177
Flaubert, Gustave: 46
Floupette, Adoré: 64
Freud, Sigmund: 40, 42
'Frisson d'hiver': 169

Gautier, Théophile: 69, 109, 113
'Gazette de la Fashion': 166
'Le Genre ou des Modernes': 74, 148, 178
'La gloire': 172-3
'Le gouffre' (Baudelaire): 51
'Grands faits divers': 202
'Le guignon': 47, 51-2, 57, 68, 154
Guiraud, Pierre: 114

'Hamlet': 134
Harries, Karsten: 152
Heidegger, Martin: 19-26, 33, 37, 42-3, 59, 81, 91-2, 169, 177, 179, 210, 214
Henry, Albert: 114
'Hérodiade': 41, 61, 66, 72, 80, 89-90, 92, 94, 197
Hesse, Mary B.: 39
Hofmannsthal, Hugo von: 223

Hugo, Victor: 25, 46-8, 68, 107, 109, 154, 210, 219

'Igitur ou la folie d'Elbehnon': 135, 162

Jacobs, Steffen: 21
'Le Jury de peinture pour 1874 et M.Manet': 204

Kaufmann, Vincent: 15
Keats, John: 156
Kravis, Judy: 86
Kristeva, Julia: 11, 14, 26, 62, 65-70, 72-3, 75-6, 81, 104, 211
Kuhn, Thomas S.: 38

LaCharité, Virginia: 85
Laforgue, Jules: 108
Lamartine, Alphonse de: 47-8
'Las de l'amer repos': 43, 56, 60, 74, 78, 80, 142, 202
Lefébure, Eugène: 110
Lefèbvre, Henri: 24, 35, 37, 81, 206, 210, 217, 219, 222
'Le léthé' (Baudelaire): 51
'La littérature': 127
'L'irréparable' (Baudelaire): 50
'Le Livre, instrument spirituel': 133, 175-6, 194
Lloyd, Rosemary: 25

'Magie': 110, 202
Manet, Edouard: 84, 148, 204
Marchal, Bertrand: 14, 37, 115, 181-2, 205
'La marchande d'herbes aromatiques': 120
Marinetti, Filippo Tommaso: 223
Mauron, Charles: 14
Marxist theory: 201
'Médaillons et Portraits': 32, 68, 73, 79, 82, 116, 148-50
'Mes bouquins refermés': 30, 111, 122

Millan, Gordon: 10, 12-3, 44
'Mimique': 102
'M'introduire dans ton histoire': 80
modal difficulty: 12, 30, 32, 34, 113
Modernism: 222-3
Mondor, Henri: 13, 44, 51, 86, 109
Mooij, J.J.A.: 152
'Les mots anglais': 110, 148, 179
'La musique et les lettres': 78, 108, 148, 150
'Le mystère dans les lettres': 63, 126, 132, 179

Nerval, Gérard de: 52
Nietzsche, Friedrich: 222
Noulet, Emilie: 13-4, 65, 72

'L'œuvre poétique de Léon Dierx': 177
'Offices': 136, 148-9
ontological difficulty: 12, 30, 33-4
'Or': 110, 113, 147
'O si chère de loin et proche et blanche': 100
OuLiPo: 36

'Parfum exotique' (Baudelaire): 54
Parkes, Malcolm: 85
Parnasse Contemporain: 45-7
Paxton, Norman: 64-5, 72, 74
'Paysage' (Baudelaire): 52
Pearson, Roger: 14
Perec, Georges: 36
'Petit air': 86
'Petit air I': 158-60
'Petit air II': 115, 155, 184
'Petit air (guerrier)': 216
'Les petites vieilles' (Baudelaire): 53, 57-8
'Le phénomène futur': 168, 172
'La pipe': 169
'Le pitre châtié': 56, 78

'Plainte d'automne': 140-1, 147, 169
'Plaisir sacré': 130, 132, 174
Plato: 12, 142, 219
'Poèmes en prose': 74, 115, 130
Ponge, Francis: 45
Poésies: 25, 29, 41, 43, 48, 66, 115-6, 123, 125, 138, 206, 222
Poulet, Georges: 97
Pourbaix, Joël: 20
'Prose': 82, 85, 98, 115, 136-8, 155
'Proses diverses': 107, 129
'Proses de jeunesse': 161
Proust, Marcel: 63, 169

'Quant au livre': 193
Queneau, Raymond: 36

Rancière, Jacques: 15
Raymond, Marcel: 52
'Remémoration d'amis belges': 94, 139, 147, 158
'Réminiscence': 131, 140, 171
'Renouveau': 49, 52, 94, 161
Richard, Jean-Pierre: 14, 24, 115
'Richard Wagner – rêverie d'un poète français': 132
Robb, Graham: 14
Rodenbach, Georges: 139
Russell, Bertrand: 36

'Sainte': 37-9, 41, 43, 92-3, 95, 99, 214
Sainte-Beuve, Charles-Augustin de: 48, 108-9
'Salut': 43, 121
Sartre, Jean-Paul: 24
'Sauvegarde': 113, 147
Scherer, Jacques: 11, 14, 37, 64-5, 72, 74, 78, 97, 107, 111
Segal, Naomi: 43
'Les sept vieillards' (Baudelaire): 53
'Ses purs ongles': 111

Shattuck, Roger: 223
'Le soleil' (Baudelaire): 52
'Solennité': 141
'Sonnet en yx': 41
'Le sonneur': 46, 49
'Un spectacle interrompu': 130, 149, 170, 175
Stein, Gertrud: 223
Steiner, George: 12, 28-30, 31, 33, 35, 42, 61, 64, 67, 111, 210
Sugano, Marian, Zwerling: 15
'Surgi de la croupe et du bond': 98
'Sur les bois oubliés': 94
'Sur l'idéal à vingt ans': 82, 136, 150
'Sur le beau et l'utile': 190
Surrealists: 35, 39, 61
'Symphonie littéraire': 68-9, 148
syntaxier: 32, 44, 68

'Tableaux parisiens' (Baudelaire): 52-3, 59-60, 109
tactical difficulty: 12, 30-4, 111
Taylor, Charles: 18-20, 24, 45, 207, 210
Temple, Michael: 14
Temporality: 37-8, 64, 93-7, 100, 104
'Le "Ten o'clock" de Mr Whistler': 134, 148, 150, 191
Thibaudet, Albert: 13-4, 51, 65, 72, 85, 87, 115
Thomä, Dieter: 21-2

'Toast funèbre': 40, 68, 95
'Le tombeau de Charles Baudelaire': 121
'Le tombeau d'Edgar Poe': 29, 40, 67, 112, 189
'Tout orgueil fume-t-il du soir': 43

Vadé, Yves: 223
Valéry, Paul: 114-5
'Variations sur un sujet': 76, 82, 131, 173, 175, 193
Verlaine, Paul: 127, 149
Vers de circonstance: 14-5, 120-2, 125, 147, 161, 181-3, 206, 216, 222, 227
Veyne, Paul: 23
'Le vierge, le vivace et le bel aujourd'hui': 37-8, 41, 91, 93, 103, 214
Villiers de l'Isle-Adam: 32-3, 86, 128
Vigny, Alfred de: 37
'Le vin des chiffonniers' (Baudelaire): 58
'Le voyage' (Baudelaire): 55, 60

The Whirlwind: 120
Whistler, James McNeill: 120
Wittgenstein, Ludwig: 21, 42, 224
Wright, George: 92

Zeldin, Theodore: 185-6
Zola, Emile: 45-6